TRUTH
SPEAKS

Answers from the Master
VOLUME 1

Bodhisattva Shree Swami Premodaya

Green Tara Press

Green Tara Press
Los Angeles, CA
www.greentarapress.com

Premodaya, Swami
Truth Speaks: Answers from the Master, Vol 1
1. Religion and Spirituality 2. Self-Help 3. Personal Transformation

ISBN: 978-1-945085-46-8 Paperback
ISBN: 978-1-945085-47-5 Electronic Book Text

Author Photo by Marshall Fried © 2022 International Centers of Divine Awakening
Cover and interior design by Lorie DeWorken

CONTENTS

FOREWORD

"The wisdom mind is not some faraway attainment.
You got it when you were born, you have it every second,
and it is always trying to get you to listen a little closer."
—Swami Premodaya, 'Beyond Self' Evening

Over and over again I've seen people come to Swami Premodaya in distress or crisis, and in just one conversation gain a new perspective and clear understanding of how to go forward. Over and over again I've seen him respond to deep spiritual questions in a way that is totally original, totally fresh, while at the same time bringing new light to what is at the core of all wisdom traditions.

In these talks from the early years of Bodhisattva Shree Swami Premodaya's public meetings you will see that he meets people where they are, at every stage of the spiritual journey, and whatever their path. Whether you come out of curiosity, as a student, or as someone who has been on the spiritual path for years, you are welcome, and your concerns and insights are valued. No matter what comes up, no matter the topic or question, he opens the field of perception and understanding to a more God-infused depth and clarity. If you prefer to use the word Reality, Truth, Source—or whatever word is meaningful for you—that's fine. These satsangs, these meetings in truth, are not about the words, they are about what is beyond the words and what will help you in whatever way serves you most.

1

For those who are uneasy with the concept of "guru," Swami Premodaya is very clear that the guru is a function, not a person or personality, and that he is a person with strengths and weaknesses just like everyone else. The true guru never impinges on someone's personal freedom. In relating to those who come for assistance, the guru-function responds, and that function is not based on the history, personality, or preferences of the person serving as guru. For those who choose to engage with that function, use of the guru is a method for going deeper and further on the spiritual path.

From the first time I attended a public talk with Swami Premodaya in 2006, I have seen for myself that his whole effort is to help you see and experience for yourself what is true and what is real, not to give you a new philosophy or new beliefs. Whether your word for the ultimate reality is God, Truth, Source, Swami Premodaya will help you connect more and more with that. His methods are practical, direct and effective.

I came to Swami Premodaya after many years as a meditator and spiritual seeker: reading spiritual books, attending spiritual talks, and all the rest. Along the way I had the blessing of being able to attend talks with many great spiritual teachers. Yet when I met Swamiji I felt a sense of something fresh and alive that was more real to me than anything in the past; I could see that here was a living wisdom, new each moment, drawn directly from a source within. Here in Swami Premodaya is a living example of the words of Zen master Musō Soseki, "The dharma spring has never run dry, it is flowing even now."

With Swami Premodaya's help, my life has transformed from one of sorrow and isolation to one of deeply-felt connection with others and with the infinite source out of which and in which everything arises. Every day brings new insights and understandings, and this deeply-felt connection continues to expand and express itself more and more. The more it expands, the more apparent it becomes that the field of spiritual growth is vast beyond anything I ever previously thought possible, and that it is available to anyone. This book of conversations with Swami

Premodaya is a doorway to that field of ever-opening love, understanding, and connection.

Shanti Natania Grace
Chief Administrative Officer (Retired)
Brain Research Institute, UCLA

INTRODUCTION

This book is a collection of excerpts compiled from public meetings with Swami Premodaya from 2006 to 2008. These meetings were recorded live, transcribed, and checked for accuracy. Then these selections were grouped into separate topic areas. Most of these public meetings are *Satsangs* ("Satsang" is an ancient Sanskrit word that means "gathering in Truth"), which is the age-old tradition of question-and-answer with a spiritual master. Swami Premodaya invites and encourages participants to share whatever they would like—to ask their deepest and most significant questions, especially those we all ask ourselves: "What is life?", "What is death?", "Who am I?", "Is there God?"—questions that if truly answered and rightly responded to, can lead to transformation, even positive life-changing results.

In all these selections, Swami Premodaya is speaking extemporaneously. He unhesitatingly answers every question and addresses every topic presented by spiritual seekers from every walk of life. His ways of working with every variety of person frequently excites and delights. A question from one person, may elicit a completely different response, when asked by another person. This is because he is always working specifically with that one person, providing the ideal method or precise direction that will work best for that individual's uniqueness—whether the goal is genuine happiness, inner peace, or true self-realization. It is always a meaningful, alive dialogue, and always for the purpose of that person's spiritual advancement. This is the essence of the Guru phenomenon, which sets it apart from all other human relationships and interactions.

These meetings present the powerful opportunity of quickly identifying what needs to be faced—and then dealing with it—once and for all. Some characterize Premodaya's work with them as a 'profound guided journey,' that above all feels 'completely safe.' All fears are surmountable in the right hands. All problems are transmuted into higher consciousness when worked with correctly.

CHAPTER 1

RADICAL SELF-ACCEPTANCE

Evelyn: I have realized lately I carry this whip around and beat myself up incessantly. When it comes to the concept of loving myself, my mind wants to tell me, "That's too easy."

Premodaya: Because you've been taught again and again that it's wrong and that it's not simple. That's how good the teaching is that everybody has received. The teaching is there for that reason, so you don't fall into self-love. You have to start looking at your own experience and hearing what you're saying. You have to start listening to yourself and stop believing what you believe, because on the level of belief, yes, it seems not right.

Evelyn: Everything reinforces "you're not good enough, you're not enough," and we take it in. What keeps coming up is: it can't be that easy.

Premodaya: Yes, that's what keeps coming up, because that's the best antidote to keep you from self-love. As long as you stay poisoned you will cooperate with society; you will watch TV, you will read the newspaper, you will spend the money where the powers want you to spend your money.

Evelyn: You're absolutely uncontrollable if you love yourself.

Premodaya: You can't be manipulated and you can't be fooled by some political philosophy.

Evelyn: I met this man who told me that for thirty-two days in a row to do this practice; he basically put me on a diet of self-love and said that thirty-two days was very important because then the mind would create a habit. In my experience that isn't what happened, but it did last for a certain amount of time. This idea that I was going to create a new mental habit—was that just another form of self-sabotage?

Premodaya: You have to see with your own eyes. Then you don't need anybody to tell you to do this or that for thirty-two days or thirty-two years, you just have to come to a point of understanding. And you've already come there—you have just got done telling us that you have seen with your own understanding how simple it is. Your mind—and you used the right words; you said, "my mind doesn't want to believe it's this simple," but what's that statement? It's saying: "I see it's this simple; I understand it's this simple, but my mind, the mental part, doesn't want to accept that it could be true." You can't get a clearer understanding than that. The only next step is to believe it, to know that you're telling yourself the truth. Yes, there are all kinds of courses you can take and seminars and books and self-help this and try that and eighteen ways to this and the seven principles of that, and that will never end, but it's just about understanding. If understanding is there, it's taken care of. It's a two-step process: (a) understand, and (b) listen to yourself, follow your own understanding. Then you don't need the seven principles of this and the eighteen guideposts to that, and what successful people do and what enlightened people do and what happy people do and what everybody does. Then you do what's right for you. What's right is what's natural.

Evelyn: I think that somewhere deep inside of me I have this illusion that to beat myself up and to make myself wrong is really the only way to ever better myself as a human being, and it's just not true. It doesn't work. The proof is in; the jury has spoken, but I guess that's just another trick of the powers that be.

Premodaya: The powers that be include our parents, include our friends, include those who are literally and truly and sincerely trying to help us and believe they are benefiting us. But that doesn't mean that their help is useful; that doesn't mean that some of it isn't poisonous. So, you have to get to a point of maturity where you start ridding yourself of the poisons and start feeding yourself on what's good. That doesn't take thirty-two days; that takes the willingness to start doing it and believing the results, believing what happens to your heart when you do that. That's all the encouragement you need to do it some more. The only thing you do need to do is to keep reminding yourself that what you're seeing, you're really seeing—what you're experiencing, you're really experiencing—because the input has all been from the other direction: "Don't believe it; if it's not complicated it won't work."

Evelyn: Today I felt so much love. I was so in love with humanity today, and how often have I tried to access that? I've been trying to make the first thought of the day some form of self-love, and everything that's flowed out of that is just so easy and so beautiful and so natural. I did not see until tonight that what keeps coming up is, "It can't be this easy, you need to work harder, try harder."

Premodaya: You're at a point where you have to make a decision; that's what I would say to you, whether you're going to start believing yourself and believing your own experience, or whether you're going to keep this idea that you have to work on something. This whole self-help stuff—I'm not in the self-help business. I don't teach you self-help; I don't try to give people self-help methods; I'm not for self-help. I'm for relaxing and transcending yourself, and then you don't need self-help. I'm for using the intelligence you already have. Self-help is about, "Hey, did you try this? Well, your way doesn't seem to be working; try this." I'm not for that. I'm for using your own understanding, not some tip by somebody who is selling something.

I'm not selling anything. You can buy things here; there are things for sale, but that doesn't mean I'm selling them. That really does mean we make it available to people. Because really to be selling something, you have to be selling an idea. If you're selling something, you're really selling a philosophy, a point of view, and I don't care what your point of view is. The only thing I want you to see is that every point of view is wrong, simply by being a point of view: Stop believing any point of view; be more open than that. You can't sell that—it's not solid enough to sell; it's not appealing enough; people won't buy it. But if you try it, then you can see the results of it. And you have done that.

You're at a point where you have to start believing what you already know. And I don't mean believe it like a belief; I mean seeing it's true instead of the "oh my God" response.

You've got to stop saying, "Oh my God, it can't be" and start saying, "Well, what really is it?" You have to start making up your mind; you have to start drawing the final conclusions, otherwise you will evaluate endlessly. I'm suggesting to you that you have come far enough that you can stop. End the evaluation phase and draw your final conclusions. The whole problem is you're staying in the evaluation, "I need to, you know— let's get some more data." Like you said, there's enough data. Start being it instead of seeking it.

Evelyn: That sounds easy too, actually.

Premodaya: Yes, it means draw your conclusions and go from there, and start living it, not questioning it. Life isn't endless; you don't need to spend more time evaluating; you've already done enough.

Leah: How did we come to this thinking that we have to try harder or work harder? Where is the origin? Where's the positive in that?

Premodaya: Are you asking that personally or generally? How did it get there for you? If it's for personal reasons, let's get personal.

Leah: I've always been taught that if you push and you try hard and you're focused then you're going to achieve, and if you don't have this self-regulation then you won't progress.

Premodaya: Does that seem right to you?

Leah: It doesn't *feel* right. But I'm at a good place in my life; I have achieved, so the proof in the external world feels OK. Things are working. It's just that the external and the internal aren't really matching up that well.

Premodaya: If the outer and the inner don't match, what does the inner say?

Leah: I guess the inner says that it doesn't feel like who I'm supposed to be. There's too much distance between me and other people. I want a different internal energy than I have, which is really constricted. I have a vision for something more open but every time I talk to people or do work, all the restrictions come up again.

Premodaya: Well, this is because the outer world will only support the outer. The outer world won't support the inner, unless it's people who come to a meeting like this or situations like this. Then there's support for the inner, but when you look to the outer world, the general world, for some kind of support for the inner life, they aren't interested. They need you to support the outer world. You're looking in the wrong place, which means you came to the right place tonight. I mean that very seriously— that sincere people who have embarked on the inner search have to find the right resources for themselves, and self-help isn't enough. The right resources that support the inner growth, because the outer world isn't interested because there's no profit in it; there's no achievement in it—it can't be measured; it doesn't have a bottom line.

You have already gotten to that point of understanding or maturity or wisdom or whatever you want to call it, that you recognize, at the very least, that the outer definition of success may be hollower than people think. What you're really saying is: "On the outside I have what people would call success, but I've gotten to the point where I realize it's not success, because something is missing on the inside." This is the real beginning of your real search—this is the good news, by the way.

I'm not giving it a positive spin. I want you to see where you're really at. Getting to *this* is the true beginning of the real search that can yield real fruit. Before this, nothing real is possible; before this, it's just about achieving by someone else's standard. But now you've gotten to the point where you recognize that isn't going to be enough for a person like you. Now you've gotten to the point where your inner wisdom says to you: There has got to be a better way; there has got to be something that's more fulfilling; there has got to be something that actually works inside, not just outside. And you're right, there is, but now you have begun the real search.

You need encouragement that this is for real, and I would like to give it to you. You need to hear the confirmation that this is not nonsense, that this isn't your mind trying to get you to not be quite as productive. This is the *real* wisdom—that productive on the outside doesn't necessarily give satisfaction on the inside. And now something real is possible, because of that.

It may seem, "Oh, now I'm taking on something big; this is scary," or, "This might be too much," or, "I don't know where this is going; it's kind of going into the unknown," but you're absolutely on the right course—this is the first step in the right direction; that's what I want to confirm for you. I'm not saying that to make you feel good. I'm saying that because it's the truth. Because most people go to their graves never having gotten to this point of understanding that you have now gotten to. Early enough, you've gotten now to a point where wherever it takes you, it's going to be more real than where you have been so far, because the outer only *seems* real. Once the inner starts having the inner hunger, you start seeing how the outer isn't really all that satisfying, and that's the best news possible. But I'm not trying to make you feel good; I'm trying to give you the confirmation everybody needs when they get to that point, because society won't give it to you; society wants you to be a drone and do your job and pay your taxes and follow the rules and whatever. I'm not saying there's anything wrong with any of that—I'm just saying more is possible. And most people never come to recognize that. At a still-young age, you've come to recognize that. That's excellent good news; you should be encouraged, no matter how difficult, painful, or anguishing it is.

Leah: Thank you. This feels the most true of what I've found so far, so that feels nice, even though it's really scary.

Premodaya: Well, the more true it is, if it's new, the more scared you'll feel; that's absolutely the truth. So, you have to see that you're in a new place. I don't mean here; I mean in yourself: You're at a new stage that has just recently begun. No matter how far back it feels like it goes, it's really recent. There will be all kinds of feelings and perceptions that you should keep an open mind about—don't decide too early, "I feel this way or that way; I'm scared; I'm this; I'm that." Yes, feel scared, fine, but take it all as a *cue* that something real is happening, or else you wouldn't be feeling anything in particular. You're in the right place; there's no question in my mind, and you're the kind of person I wait for. And these are the kind of people who can support you, but this isn't a support group or a self-help group; this is an exploration group, people who are open-minded enough to explore what's real and what's true. That's really why I say you have come to the right place, because you're clearly of that ilk.

No matter who needed to hear what was said tonight, no matter why it came out of my mouth, the truth is we all need to hear this; the truth is that all of us have been told from the very beginning that somehow, some way, we need to earn love. If you're here, if you're breathing, *you have already earned it.*

CHAPTER 2

WHY WORRY?

Premodaya: There's really no such thing as "your question," "his question," "her question," "my dilemma," "your problem." These are all shared. There's only a pool of so many problems, so many circumstances, so many dilemmas, so many things to be worked out and understood, and everybody takes their little pile out of that common pile. Anytime you think of something as yours, the wiser understanding is that it's not yours at all: It's everybody's. You just grabbed that one for now. It's like reaching into a grab bag with your eyes closed. You pull out something and then that gets to be yours for a while. Understand well that it's a common bag. If you're thinking of it as your problem, you're already in the wrong direction because you're already misunderstanding that your problem is everybody's problem. You aren't that different from everybody else. If I wanted to say it more controversially, I would say you're exactly like everybody else.

There really aren't big differences between people. There are small differences, certainly, but big differences? You would have to argue with me for a while to convince me. I have been working with people for thirty years; I have yet to see any big differences. Young, old, tall, short, black, white—I have yet to see any big differences. But we walk around thinking there are differences. We walk around thinking that I'm this way and she's that way and he's that way. If you look a little more intelligently, a little closer, a little deeper, then you start to see very quickly, very easily that these so-called differences are not only clearly superficial, but they may not amount to any real differences at all.

The wise approach, if you ask me, is to consider yourself the same as everybody else. I'm saying to you, any time you consider yourself as "different"—whether better or worse, higher or lower, smarter or not as smart, more successful or less successful—whatever comparison you're making, the wiser approach is to assume you're wrong in that comparison. Because you will be, because there's no correct comparison. Comparison means, "I'm not seeing clearly." You're only seeing part of something. You aren't seeing the whole package. You're only looking at one aspect and saying, "Ah, there's a difference." But if you broaden your looking and look at the whole package, the difference will disappear.

It sounds simple enough—it sounds easy to accept. Intelligent, spiritual-minded people like everybody in this room will probably accept that readily. But has it permeated everything you look at? Does it come to mind when your mind says, "Oh, now I have this problem. Damn." Does the thought follow right after that, "Oh, wait a minute; if it's my problem it's probably everybody's problem, or at least a lot of other people's"? Until then, until it's automatic to recognize the commonality of all things, then you're probably falling victim to the errors of comparison, the confusion of seeing yourself as not like everyone else.

The amazing thing is that you will be right so much of the time when you look at it that way, that you can use it as a rule. You will be wrong once in ten years, if at all. Since it's ninety-nine point nine nine nine percent of the case, why not just adopt it as the case? Then a whole lot of things get taken care of just by that. A whole lot of problems, issues, dilemmas, suddenly don't have the same shape. If they are recognized as common dilemmas, as everybody's dilemma instead of "my dilemma," that's completely different. Suddenly you aren't alone; suddenly you're not different. Suddenly everybody else doesn't have it better regarding that one thing. Suddenly maybe you don't have it so bad regarding that one thing.

The wonderful vantage point of sitting in this chair is you get to see only one person. Whoever it is, it's the same person again and again. Whatever the question, it's the same question again and again. Everybody should sit in this chair for at least a day. You will be amazed. You will be amazed at how everybody is confused; how everybody thinks it's them, when it's so clearly everybody.

This is what all worry comes from. The word "worry" is very significant because most people are caught in it. It's not possible to worry when you really recognize, when you get it completely that what you're worried about is everybody's concern. It's only worrisome, it only troubles you, it only anguishes you, when you think it's *yours*. If it isn't yours, how big a problem can it be?

This is all very basic. I'm not saying anything really complex or hard to get, or new. You could probably say the same thing, never having heard it tonight. But the question is, has it permeated you? Has it permeated your life to the point where it's recognized again and again, easily, quickly and instantly, every time a dilemma arises, every time you feel stuck in something, every time you start to feel like a victim—every time life becomes difficult, which is always going to be the case.

Has it started to permeate your understanding so that it becomes a basis for that understanding? So that it becomes difficult for you to personalize anything? That is neither hard nor far away. It's not terribly difficult; it's not climbing Mount Everest to get to that. Everybody in this room can get to that. Maybe you're well on your way; maybe you're halfway there; maybe you're ninety percent there. All I'm saying is, get all the way there. Get all the way to "depersonalizing" life. Depersonalize your life, so it's not "my life"; it's "*life*." Everybody in this room can live a depersonalized life where your anguish isn't yours.

Now, there's a price to pay for that, because if your anguish isn't yours, then ultimately, probably further down the road, the day will have to come where you recognize that your joys aren't yours either. Everything will have to get depersonalized. You'll have to take the personal out of everything, not just the stuff that's hard, but the stuff that you'd never trade for anything. Eventually the day has to come, if you want to go all the way down the path, when you don't feel *anything* belongs to you—no matter how personal it is—no matter how much you see it in you, but nowhere else. How could you, *just you*, have it? How could it come to you, if it isn't coming to if not all people, and if not even most people, at least many other people? How could anything just come to *you*? How could you have it so bad that it's worse for you than everybody else?

Now, that's easy to say, that's easy to remember when everything is fine, but when your life is falling apart, when you feel terrible, when you're in one of the worst moments of your life, the proof is when it's clear to you in those moments.

At the very least I'm suggesting—in fact, I'm reporting and guaranteeing—that you can get rid of all worry. No matter how big a worrier you are, worry can just leave your life. It doesn't mean you don't get upset, it doesn't mean you don't take care of business, or don't have to pay the rent, or if a hammer falls on your toe it won't hurt. It simply means you don't worry about it. It doesn't even mean you accept everything or say yes to everything. It only means you don't worry about it.

"No worry" just means *no worry*.

It doesn't even mean everything turns out fine. Everything can turn out horrible. But you didn't waste any time or energy worrying about it. As everybody knows, worry doesn't change a thing. Things turn out however they turn out whether you worry about them or not.

Most people will identify themselves as big worriers. What's amazing is big worriers will identify themselves as big worriers, and not-big worriers will identify themselves as big worriers! It's easy to see the difference when they start speaking. You may think you're a big worrier, and you may be. You may think you're a big worrier, and not be a big worrier at all. Whichever you are, don't worry about it!

This is never said, even in spiritual circles I don't hear this said very much, that the base minimum is you can simply get rid of worrying. It can be not part of your life. It can be not part of your habitual mental apparatus that you go into a worry mode. There's that old folk song, "It Takes a Worried Man to Sing a Worried Song." I never thought about it before, but it's true. First you have to be worry-prone to worry. You can't sing a worried song if you aren't a worried man. It doesn't matter what happens; the *worry precedes what happens.*

The tendency to worry about it is there, before there's something to worry about. And if there's nothing to worry about, you still can worry a little anyway. You can pick something, which is what we do.

I'm trying to remember how worry ended for me, but I can't remember. Because eventually you forget that you ever worried at all. Eventually the mechanism of how to worry gets forgotten. You forget the trick of how you make yourself worry. And before, I would have, if asked, have told you I'm a big worrier. And I would have been right.

Anna: What's the difference between a big worrier and not a big worrier?

Premodaya: A not-big worrier is somebody who, if you ask them, says they worry a lot. But if you listen to how they talk, you see that they don't. There's more positive there than they realize. They don't really give evidence of being big worriers. It's just evident.

Anna: They don't have sleepless nights?

Premodaya: They don't have sleepless nights due to worry, but they think they do. There *are* big worriers. There's no question. But there are also many people who believe they are big worriers, and they aren't.

See, worry isn't about trusting. The opposite of "worry" isn't "trustful."

The opposite of worry is *not worrying*. It's not esoteric; it's not a complex subject. It isn't fed into by lots of psychological and emotional complications. It's just worry. It's a habit. It's a learned behavior. It's not even psychologically deep or spiritually deep. But you have to hear that it's possible to literally never worry. You have to hear what most people never hear in their lifetime, that you don't have to be stuck in worry, that worry doesn't have to be your mental or emotional response to most things that you don't like, or that aren't the way you would like them to be.

The only reason it comes to mind tonight for me is how easy it is for most people to get to a point of being a non-worrier. It amazes me that more people don't get there. I think part of the reason is nobody ever told them it's possible.

I'm telling you more than that it's possible. I'm telling you that it's not even hard. But first you have to recognize that worry, as a tendency, isn't this big bear we think of it as. It's just a little bear cub.

Grant: When worrying leaves you, does it leave you little by little, or all at once?

Premodaya: I don't remember. All I remember is noticing one day that I hadn't worried about anything in a long time. And then I suddenly realized: I don't worry about anything anymore. I was a little taken aback, because I hadn't noticed it. I don't know if I'm the typical example, but I certainly know that all of these kinds of things can end either dramatically or undramatically. You can suddenly feel them leave you, or you can wake up one day and without any big fanfare recognize that: Wait a minute, what was there for thirty years doesn't seem to be there anymore, and I don't think it has been there for a year or two, and I have never noticed before.

This is possible with everything: everything psychological, emotional, and even spiritual. There are only two forms of spiritual change: sudden (and more dramatic therefore), or gradual (and you notice it after the fact). The answer to your question is, both are possible. And it doesn't matter—what matters is getting to the point where worry has left you (or whatever it is), it doesn't have to be worry—whatever is plaguing you. Whatever is taking your energy needlessly can be not any more part of your life, part of how you habitually experience.

People often get caught in this question of, "How will it happen?" Does it matter? Does it matter how it happens, if it happens? People always want to know. That's probably natural. People want to know ahead of time, "What will it look like? How will it feel? How does it happen?" I'm frequently saying to people: What does it matter? It will happen for you this way, it will happen for him that way, it will happen for her that way. Because you're not him and you're not her. This universe is so free! You're free to sing a worried song as long as you like.

Anna: I would like you to summarize what helps you not to worry; I would like to have an example. I like theory and abstract things, but sometimes it's good to be pragmatic.

Premodaya: This isn't a theory; this is a testimony. I'm giving you my testimony that worry can end for you.

Anna: You have to deal with certain issues, right? So how do you deal with things?

Premodaya: By dealing with them. You're able to put it so clearly, and not see your own point.

Anna: My point is, maybe there's something positive in worry, if it's not over-excessive. For example, you might get better organized, or hurry, or don't take things too easy, or think about things you might forget—if you're worrying about it.

Premodaya: Be sure you aren't talking about concern. Concern and worry aren't the same. Worry is a kind of a low-grade anguish, a low-grade misery, a small suffering. Being concerned with something isn't necessarily a suffering. You're making it very clear. The confusion is: What exactly is worry? Let's define our terms: worry is a low-grade suffering or misery of unneeded concern about things that will turn out the same whether you worry about them or not.

Beth: Would you say, in actuality, that it's the law of attraction? What you're worried about is going to turn out in a negative way, if it's in a negative vein?

Premodaya: No, I'm not saying that. I'm saying worry is all in your head. And all you're going to attract when you worry is more worries. It's a process, a habit, a groove. If you start worrying about every thought you have and what it's going to attract or repel in the ether out there or what it brings to you or doesn't bring to you, eventually you'll go nuts!

What I'm suggesting is, worry is a very simple subject, although if you're caught in a reasonable amount of worry, the average amount of worry, it seems like a complex subject. All I'm trying to clarify is that worry, in and of itself, doesn't have these tremendous powers that people ascribe to it. It's a small problem, that seems big when you're in it—just like water seems very wet when you're sitting the middle of the puddle. But when you have gotten up and stepped out of it, there's not a whole lot of wetness. It quickly dries off. Worry is just like that. When worry starts to drop away from you, it's easy. It evaporates more and more by itself. But first you have to hear that that's possible, that you don't have to live a life that's really stuck in a groove of worry as a constant companion.

I'm not trying to teach you methods to not worry, because the methods are endless. You can find your own method. First you have to accept that it's possible. I'm just trying to get you to accept that it's possible. And that's difficult, that's very difficult. If this was a room of average people off the street, most people would be yelling at me by now, saying, "What are you talking about? It's not possible to not worry. Some things are going to make you worry. That's how it is." I want to make sure for you, those who know better than that, that you actually get it, that you get that it's possible, that you don't get caught in all of these other questions and concerns about, well, what happens if …?

All that happens is: You don't worry anymore. You still have all your same concerns. You still have all the same problems. You just don't worry about it. Worry is an add-on.

Dylan: That's the part I'm not getting. How a concern is different. Then how would one respond or react to things that we, in our worry state, would think would be absolutely crises—like a health crisis, or all of your money's gone in one day.

Premodaya: You just did. By seeing it as a crisis and not seeing it as a worry. Crises are real. Worries aren't.

Dylan: Are you saying that the person that it's happening to wouldn't be upset?

Premodaya: No. They could be upset, but they wouldn't be worried. Worry and upset aren't synonymous. Worry is an add-on. Worry means you go on to a track where you think about it, concern yourself with it, hash it over again and again, and feel bad about it, and all of that isn't necessary.

Felix: What you said earlier, about depersonalizing life—what is it that you have to accept in order to depersonalize?

Premodaya: That it isn't yours, that it doesn't belong to you personally, that you aren't any different from anybody else, that whatever can happen to you can only happen to you because it can happen to anybody.

If it can't happen to anybody, it can't happen to you. If it happened to you, it means it can happen to everybody and anybody. There's no thought you can have, that everybody else can't have. There's no feeling you can go through, that everybody else can't go through. There's no set of circumstances or life conditions that can be there for you, that can't be there for anybody else. If it can happen to you, it means it's not yours; it means it can happen to anybody. And this is simply a matter of understanding, of seeing it rightly, that nothing is yours. I'm not stating that as anything other than a fact. Nothing is yours.

The value in stating that is because the mistake we all make is personalizing it, saying it's *mine*; feeling it as, "Oh my God, look what's happened to me." But it couldn't happen to you unless it could happen to anybody.

To depersonalize your life, you have to start seeing that whatever it is, can happen to anybody. You weren't the target. God didn't look down and say, "Aha! I'm giving it to *him* today!" It just circulates.

I witnessed an accident this morning. This man was innocently driving, following the law, following all the rules of the road, turning only when he was supposed to turn. But he got creamed. His brand new beautiful car was destroyed.

The only reason that happened, is because it could happen to anybody. Today was *his* turn. Ten years ago, maybe it was *your* turn. Ten years from now, maybe it's *your* turn. Everybody in this room, if they live a normal life span, won't leave this life without having been in a car accident. And that's because, if it can happen to one, it can happen to anybody.

So why worry about it? It's going to happen. Worry is, "Am I ever going to be in a car accident?" Concern is, recognizing that sooner or later, you will be in a car accident. Which one seems real? The only way to worry is to live a personalized life. Worry means personal. The concern means impersonal. Concern means, "I recognize this is possible," or "I recognize these things happen," and it's not personal.

Anna: To identify worry, maybe also, the difference between being upset or being worried is actually these "what if" thoughts.

Premodaya: Of course. You hit the nail on the head, absolutely right. Every worry is "what if" and every "what if" isn't real.

Anna: It's more about being realistic or thinking of probabilities.

Premodaya: Thinking of any probabilities is worrying because the probabilities don't care what you think or how much you worry. They'll happen as they happen. You can't figure out the probabilities. You'll spend your whole life figuring them out. That's called worrying.

The truth is, you never have to worry about anything, because you're worrying about what *isn't real*. If you can call it a worry, then it isn't real. If you can call it a worry, then it's a "what if." It's a hypothetical case that you made up in your mind that doesn't really involve anything real or doesn't even really involve you (it involves some mind trip that you've fallen into). The trouble is we all do this chronically. We all chronically have this tendency. My suspicion is most of us are taught how to do this. You have to be taught how to worry. It seems valid. Somebody said earlier: It seems like there's something positive in it. It seems like there's at least something to be gained from it.

But think about it intelligently for more than a minute or two and it's obvious there's nothing to be gained by it. Worry is anguishing yourself needlessly. Now, I suppose ICODA could mount a workshop, "How to Stop Worrying," and that would be fine. But I'm not interested in it. Because I believe you can find your way to stop worrying. But I don't believe you can until and unless you accept that that's possible for you. That it's not climbing a mountain to be free of worry. It's just a small hill. That's really all I want you to hear. What's important to me to impart is that you hear it clearly and understand it, that this isn't a bear that you're wrestling with. If worry is an issue for you in any way, you aren't wrestling with a ferocious bear, although it seems like it when you try not to worry. You're really wrestling with yourself. You're wrestling with your own tendency to anguish yourself needlessly by focusing on what isn't real, by playing out scenarios in your head that not only have not happened but aren't likely to happen. When you're worrying, you're playing the probabilities game, and it's a losing game. You can't win.

A worry-free life is not a grand goal. It won't take you to the mountain top; it just means you won't worry anymore. It's certainly good. If worry is there in your life to any significant degree, it's certainly a good place to get to, but it is not a great spiritual achievement. It's not even a great psychological achievement if you ask me, but I think most psychologists would disagree.

Worrying is its own animal. It has its own shape and it's its own groove, and it has nothing to do with anything else. Certainly, those who have a tendency to be anxious have more of a tendency to worry. But worry can stand on its own. Worry is really a specific subject. It's not this psychologically complex topic like people want to make it. I know how possible it is for reasonable people to get beyond worry. If you're reasonable, if you're intelligent, and if you can accept that there's such a thing (and it's not even a big dramatic deal) to have worry not be a part of your life, that's the beginning. But first you have to hear it, believe it, and accept it. And when I say believe it, I mean believe that it's possible for you.

Casey: I have a comment. I considered myself ninety-nine point zero percent worry-free. And then I recently moved to L.A. from San Diego County. It's only been three weeks, and three crises have happened already. And I know that I was called here this evening, because even though I was keeping myself as centered as possible, I was starting to get into the worry mode, which I have let go of, most of. The crises were happening, and I was observing them, but something else was going on inside of me. Now I found myself here, and it's like—OK, don't go into that worry mode.

Premodaya: Don't add anything on. Deal with the crisis, see the crisis, do what you have to in response to the crisis, concern yourself with the crisis to the degree you need to concern yourself—if there's a pain in the crisis, you will experience the pain of it, if there's an anguish in it, maybe it's unavoidable to feel the anguish of it, but don't add worry into it. Don't add this round and round, merry-go-round of mental hashing that goes nowhere except more round and round.

The good news is that you're sitting here saying, "I'm ninety-nine percent worry-free." You're the proof of what I'm saying. If you ask me, ninety-nine percent is good enough. On that issue, a hundred isn't needed. The only thing that's happening is you're worried about that one percent. You must be a little bit like, "Why can't I get to a hundred percent? Look, I started worrying—that shouldn't happen." That's an added worry right there. Ninety-nine percent puts you ahead of most of the human race. It's plenty more than good enough. What if your whole life goes into upheaval, which it does every time a person moves, and especially if you move into another city, and a moment of worry happens—so what? Ninety-nine percent? Good for you. Fantastic. Don't look for one hundred percent. Because that hundred percent, that one percent missing becomes the worry itself.

Casey: Yes, I started feeling a little guilty.

Premodaya: All kinds of things start to be felt. Recognize the rarity of being able to say, "I'm ninety-nine percent worry-free." And, be glad. If a moment of worry happens here, a moment of worry happens there, so what? How different is that from most people, who have some kind of worry every single day? You had to have three crises happen to have worry come up. Good for you. And I'm not giving you positive talk. It's the truth. I'm not suggesting you take a positive attitude. I'm against "positive attitudes." I'm suggesting you look at the reality of this. You're a human being who has gotten to a point of life where you can say, "I'm ninety-nine percent worry-free." Wow! Stay with that, that's some good stuff. And if a moment of worry happens in a time of particular difficulty, so what? That doesn't negate that you're ninety-nine percent worry-free. Have that one percent. Enjoy it! Seriously.

Darshana: It seems like worry is often used as a distraction? For instance, right after my father died, we were also waiting to hear on an apartment, and staying at a hotel at the time. My worry was at a peak that week which I found so inappropriate. My father had just died, and it was really painful, and here I was caring so much about whether we got this apartment or not. It seems like the amount of worry you would be able to get rid of would equate to how much you still would need to use it as a distraction. Does that make sense?

Premodaya: Well, that's certainly possible, but what's more common is how much things are being personalized. Worry is just extreme personalization. But of course, what you're saying obviously has to be true for some people; it's used as a distraction. For some people, worry comes in handy in many situations. That doesn't make it a benefit; it just means you can use it to shield yourself from something else. And that something else you're shielding yourself from, in those cases, will always be something that would come as an even bigger worry. But it always amounts to energy that goes into going round and round instead of dealing with whatever has to be dealt with.

Your story is really an example of how worry is its own track. What you seem to be suggesting is, "Well, my father had just died; why wasn't I so mired in my grief, or so concerned with that situation? Why would I be so worried about getting this apartment?" Because that's what you were worried about. Because worry is its own track, and it doesn't matter what else is going on. It doesn't matter if your father just died. It doesn't matter if you just lost all your money in the stock market. If you're already worried about something, you're perfectly capable of staying on that track as much, and as long, as you like. Worry is self-perpetuating. It's a track. It's a groove. But it's always a groove of extreme personalizing. Me, mine, I.

Malik: I thought you might be suggesting that you were using it as a distraction maybe to not feel the grief. With my whole avoidance issues, I might have that worry playing to avoid. That might be my distraction.

Premodaya: I'm suggesting the exact opposite. I'm suggesting that worry is not a defense that people use to avoid something else, or stay distracted in difficult times, or to accomplish any other purpose. I'm suggesting, if that was the case, it would be more of a bear than what I'm trying to communicate. I'm suggesting it's not a bear, because it's so small. Because worry is just about worrying itself. It's not about using it for greater purposes—even if they are psychologically avoidant, it's still a greater purpose. I'm saying worry is just worry. That's why it's possible to get to the point where you can say, "My life is ninety-nine percent worry-free." Because it's not this big hairy thing that has to be contended with and wrestled with and overcome, and a million things have to happen before it's possible. It's actually a small problem, believe it or not. But it's a big problem if you haven't started yet to move beyond it.

The ninety-nine percent lady, do you agree from your own experience, that, when you're ninety-nine percent you see how small the problem really is? That it's not this huge thing that overshadows your life?

Casey: Absolutely. I do have to say, though, that it was a big problem that brought me to this realization. And then I started realizing that none of this other stuff is important.

Premodaya: Yes. But the realization was not the big problem; the getting there was not a big problem; the catalyst may have been a big problem. What I'm saying is you don't need a big catalyst to get there. For you that's how it worked. Fine. Whatever happens, happens. But it's not a requirement, is what I'm saying. For you it doesn't matter, because it's already ninety-nine percent. But for everybody else who can't say that, it's important to hear that you don't have to go through a terrible crisis to find the way out of worry. It doesn't have to be a big deal. It can be a simple, easy road.

I wasn't even trying to be a non-worrier. I was quite happy worrying all the time. I enjoyed it, like most big worriers do. It's an ego fulfillment. Because worry is always *you* at the center. I wasn't looking how not to worry, which is why I was quite surprised when I realized, "There doesn't seem to be any worry ever anymore. How did that happen?" And based on that is why I can say to you that it doesn't have to be dramatic.

Benjamin: It could also be a push to something better. I realized that worries are for something that is not of the present; my perception of what were the worries, actually became challenges that I was eager to accomplish.

Premodaya: The delusion is that the worries got you to that understanding. The worries didn't get you there; the seeing that the worries weren't necessary is what got you there. The seeing that the worries don't add anything, don't benefit anything. What would have been even easier on you is to have gotten there without having to worry.

Benjamin: That's what we're all trying to accomplish.

Premodaya: I don't know if anybody in this room is trying to accomplish it or not. It's just the subject that came up tonight. But it's a topic that if you bring it up, most people will say that they have an issue about worrying. So, I probably can't go wrong on that topic.

Benjamin: You said earlier you had something against positive attitudes.

Premodaya: What I have against it, is that what most people mean when they use the term "positive thought" or "positive attitude," is not really a positive attitude. It's a replacement. It's a self-delusion. And it's an adoption of a phony stance. "I'm going to be positive about this even though it's terrible." It's a cover-up. There's a huge cavernous difference between real positiveness and "adopting" a positive attitude. If you can actually adopt a positive attitude, perfect. I'm all for it. But that isn't what most people do when they say, "I've adopted a positive attitude." Most people are simply fooling themselves. Putting an overlay, hiding from the real feeling, hiding from the real situation, hiding themselves from meeting it, feeling it, experiencing it, dealing with it.

That's why I'm against "positive thinking," because it's usually phony. It's usually self-avoidant. Every time you deal with something for real, literally every time—every time you meet it one hundred percent, and experience it one hundred percent, and move through it, it will naturally take you to the positive. You will always come out the other end—there's always the positive end. The end of everything is positive. But if you short-cut the process by phonying up a positive attitude, you will never get there. I'm not against really positive thinking. I'm against unreal positive thinking.

True, positivity of mind happens to you; you don't adopt it. It's a result of not avoiding what has to be met. And one of the great ways to avoid what has to be met is to worry about it instead of meeting it. Worry is always a form of procrastination.

The good news is, in a random assembly of spiritually sincere people, there can be one person—which is a big proportion out of such a small group—who can report that "I'm ninety-nine percent worry-free." If that doesn't encourage you to accept that that's completely possible for you, then I don't know what can. And I suspect there are other people in the room who could say they're ninety-nine percent worry-free. But until everybody in the room can say it, it's probably valuable to discuss it a little bit like we have tonight. Don't think of worry, and the tendency to worry, and how worry operates in your life, as a make it or break it issue, as one of the bears that you wrestle with to try to evolve into a better life, an easier life, a more spiritual life, whatever it is. Think of it rightly as a small roadblock that can be overcome without gargantuan efforts. Think of it as something that absolutely can leave you. And consider all the knowledge, all the understanding, all the insight you already have about it.

Numerous people tonight indicated a very clear understanding of how worry is an add-on, how it isn't necessary. How it's a self-propelled anguish, how it doesn't go anywhere, how it's about the future, the past, never about what's real right now—there's no lack of understanding in the folks that are here tonight. I'm just saying start using that understanding. If you really start using it, it wouldn't surprise me if worry starts to lessen and lessen and lessen more for you. You don't have to go to a special workshop, "How Not to Worry." You just have to start living what you already know a little bit more, from the understanding that it's completely possible for you, that it's not a big deal, that it's not the drama of all dramas. If worry ends for you, that won't be the most dramatic moment of your life or the greatest psychological or emotional achievement of your life. It just means you won't have a whole bunch of worries anymore. When things are upsetting, you will still get upset, more than likely. When things are difficult, they will still feel difficult. When something is critical, it will still feel like a crisis. When life brings troubles, you will still be faced with troubles. The only thing different is you won't worry about it. You won't add on one more layer of self-suffering.

CHAPTER 3

WILLINGNESS

Premodaya: Whether it's here at ICODA, or anywhere else, do you think you can get what you're after?

Maurice: With time and a lot of strenuous work, sure. If I will it, right?

Premodaya: No. Lots of people "will" lots of things and they don't happen. That's the bad news. The good news is it may not take any time and it may not take strenuous effort.

Maurice: I always expect the worst.

Premodaya: Well, stop that. Sometimes we think it will take gargantuan efforts to get to that spiritual place, or that emotional place, or whatever we're believing we have to get to. We see it here all the time. People in an hour, in an afternoon, in a split second [snaps fingers] get to these amazing places, and burdens of decades drop away. They come back, again and again. They come back six months later, a year later, and report that it was permanent. It really happened for them. So, you really don't know what's possible. If you're sincere and willing, then it's absolutely possible. The master key is "willing." Now willing doesn't mean that it will necessarily be exactly your way. Willing means you're willing for it to come any way that it comes, even if it doesn't vaguely resemble what you want. Is there that kind of willingness? Are you willing in that way?

Maurice: I think so.

Premodaya: Wonderful. Then everything is possible for you. Absolutely. If that's true, everything is possible. It has nothing to do with your will. It's your willingness, which is a vulnerability, an openness.

GOING DEEPER INTO INNER SPACE

Priya: I do feel more frequent awareness of being within, and I feel hesitant to say because sometimes when you say something, you lose the actual thing—a little bit more feeling within up toward the heart area. Occasionally you can see when you look at something that you zoom out there and you forget everything else, but sometimes you remember to remember, and there's that and an awareness of the place you're looking from, and big space; both are there together instead of just one or the other.

When there's just a space, it's almost like both things disappear. It seems like just awareness and not separation. When you try to look at things or close your eyes and think, "What is it? What's here, what's real, what am I, what's going on, what's now?" there's this feeling of "I'm looking" that interferes with the looking. It feels like less of that interference.

Premodaya: Are you happier?

Priya: I think so; it's not like a continuum.

Premodaya: It doesn't matter, does it?

Priya: No, it doesn't matter.

Premodaya: That's the proof that it's real. It's not about bliss or not bliss. It's not about a feeling state. Feeling states come and go, and we don't control them anyway. It's not about latching on to some preconceived idea of how it's supposed to feel or how it's supposed to be. When it's real, when more awareness really comes, when more presence really comes, when you really move higher, move closer to the Divine, you don't care what goes along with it, because the Truth is the Truth. You don't care if it feels this way or that way. If you care, then you're deluding yourself; then you haven't really opened more, but you have clearly opened more since you were here last time, a few weeks ago. Clearly. I'm just confirming it for you that it's real.

Priya: I noticed, at least one time that in feeling afraid, having that switch happen extinguished that fear for that moment, which seems like a feeling related thing.

Premodaya: Actually, it has nothing to do with feeling; it's attention; it's where your attention is. So now your attention goes in both directions, outward and inward. It's much bigger. Normally your entire life your attention goes up and looking out, and your entire training as a human being from the moment you're born is "go that way." Your energy is always moving in one direction and one direction only: out. What Priya is explaining very clearly is that it never goes inward. What you're describing is suddenly it's not just going out; it's also going in at the same time.

That's a radical turn. When that radical turn happens, everything changes; that's the beginning of everything changing, because for the first time you don't forget "you." For the first time you're part of the equation. For the first time, the inner landscape is included, not just the outer landscape. For the first time, the energy is actually moving in, and the inner space is as vast as the outer space; in fact, they are the same, but until you have a taste of that in your actual experience, you're stuck; you're caught in the trap of the outer. But all that has to happen is you bring the arrow around—even by force of will you can sometimes bring it around—and point it in; you turn your eyes inside out. That's what has happened for you, more spontaneously—spontaneous is always good—but it can be done with effort too. Many meditation techniques, many yoga techniques, are about turning the arrow this way.

Now it will get very interesting. You're correct that once the arrow turns this way at all, even a little bit, but for real, it brings you more up into the heart. Everything you're saying is true. If you have any doubts about it, I'm telling you: don't have any doubts. But you know in your experience it's real; you don't need me to confirm. Now just watch it; don't do anything. Watch how it works; watch how the attention goes back and forth and sometimes in both directions at the same time. Sometimes you'll see you're more inner oriented, and sometimes more outer oriented. Don't worry which it is; don't worry where the arrow is pointing, because it's happening spontaneously—that can be trusted. Allow it. It will take you deeper and deeper into the heart. Deeper and deeper into the inner space, and it will get sweeter and sweeter. Very good. Wonderful. You weren't looking for that when you came last time, were you? You were looking for a release from pain?

Priya: Yes, I thought it was seeking enlightenment but—

Premodaya: But you talked about having experienced a lot of grief; your husband recently passed away; you've been through a very difficult year; many difficult things have happened, and you've really been through the wringer. There was a lot of pain and a lot of anguish and a lot of grief that you felt you were carrying, and I think at least on the surface that's what your motivation was. This is not directly related to that; this is much better. This is a prime, living example of what can happen if you're sincere, if you're open, as you are—and many people come this way. You come to get rid of something. You come to a meeting like this or to a teacher, or to a spiritual group or to a book or to a church, or whatever it is. You come because the feeling is there that something has to be gotten rid of; something isn't bearable; something isn't tolerable and somehow it has to be pulled up and thrown away. It's a legitimate feeling; I'm not saying it's not. Who hasn't felt that for whatever reason at some point, if not much of their life? But the amazing grace of it is that often people come for that and end up getting something else; something that has nothing to do with pulling out the pain and throwing it out the door; has nothing to do with changing the experience of life; has something to do with falling more into yourself, more into what's real.

Who can say how that happened? That was the first time you'd come to ICODA, a few weeks ago; you came up in the chair and you talked about your grief and how you lost your husband and all the things you have gone through; and now you're reporting an opening of the heart, that's your sincerity. I said to you then: Your sincerity will take you where you need to go, and that's what has happened. Your sincerity took you further into your own heart. That's better than healing. That's better than getting rid of some unresolved grief. That's more profound and more true and more real than changing how you feel.

Priya: I want to be able to live with the awareness of the feeling that's there; I don't want to lose it.

Premodaya: Be willing to lose it, because if you try to hold on to it, if you tell yourself I want to keep this, it will veer off in some other direction. Then you're stopping the spontaneity of it. This is grace, and grace can't be grabbed.

Priya: You can't bargain with it.

Premodaya: You can't bargain with it, and you can't say to the sponta-neous flowering of awareness, "Hey, I want you to stick around, and I want you to be here at least six hours every day, and especially after dinner when I kind of get a little low energy. I want you to be there and perk me up." You can't make any bargains with the Beyond. What you can do is be grateful that this opening has happened and watch what form it con-tinues to take. Watch how it continues to evolve, and don't try to grab at anything.

Priya: What I meant was that the grief feels like a connection.

Premodaya: Absolutely. See, you don't need to grab anything, because your wisdom will take care of you. The grief is absolutely the connection. Don't push away anything and don't pull anything towards you. If grief is there, grief is there—accept it. If sadness is there, sadness is there—accept it.

Priya: And don't cling to them either.

Premodaya: Don't cling to them, don't push them away, and don't pull them in closer. That's how you let go: by not pushing away and by not pulling toward. All day, every day, seven days a week, three hundred and sixty-five days a year, the society is telling us, "push this away," "pull this in." Our own feelings are telling us, "if it's pleasant, pull it in; if it's un-pleasant, push it away." That's the basic mistake; that's the basic pushing away of life; that's the basic rejection of the Divine, of the Real. Because you're saying, "I want it my way," and the Divine isn't concerned with your way. In that moment, you're the barrier.

What you're really saying is somehow this has happened for you, this opening, and you see much more clearly how everything that's there, pleasant or unpleasant, wanted or not wanted, is part of it. That's an actu-al letting go; that's *acceptance*. This is tough to grasp until you see a living example of it: Acceptance and letting go are the exact same thing; they are two terms for the same thing; they aren't different. If you take nothing else from this evening, if you get that and get it fully, your whole life will change. This is the fruit of your sincerity.

As far as I'm concerned this is literally a miracle. A person comes one time, sits in the chair, bares her soul—and out of that willingness to be open, to be naked, to face whatever is real—grace descends and opens her eyes, is one way to tell the story, one way to characterize it; you can characterize it many ways, but what's better than that? How do you explain that? That's the mystery of the Beyond. That's the Divine, the Eternal, the Unknown, in actual manifestation.

We think it's something far away; we think it happens to somebody else; must have happened to that guy sitting in the big chair; it happened to Jesus, whatever; but it's not like that. It's not far away, it's not remote, it's not ancient, it's not something that happens to somebody else; it's something that's happening to you right now. The question is, can you plug in and see how it's happening and to what degree it's happening, and how you're either preventing it or supporting it, whether you're honoring it or whether you're denying it?

Because really, what is she saying? She's saying life is happening. Well, who in this room is life not happening to? That's all these people are talking about when they say, "Be fully in the now, and that's all it takes." It means, you're already there. It doesn't mean you go somewhere; it means you can't be anywhere else. How can you be anywhere but in life right now? You've never been anywhere else. You didn't put yourself there. You didn't fill out a form and say, "Yes, I would like to be in life, and I would like to be there from about 1946 to about 2088." Yet somehow, here you are. So, that "*here you are,*" can be trusted, because here you are. That's now. Forget everything else and put all your attention into that, all your energy of life into that, because there's nothing to lose, because you're already there; you have never been anywhere else. When have you never been in life? Show me a moment since you were born that you weren't in life, in you, a moment that you weren't you and that you weren't life itself. Let's say it that way: *You are life itself.* You are not a body that's alive—you're life itself. You are not this body—you're the life that this body represents.

"Waking up" just means knowing that, not having any illusions that you're anything else, not having any weird self-induced trances and ideas, and borrowed beliefs and cultural ideas, that you're anything other than existence itself in that chair where you're sitting. When you really start to get that, that swallows you up for real. What you're experiencing is how it's coming to swallow you, and that's fearsome. Fear may happen; anguish may happen; agony may happen. It can be painful. It isn't just love and light and bliss folks. Something is trying to swallow you whole. But if you let it, you won't be sorry, because it's the Beyond that's trying to swallow you; it's the Divine that's trying to swallow you, the ultimate letting go. All the other letting go's are little practices for the ultimate letting go, which is, "OK, swallow me, I give up."

SIMPLY *ALLOW*

Vivian: Do you teach any techniques to transcend the mind?

Premodaya: That's all I teach, but not through techniques. Through accessing that which is trying to access *you*. In the way we work here, it usually has to do with developing more willingness to allow. To allow what is. We do a lot of work here on willingness and allowing.

Vivian: Using techniques?

Premodaya: The technique is, allow more.

Vivian: I understand there are techniques that you use which automatically allow more. It connects you with this Truth, the Source, What Is.

Premodaya: We don't bother with the in-between; we just go right to allow.

Vivian: Without using any techniques or any practices specifically designed for that purpose?

Premodaya: The technique is allowing. Anything that stands in the way of bigger allowing, we deal with.

ACCEPTANCE IS THE MASTER KEY

Jesse: I made a New Year's resolution and it's just one word, and it's "acceptance." I had it printed on a leather band so I would remember: Acceptance.

Premodaya: That's the magic word. Even just in these few words you're expressing absolute sincerity. I sense you're expressing how significant and important and real this is for you, so I want to do whatever I can not only to honor that but to take it as seriously as you're taking it.

Jesse: What I was going to ask is, up until a couple of years ago I basically occupied two states, if you will. I like to use the analogy of being in a prison: One state would be with me as the prisoner and the other would be with me as the warden or the judge. Basically, that was it, it was those two states that I occupied, and I can go back and forth like that, and right now I'm the prisoner. I was fortunate enough to escape those two roles a couple years back.

Premodaya: How did that happen?

Jesse: I actually had a breakdown, I ended up at psych hospital for four or five days and I came out and it cracked me open in a way I couldn't have done on my own. I spent a lot of time free, but then gradually back into those roles, back into the two. And occasionally I still am free or open or connected but few and far between. I have seen it now; instead of two, I have to worry about three different roles, but I certainly prefer the latter. I was wondering how I can apply acceptance to that? I know accepting myself, accepting others, accepting the world, not fighting reality; I intellectually know too much, but knowing in the gut is a different story.

Premodaya: So, what do you know in your gut right now?

Jesse: I know that I'm nervous. If I'm in the judge or warden role I'm not nervous. If I'm free I'm not nervous, but I spend so much time in this prisoner role. How would I apply acceptance to this? Accept the judge, accept being the prisoner?

Premodaya: I'm curious a little bit how you got to acceptance. You said New Year's resolution, so what's the thinking or whatever the process is, that got you to the idea of acceptance? Maybe you read it somewhere, maybe you heard it somewhere, maybe you came up with it—whatever it is, I'd be curious to hear how you got from wherever you were to acceptance.

Jesse: I read it; I heard it; I came up with it; all three of those. What I found in the last two years is I'm rarely critical of the outside world like I used to be. I've compared it to being in the middle of a sphere where the interior of the sphere just *mirrors* and everywhere I look it's right back at me, so I think that accepting is now geared towards myself. As I become more accepting of the outside world and the outside people in my life, it's more accepting of myself. I think that's where I'm at and why I came up with the resolution. Even if I wanted to, there's no going back.

Premodaya: I would call that wisdom. Would you call that wisdom?

Jesse: It's something I aspire to. That particular statement, I'd call it progress. But I'm not too good at complimenting myself. Having experienced it, I know it's true. I know it's real.

Premodaya: That what's true, what's real?

Jesse: That place, if you will, that state of being connected, of being open, of being not nervous in situations that might otherwise make me nervous, of being at peace, of being comfortable—I don't know how many words there are.

Premodaya: Good. You already know and accept that it is, in truth, really truly possible for you? Or is there some vestige that still says it's a pipe dream?

Jesse: Society, people, the everyday world, and I'm tremendously outnumbered, including all of my family and my friends, so it makes it seem a little challenging, but it doesn't take away from my belief that it's the truth, that it's real. It just throws me back in that prison setting.

Premodaya: That what's real? That you could find peace, is that what you're saying?

Jesse: That there's something beyond the self, beyond the ego. To feel detached is just amazing. This I think is the largest obstacle in my life, this "judge work," as I call it.

Premodaya: You're saying to me that you know beyond any doubt that you can get there, that it's possible for you to find that beyond self, that beyond selfness? Your friends say either it doesn't exist, or you can't do it; your family says either it doesn't exist, or you can't do it—whatever form of "no" they're saying. Nevertheless, you know through the fact of inner knowing that this is absolutely possible for you and it's absolutely the truth. Is that what you're saying?

Jesse: Yes.

Premodaya: FANTASTIC. With a capital "Fan" and a capital "Tastic."

Jesse: Now can you show me a shortcut on how to get there? It seems that everyone else is in their own prison also.

Premodaya: Don't go there. For just a minute stay at: You know it to be possible for you. How many people do you think there are on planet earth out of six point three billion people who could say that they know absolutely, and without doubt, that it's possible for them to go beyond self, that they know, whether they reach it or not—they know it's possible to find Truth, or to find peace, or whatever is the right phrase?

Jesse: A small percentage.

Premodaya: So small that it takes your breath away. Here is my welcome speech to you: Welcome to the tiniest minority in the world—those who have heard some call of the deep inner voice and have had the wisdom, the intelligence and the sanity to take it seriously, to listen to it, and to start following it. You're quite right; your family probably will not support you. You're probably very accurate that your friends will not be a help to you in this. When the real search begins, and you have crossed the threshold—as you have—that's characterized by the singular statement of, "I know there's no going back"—then it's very important that you understand (and I'm glad you see it) that it's not a road you go down with a whole lot of cheering fans; your family and friends won't cheer you on. The first part of acceptance that I would encourage you to recognize is the somewhat solitary nature of that road. The real support, the real friendship, the real possibility of someone holding your hand as you go down that road is people who are also your like-minded, folks who are on a spiritual path. So I think you've come to the right place. I think any place you would have come would be the right place, because I think you've come to that point where you can actually start to trust your inner knowing. That's what I would encourage you to start doing as of now: Whether the judge is there or not, whether you experience yourself as a prisoner or not, whatever state, as you rightly call it, is operating to, at the same time to recognize that the inner knowing is not false, that the truth of how it feels is, as you say, *real*—and to really get that, to really let that live you more.

Having said all that, let me go back to your question. Let me say to you as absolutely the first thing, and have no doubt about it: You have found the master key. Acceptance *is* the master key. The fact that you can walk in here tonight and say, "Could you help me with acceptance? I've made a New Year's resolution. I don't usually do that, but I've decided acceptance is the key—I've made this band to remind myself"—well, you won the lottery. You have found the master key. The rest is all going to be about how to live it. The rest is all going to be how to make it happen. You're asking the right questions, and I'm happy to help you in any way that I can with fleshing out the answers to those questions, but you have got to get it—I want you to get it now, right here, right now—that you have found the master key. Have no doubt about it ever again. All the inner knowing that tells you and has told you and is still telling you that that is right, is right. That's why I said to you, you can really start trusting your inner knowing because it got you to this; it got you to *the* master key—you found it. Judge, no judge, prisoner, no prisoner, you found it. Start by knowing that absolutely, take that in absolutely, trust that absolutely. Can you do that?

Jesse: I'm just kind of happy about it, actually. It has been a long road.

Premodaya: You should be happy about it. No matter how long the road ahead is, you have found the master key. Tiny, tiny, minority of humans on this earth get to the point you have now gotten to, so I don't care how many breakdowns you have had; I don't care what horrible experiences life has put you through; I don't care how many judgments and criticisms you have of yourself, of everybody else, of the world, of me, of whatever. What matters is you have found the master key, and to know that and cling to that, attach yourself to that, get attached to that, and then everything is possible for you.

WITHOUT ACCEPTANCE, NOT MUCH IS POSSIBLE

Premodaya: What brought you?

Eric: I'm interested in change, in personal growth, in transformation. I have read quite a lot of your website and it seemed to be a place towards achieving that.

Premodaya: Transformation means many things, and often people have varying notions of what it means for them and varying intentions and varying motives. What's your motive for transformation? What are you looking for?

Eric: A huge thing for me is resolving a lot of the pain traumas of the past and becoming clear on what my purpose is here. I have gone through enough to know that change is possible, that you do get clear.

Premodaya: What if none of that happened for you? What if this life continued just as you know it now and there was not any big change, significant transformation, any further healing of any trauma or pain. What if it stayed just the way it is?

Eric: I can live with that.

Premodaya: I love that answer. I love it when somebody can say that. You said it with clarity. That's quite something, for a person to say, "If it never goes beyond what it is right now, that's OK. I'm not in a complaint mode about it; I can live with that." That's standing on a firm ground. That's a certain spiritual maturity, a certain personal maturity that only comes from someone and can only come to someone who is sincere about change, who means it, who isn't just shopping or, "Let's see what's out there, let's see what's possible. Maybe I can change this in my life; maybe I can improve that." It's really only possible to say what you said, from a much deeper place than that. It's not a statement everybody can make. It means—and maybe you know this better than I do, but I want you to hear it in case you haven't thought of it this way—that a really very advanced degree of acceptance has already occurred, and that's the coin of the spiritual realm. Without acceptance, not much is possible. With a level of acceptance that says, "If nothing happens, if it's just like this for my remaining days and who knows beyond that." If there's enough acceptance for that statement to be real, and I heard the reality in the way you said it, what I want to suggest to you is one of the most important transformations that could ever take place has already taken place.

Eric: I know what you're talking about.

Premodaya: I love hearing that, because most of the world doesn't have anywhere near this level of acceptance. Most of the world is striving; most people are struggling to get something, to be something, and the very struggle is the misery. The very striving is the suffering. The medicine, the antidote of acceptance, is never even considered, so it's a powerful thing to speak with someone who can show acceptance. We're lucky that way at ICODA. We just keep having these meetings and events and these amazing people show up who certainly have as much to teach as to learn.

HONESTY IS THE BEST SPIRITUAL POLICY

Premodaya: These 'Beyond Self' Evenings are more of a question/answer format, so if anybody has a burning question it would be good to get it on the table.

Dylan: I'm interested in your thoughts about how one maintains equanimity and one's realizations and one's stability, to whatever degree one has in Truth, when the physical body is a factor—when the body is ill or over-agitated and metabolically, energetically, out of balance. I admire those sages that I've heard of that can have horrendous physical sufferings and can still be well established in the Truth and equanimity without any real effects psychologically. Just wondering what you have to say about that general topic. Any recommendations?

Premodaya: My recommendation is that you forget all about it.

Dylan: About the physical?

Premodaya: No—about everything you said. My recommendation is that you recognize more truly that any idea of equanimity, or impression of equanimity you see in someone else, is an assumption. And any equanimity you think you have when you're feeling fine and there are no issues of health, or bodily state, or anything else, is also an assumption—is also a nonrecognition of the grandness of everything going on inside you and outside you. The idea of equanimity is our hope superimposed on what's really happening. Equanimity simply means: you think you're in balance. Non-equanimity means: you think you're out of balance. The kind of folks you're referring to—if they're the real deal—have come to the point of understanding that it's not about how it looks or being in balance. When that point of understanding is completely understood and achieved and becomes your true understanding, then there's no question of equanimity or non-equanimity, because then the flow that you call "you" is not in any way trying to resist the flow that you call "not you."

Then sickness isn't a tremendously different condition than health. Then stumbling isn't a tremendously different experience than walking straight. Then what matters isn't, "How do I feel?" or "How do I perceive myself?" or "What's going on with me?" What matters is *what is,* and not taking a stance toward *what is*—or you can call it "Truth," or you can call it "Reality," or you can call it "Existence," or you can call it "God." You can call it about one hundred and eighty other things, so take your choice, but call it something.

Call it something, because most of the world doesn't call it anything, doesn't recognize it. If you recognize it, then it's just a matter of what your stance is towards that—not what your stance is towards whatever conditions are going on around you or in you. The concern for equanimity is the mimicry, the imitation, of accepting life as it is. I would rather see you living life as it is, rather than your idea of life how it should be. If those folks you admire have achieved that, then that's what they're doing, but it's not about, "How do I find equanimity?" It's, "How do I find Reality?" If Reality includes equanimity—OK. But more importantly, if Reality *doesn't* include equanimity—OK. Is that intelligible?

Dylan: Yes. Are you saying that a radical OK with what is, would be what would be, if one gets to that point?

Premodaya: No. I'm saying: Lose all concern for the conditions that you're concerned with and then you'll be in tune with what is. Your concerns come out of your assumptions, your experiences, your interpretations, your expectations. I'm saying: Transcend the expectations. If you expect to be healthy, you're going to be upset if you're sick. If you expect to be in a state of feeling good, you're going to be upset if you feel bad. Every life that has ever been lived on this planet (or ever will be lived on this planet) has included in it both sickness and health, both balance and imbalance, both good days and bad days, both things you like and things you don't like. That's the higher understanding. The higher understanding is: If I choose, sooner or later I will always be disappointed, because life is going to bring what life brings, whether I'm choosing or not. My choosing is the problem. My choosing is what sets me up to say, "Equanimity is good. And non-equanimity is a problem."

Who said non-equanimity is a problem? I'm saying: See beyond that. See how that's a self-created problem. Your idea, in terms of the "sages" you're referring to, is that somehow they have reached some state or some ability, some special category that isn't available to you without you having traversed a great road and climbed a very high mountain.

Dylan: I do believe that. That's a functioning belief.

Premodaya: That's a problem. Because if it's believed to be or held to be that far away, there's no way for you to get there. Then it's something that happened for this one, three hundred years ago, or that one in India, but it really can't happen to me. I can't find what I need to find. I can't be in Reality in the same way, or in a similar way, because it's a high achievement. Maybe I'll make it, or maybe I won't. I believe these guys made it, but they're on a different level from me. That sets up an impossibility for you.

Dylan: How would I come to a reasonable conclusion about that? It could be just that I didn't try as hard as they did yet. That's kind of the way my mind works.

Premodaya: It's the way everybody's mind works. These are all ideas. These are all your assumptions. These are all your expectations. These are all self-created. These are all things that come from your mind or from your feeling and have nothing to do with the truth of what is. Have nothing to do with the conditions of life in the raw—meaning: what life brings. Life brings what life brings. Existence brought you. You did not have anything to do with it. In the same manner, existence brings whatever it brings in this life. The whole problem—literally, the whole problem!—is that we want "one from column A, one from column B—and *nothing*, don't give me anything out of column C." If we didn't have that list, if we didn't have that set of preferences, if we didn't look at life as a menu of good stuff and bad stuff—where's the problem?

Dylan: It would be a lot easier to live? Are you saying that?

Premodaya: No. Because it may not be easier to live. I'm saying it would be closer to what's true. That may turn out to be easier. That may turn out not to be easier. See, this is a subtler permutation of the same idea, "Well, if I achieve, this life will be easier." Who knows? It's the same choosing. "OK, I can accept that idea, but life will be easier, right?" Because now it has moved to a little subtler level of, "Well, I will accept that some may be bad, some may be good, some may be pleasant, some may be unpleasant—but at least it's easier." It's the same thing—easier versus harder. No guarantee.

Dylan: Does what you're saying imply that this sort of longing for the Absolute or whatever it is, is somehow intrinsically false?

Premodaya: That's not the longing for the Absolute. That's the longing for an easier life. You have to be honest with yourself about what you're striving for. If you look at what you're really saying, your questions are all built around striving for some preference of yours.

Dylan: Yeah, for not suffering. Which seems to me to be normal and natural. That's why I'm trying to understand exactly what you're saying that is not correct or false about it.

Premodaya: No, it's just a question of telling yourself the truth. Here is what you're really saying: at the level you're experiencing, it's not the longing for the Ultimate or the Divine—it's the longing for the end of suffering.

Dylan: Right.

Premodaya: And that's a preference.

Dylan: I guess I was equating the two. That if there were a merging or full realization of the Absolute or God or Truth, that it would equal not suffering.

Premodaya: I'm saying that's your idea. What if knowing God fully leads to more suffering than you ever imagined?

Dylan: Then I will go down to the bar or whatever, you know. Honestly, I'm not clear about that in myself.

Premodaya: That's all I'm saying. I'm saying—throw away, get rid of, eject all these preconceived notions of, "If I go higher, what is it going to look like? If I get closer to Truth, how am I going to feel? If Reality gets more real in my life, what is it going to bring me?" Who knows? Maybe a worse life than you ever imagined. Who knows? This is the whole illusion we create for ourselves—that we have ideas about how it will look, how it should look, and how we want it to look and, unfortunately (I guess it's unfortunate), Reality has nothing to do with what we would like it to be. Reality could not care less about what you or I would like it to be.

Dylan: How I'm structuring my relation to it is going to have a different effect in how I live my life. That's what I'm saying; it doesn't seem that the type of aspiration that I'm talking about is not right to have.

Premodaya: I'm not saying any of it is wrong to have. I'm saying—see it correctly. See it correctly.

Dylan: Can you help me understand a little more?

Premodaya: Seeing it correctly means, if your desire is for less suffering, don't tell yourself that's a desire for God. Or don't tell yourself that's a desire for Truth, unless and until you can say, "Less suffering, more suffering—either one is OK with me if it brings me to God, if it brings me to Truth." That's the only reliable measure of how much you might be deluding yourself about what you really want. You have to be clear about what you want. What I'm suggesting to you personally is that some of the things you say you want—there's nothing wrong with them, but understand them as your wants, not as the road to the Divine.

Dylan: Yeah, I've been under that belief. You're correct. I equate that, in other words the nirvana, the paradise, the extinction of suffering, and so on.

Premodaya: Those are preconceived notions about how it should look. I'm saying that no one knows what it's going to look like for you—least of all you.

Dylan: In the face of that, then the bottom line would be to drop the desire completely?

Premodaya: No. See what you really want and what it is, and don't tell yourself it's some other ideal that may be totally sincere, but don't fool yourself about it.

Dylan: I could be at a level of still fooling myself—that I'm not aware. What's the next step to eliminate that?

Premodaya: By really being honest with yourself. By asking yourself if you're being honest. The problem is we experience what we experience, and we have absolute freedom in that—a freedom that is mind-boggling. So free that you can suffer as much as you want, in any way you want, over anything you want—real or unreal. So, you can be the emperor of earth, you can have fifty thousand wives (the most beautiful women who have ever lived), you can live in the greatest palace that has ever been, you can eat the best food that anyone has ever eaten, and you can suffer like nobody has ever suffered, because you're that free. You have that much freedom that you're able to choose that. You are able to live that, if you so choose. You're able to convince yourself of anything you really are adamant about convincing yourself of. That's the power of the mind.

Everybody knows this. Everybody has met, has seen, has interacted with, has even seen up close, people who are tremendously disadvantaged. People who have nothing. People who probably will never have anything, who suffer almost not at all and are tremendously happy—and they radiate that happiness; they generally show a very good mood. And I think most of us have met people who seem to have the world on a string (as they say). Who may have fortune and fame, or whatever it may be; may have a better car than you and me; may have a better material life than you and me; may have the adulation of many people—and you can see it—and they will tell you that they are miserable and depressed.

This has to give you a clue that the measure of suffering isn't my measure, Gabriel's measure, Christopher's measure, anybody's measure. The measure of suffering is: If *you* say it's suffering. Because you can have diamonds and call it "suffering," and someone else can have diamonds and call it "joy." The whole dilemma is that it's so left in your hands, and it's left in your hands because this is the degree of freedom that's available in this existence. This existence is generous beyond comprehension. The proof of that, if you want a proof is: Have you ever gotten anything that you really wanted, that you really enjoyed, that you really coveted, that really meant a lot to you, that you can't in a few seconds of thinking about it recognize as a gift from life? Not so much something that you somehow got, although you may have taken steps and gotten it, but that it's actually, simply a gift from existence. That's the generosity of existence.

This universe is a generous universe. So generous, so giving, so open, that if you prefer suffering, "Be my guest," says the universe. "I'm not going to prevent you. I want you to know your freedom." That's what the universe basically says—"I want you to know your freedom. In that freedom, if you want to suffer, I'm not going to stop you." We can spend many nights (if not all the rest of the nights for the next hundred years) trying to come up with a valid definition, objectively, of what is "suffering." Buddhism has come up with some very useful ones, but, ultimately, you have to come to a point where you come to terms with *your* suffering, and that will take a completely different road for me, than for you, than for him, than for her. Nobody can do it for you. Nobody can make you do it. And nobody can give you the definition that's right for you. You can get some insights along the way from various traditions and various paths and various teachings and various brilliant gifts that have been given to humanity, but, ultimately, it's what you come to yourself—maybe with the aid of those gifts, maybe with the aid of those pieces of wisdom—but ultimately, it's you facing the simple and horrifying fact that you're here; suffering is here, and it's totally up to you what happens with that.

Now, what most people do (not the kind of people that come to a meeting like this) is to blame something or someone other than oneself. The other basic tendency is to blame oneself in a way that is absolutely not legitimate. Either you take it out on yourself, or you take it out on something or someone else, but the cause is always seen as a rational cause. As: A causes B. And suffering doesn't work that way. This is not a mind problem. This is not something people can figure out, although people try to figure it out. This is an existential problem. This is a problem that involves your whole self and your whole relating to existence. The wise man is the one who faces it. The wise man is the one who says, "I'm going to go into this and I'm going to find the answer that is the actual answer for me." Everybody who has ever done that has done that in a different way—because everybody is different—but ends up finding themselves in the same place. That's how traditions get born because the place is recognizable.

Dylan: So out of those realizations, can there be then some general principles that are valid for all of us?

Premodaya: The principles are the same for everybody. One principle I have already elaborated on is being brutally honest with yourself. Getting to the practice of not fooling yourself quite so easily, quite so habitually.

Dylan: Is it necessary to find out why you're suffering or can you just turn around and go towards a brighter day? Focus on what you do want?

Premodaya: You can drop the whole thing in a heartbeat. It's an absolute possibility. You can drop the whole thing in one second, or you can come at it from endless other directions.

Dylan: When you say drop the whole thing in a heartbeat, do you mean drop it never to be picked up again? You're saying a person has the ability to do that? Would that ability have preconditions of a certain amount of awareness?

Premodaya: No. The precondition is you're willing to drop every idea you have.

Dylan: I'm trying to understand what exactly you mean. If I understood it more—

Premodaya: That's why you're not going to do it, because you have a precondition. "First, I have to understand it. Then I'll do it." Whatever way I explain it to you, you will come up with a precondition to fool yourself of why you can't do it, or shouldn't do it, or won't do it.

Dylan: OK. I will go with that for the moment. Then what would be my alternative?

Premodaya: To stop lying to yourself that you're really looking for the answer—because the answer has been given. But your mind, and I don't doubt your sincerity one bit, comes in every time. That's what I mean by honesty. I mean: *see that*—that the mind comes in every time and sets up a condition, sets up a preference, sets up an idea of how it should look. This is the idea of how it should look: If I understand it first, *then* I can do it. That's your idea of how it should look. It should look like "understanding." Help has been given. Struggle with the question now. Struggle with that notion that it will be beneficial to you to become more honest with yourself.

There's a real problem here. When people say, "It can all be dropped in a heartbeat," you have to be very careful, because then people often get into a self-deprecating self-talk of, "Well, I have a sense that that's possible, and there must be something really wrong with me if I can't do it or if it hasn't happened for me yet or if I feel like it may never happen for me in this lifetime," or whatever form that thought takes. You have to be very careful. You have to understand very intelligently that there's no meta-method that is being missed. There is no magic bullet, magic key—magic anything—that, if you could just get to it—bingo bango! "I'm there!" There's nothing wrong with you if you can't plug into that, or make the statement that, "Yes, I've achieved that." You haven't failed at anything if that's the case. It's not that, "Oh, these great saints and sages achieved, succeeded, and poor me! So far, I want that. And so far, I've failed." That's a very real spiritual trap because, again, it's like we were saying earlier—it says the mind is then saying to you, "This is for someone else." It's self-victimization. "This is for someone else—not for you." We fall into that so readily that any time I make a more radical statement like the one I made, I feel a need to qualify it this way, because people misuse this as a way to beat themselves up, as a way to see themselves as somehow spiritually "less than," and I very much want everyone here not to fall into that trap.

It can be done in a heartbeat. It can be done in a lifetime. It can be done in ten thousand different ways. It can be done starting through the mind, and it can be done starting through the heart, and it can be done starting through behavior—there's no limit to how the path is traversed. Certainly, many people, if not the majority, come to the spiritual path initially because they are looking for a way to suffer less. They have gotten mature enough that they can say to themselves, "It appears that my intellectual ideas, my worldly understandings and my material strivings and whatever else aren't going to take care of the job. Those aren't the answer." People start looking more into the spiritual realm. They start looking for a different road. They start exploring what maybe hasn't been so much explored before. Then they end up at a meeting like this, or they end up reading certain books, or they end up going certain places, or whatever it is. All that is good. I'm for all of that.

Don't ever exclude yourself in any way, is all I'm saying, because then you're setting up, needlessly, yet another barrier for yourself. Your job is to include yourself, and to love yourself, not to criticize yourself for what you think you haven't achieved yet, because that simply becomes yet another barrier. These traps have to be understood. These are traps. Now, this subject is interesting to everyone. At Thursday's darshan, my heart leapt for joy when I sat in the back and heard you, Terrence, say, "Well, for me at least either suffering has ended completely or has wound down to the point where I'm not even sure I can call it suffering."

I'd like you to say whatever you can say about what you meant when you said that, and what your experience has been of how that happened for you, because you're the living example right now, and I think you have something of value to share.

Terrence: Suffering certainly did get me into spirituality to begin with, and a sincere willingness to not want to suffer and knowing that there wasn't a way out by my own means, by my own power. I had to really be honest with myself: I enjoyed suffering. That was a part of what perpetuated the suffering, because it strengthened my ego.

I didn't know I was creating it, and I came to the point where I had suffered so much that I was willing to listen to someone else, like Premodaya, who could see what I was doing, and just take it in and not say, "Well, yeah. But …" and not defend. I let it sink in when he was telling me that I was someone who was perpetuating it by enjoying it, by self-criticism. When I would start suffering, I would criticize myself for suffering. It made me feel different when I suffered. It made me feel like nobody could understand me. I was constantly taking my emotional temperature all the time.

I had to see all of that fully. I had to really see it and not do anything with it. When I started to see it in myself and be more aware of it in myself, I was bringing it up to the light of day and seeing it with awareness so it wasn't unconscious anymore. It wasn't something that was taking me over. What used to be something that was happening to me in the darkness, in unawareness, which was causing more and more self-criticism, became something that I could see and laugh at almost. It became funny after a while to watch how I was creating it. And when the mind starts to do what it does—what it had done my entire life—I just see it. The more my awareness has been on it, the more it can't do anything.

Premodaya: What is it like to live without suffering?

Terrence: It's light. It's enjoyable. I see that there was just this unneeded burden that I was carrying around. I'm more able to be less, to be no one, and not have to do as much, just relax. It's relaxing.

Premodaya: If we could bottle it you would give it to your friends? You don't see any drawbacks to it so far?

Terrence: Absolutely, no—it's easier to not suffer.

Premodaya: I know you gave a complete answer but how did this happen from the perspective of the real "how?" Not I talked to you and then that happened, and that happened, and "I saw this, and then my awareness went on that, and this came up to the light of day," but just, what's your real explanation of how this is possible? How could it be that suffering isn't there for you anymore? How is that possible?

Terrence: Not suffering anymore has been possible by letting go. Letting go of suffering has been possible by surrendering, by relaxing, by dropping it, by letting it go, by seeing that I was clinging on to it. When I saw that I was clinging on to it, I let it go. But I had to see it first.

Premodaya: You have no doubt that that's happened in actuality for you?

Terrence: I have no doubt.

Premodaya: Now that you see how it happened for you, and now that the feeling is really unquestioning, there's no doubt in your mind that this is for real; suffering really is dropped away. Can you see how this is possible literally for anybody?

Terrence: It's the easiest thing in the world. It's hard to hold on to. That was the hard work—thirty-four years of work.

Dylan: Has it had any testing experiences yet like things going wrong in your life?

Premodaya: Every day is a testing experience for this. Every breath is a testing experience. When the suffering truly ends, you know it. Here's what's interesting—Terrence could say this to the Rotary Club or the teachers' convention or whoever, any group of people, and I guarantee you there would be a huge proportion of people who would just say, "This is complete bunk. There is no way that suffering ends for a person. There is no way that a life can come to a point where suffering isn't included." Buddhist philosophy says suffering is the definition of life. So even when you take an intelligent, clearly not delusional, clearly not psychotic, clearly not somehow impaired, clearly not drunk, clearly reasonable person—and most people can see that readily and easily—and this intelligent and reasonable person actually stands up and testifies that, "Hey, it happened for me. And now that it's real, it's very easy for me to see that this is not rocket science. This can literally happen for anybody if they're willing," the amazing thing is most people simply will reject that out of hand.

There's another level (and that's more in spiritual circles) where people will say, "Well, it can happen," and this is what we talked about a little earlier, "Apparently it happened for him. I'll take it on faith; I don't know for sure. He seems honest and reasonable, but it probably can't happen for me." What I want to say to you is: Believe him. Believe this testimony. Believe that there's no one that this can't happen for. I mean, sure, if you have a brain disease or you're somehow "not all there," it's not going to happen. But assuming that you're intact in every major way, relatively speaking, this is possible for anyone and everyone. The key factor, the single operative element that makes all the difference in the world, the single thing that has to change no matter what else does or doesn't change is: absolute willingness. Absolute willingness to be the self-experiment of the end of suffering in your life. The willingness to have suffering end in your life.

The amazing fact is most people aren't willing for a variety of both comical and very valid-sounding reasons. This is where the honesty comes in. You have to ask yourself, "If I believe in what these guys are saying, if it has any merit whatsoever, am I actually willing for suffering to end in my life?" If you look deep enough you will probably find a "no" somewhere. It's counterintuitive. We think, "Of course I want it to end! Of course, I don't want to suffer. Of course, I would accept it. Of course, I'm willing," but then you have to look all the way in and see if there's any kind of objection—any kind of "no." Because most of us want some kind of sympathy; most of us want some kind of hand-holding; most of us want some kind of payoff that suffering gives. *Suffering gives a payoff.* We wouldn't cling to it for no reason. We aren't that stupid. You have to see what the payoff is. At the very least, you have to begin to see what the payoff is, and you have to begin to see whether you're truly willing, and if you find you're not, that's the beginning of having the chance to develop the willingness.

That's the long and the short of it. No lie. It's all about willingness. There are a hundred other factors for each individual, but the one that makes the difference is the willingness. All the rest can be dealt with, if the willingness is there. If the willingness isn't there, you can spend your whole life, every minute of it, dealing with all the other factors, and your suffering will continue to go round and round. The wheel will continue to turn.

Darshana: I don't know if this helps, but I was kind of in an intermediary between Terrence's lovely place and maybe at the very other end of it. I have these moments of, "Dude, let it go!" And you're buoyant! Then I wake up the next morning and I'm hungry, and I'm late, and something happens, and I'm completely mired back into it again. Then somehow, I bring it back up to—as Terrence put it, "the light of day," and you realize, "Oh, this isn't important at all," and then, again, you become buoyant.

I think to some degree I'm still completely married to the necessity of suffering, but it's not like one day there's a flip switch. But it's becoming into a practice, maybe a quick self-examination, just like, "Is this really that important?" Realizing that, it can evaporate, and then making that into a practice. That's where I fall off that train on a regular basis.

Premodaya: As a practice, you will always fall off the train—no matter who. I don't mean "you." Anybody. As a practice, there's no way to carry it out—day in, day out, moment in, moment out, and not fall off the train. It's not possible, no matter who you are or what level of consciousness you think you're at. There is a switch and when that switch is flipped, it means you've reached a threshold. That's what Terrence described. You've reached a threshold where you just can't do it anymore. It's not you have let go of it, although that's an accurate description, but what has really happened is that it has let go of you. All the striving in the world may get you there and it may not.

What has to be absolutely guaranteed, what has to happen without any equivocation, is that you completely go into the willingness question. You have started that, because here you sit, in a group of people, actually admitting that you're married to your suffering. What does that translate to in the terms that I'm talking—"I'm not willing." If you can admit that, you're on the way. Until you can admit that, there's no hope. Most of the world can't admit that, or won't admit that, or doesn't recognize—that's once again the honesty—that they aren't willing. When you can sit here and make the statement, "I see that I'm married to my suffering," you are working very for real on the level of willingness, and this will get you somewhere. That's the good news.

Now start to see what you just saw. Start to see it in your life. Start to see how you're married to suffering. Start to see what you enjoy about it. Start to see what the payoff is. Start to see why an intelligent person would cling, would try to hold on to it. Because there are really reasons why, so see it more clearly. Start to go into it much more deeply. See your part in this—not as a self-criticism, not as, "Jesus Christ, how can I be doing this to myself?" But as, "This is everyone's dilemma and this is good news that I can start to look at this." But I'm telling you, plain and simple, there's a threshold. There's a threshold where it all flips. And that's what happened to Terrence, and if you're going to get there, that will happen to you. There's no other way. You will experience that flip. You will be amazed. It will be like, "What?" You won't believe it. You won't. Nobody does. It's like, "How can this be?" That's why I asked Terrence, "How do you explain this? How can this be?" Because it doesn't go with everything that's has come before.

Dylan: I would like to talk to him, if he wants to talk to me.

Premodaya: Your time would be better spent challenging yourself on this issue of self-delusion and honesty.

Dylan: I heard it. I'm taking it in.

Premodaya: What more hopeful thing can anybody say than it's possible for suffering to end? Does it mean your personality will be great? I don't think so. Does it mean you will never raise your voice, or be crazy, or take a misstep, or offend somebody, or feel bad about something? No. Does it mean you will become some kind of perfect person that you never were before? You'll be the exact same person. [To Terrence] Are you the exact same person?

Terrence: Yes.

Premodaya: You'll be the exact same person with all your strengths and weaknesses, all your good points and bad points, all your nonsense and all your wisdom. The difference is—you won't be sitting in a tub of suffering anymore. When something feels bad it will just feel bad. You won't infuse it with this other layer called "suffering." You won't turn it into this needless drama that we all do. Pain will just be pain, disturbance will just be disturbance, anger will just be anger. You won't become perfect if suffering ends for you; you will just become a person who isn't suffering. You will see the perfection that is, and that will be enough.

Terrence: More than enough. Yes.

Premodaya: A living guy (not just me) can verify it. You can hear the truth of it. This is what I meant by, "It happens differently for different people, but when you get there it's the same place for everybody." It only has one quality, and it's what he's agreeing with me about. It doesn't seem possible until you start to get close. Part of the dilemma for sincere spiritual seekers, and people who are really willing to work on themselves, is it doesn't look more promising until you really get much closer.

Jocelyn: For me the gratitude just becomes more and more profound. Every challenge, every hardship, that arises is a gift. It's like, "Are you sure you don't want to suffer?" And each time you push it away, there's more gratitude. When everything's smooth, it's just smooth. But when the "shit hits the fan" is when the gratitude is the most overwhelmingly powerful. I think I'm explaining it properly—the harder the challenge that comes, the more gratitude.

Premodaya: The more you're in awe of that, "This has happened to *me!*" That somehow, this gift has landed on my head. That I can be living this event or this condition or this set of circumstances, and—lo and behold!—I'm not in any great suffering because of it. It's awe. You can only feel awe in the face of that, because you know it's not about you. You know you didn't do it.

Jocelyn: Also, what you were saying about the "personality doesn't change." All those things that were familiar to me my whole life, that triggered a mental suffering—still happen within the body, and everything is included. There's nothing excluded. Which is why other spiritual teachings always got me so frustrated. Because you have to "do this, and do this, and do this practice, and this practice." It was always about trying to get you somewhere else, to not be uncomfortable. Not to be with what is.

Premodaya: This is the real understanding, and this is what people don't get, until they get closer—that nothing will change. If suffering ends for you, nothing will change. The only thing that will change is that *you won't be suffering*. People have this preconceived notion; non-suffering means it looks a certain way, "I will be happier; I will be more blissful; I will be richer; people will like me better; I will be easier to get along with." Whatever. None of that's the case. It may happen. I'm not saying it can't happen. I'm not saying it doesn't happen. I'm saying: there's no preset way it's going to look, other than you won't be suffering.

Jocelyn: And in the willingness and in the honesty, it came to a point where, "I don't care if it's going to be good, or it's going to be bad, or it's going to be horrific, or it's going to be euphoric. I don't care. I want the Truth. That's all I want. I dedicate myself, my life, my being, one hundred percent. That is what I want. If it means I drop dead, OK. If it means everything falls to pieces, OK." For a good part of that, going through that process, everything did fall to pieces, but here I am, so I recommend it. If it's really falling to pieces then—

Premodaya: That's a good sign.

Jocelyn: Then that's a good sign.

Dylan: Why doesn't it get better? It seems to me, she seems happier. He seems happier.

Premodaya: Because that's your idea of how it should look—that's why. Your idea is: It should get better. Reality *is* whatever it is. She just described to you, with great honesty, that there was a period where everything fell apart and felt awful. Now, had you been commenting or looking at it when that was going on for her, you would say the same thing. You would say, "Why isn't it better?" But she went full circle and gave you the outcome. The outcome is: It includes everything. The outcome is: It includes feeling bad. What you have to see (and you are immensely capable of seeing it) is that this whole thought that happens for you of "Why isn't it better?" is your own idea and nothing else, your own preconceived idea that it means it will be better.

All I'm saying is: No. It may not be better. Take out your preconditions, and then you get a shot at it. As long as you're looking through the lens of your preconditions, nothing significant can happen because you're only following your own idea of it. This is *real*. Following your idea of it isn't, and so you'll go round in circles. It doesn't matter what the definition of *is* is. What is, is. My idea—your idea, his idea, her idea—of what is, doesn't matter. That's just our idea. Suffering can end when you're willing to give up your ideas of what "suffering ending" should look like, or feel like, or be like. Before that, there's no realistic possibility, because you're still working on getting it to how *you* want it—which isn't the end of suffering, which guarantees *more* suffering.

THE END OF SUFFERING

Premodaya: Someone asked: Is the process of "the end of suffering" the same for everyone? Are the stages predictable? The process of suffering is not the same for everybody, but the contents are the same for everybody. Everybody is an absolute individual, so no process of any kind can be the same for one person as for another person because you will change the process when it is going on for you. It will have *your* flavor; it will have *your* spin; it will have *your* touch. But the nature of it will be the same, no matter how different any two individuals are. Not because, as the second part of the question says, the stages are predictable; not because there are necessarily stages—but because there are thresholds.

Certain things have to happen so that other things can happen. Until those criteria are met, if there is a stage, you cannot go to the next stage. How those criteria get met is not a set thing. If there are five criteria in one area—let's say one stage, one level, one part of the happening—one person may go through those five criteria in five seconds, another person may take twenty years. There's no way that your individuality can be taken out of the equation. There's no way that you can map what it looks like ahead of time, because every individual creates the map as they go. The map is personal. The map is your flight—your flight plan, your flight pattern—but the thresholds have to be reached. How you reach them is up to you, but reach them you must. You can't skip a step. You can't take a shortcut. You can't not spend enough time on something that requires your time—or not give your all to something that requires your all. The requirements are intrinsic. The process is self-fulfilling, self-regulating—but *you* determine how, when, and why.

"Is the process of the end of suffering the same for everyone?" In one sense it is. In one sense it's the same for everyone. The same way as if you're taking a trip to Iowa [pointing to individual attendees in the room], you can start from New York; you can start from Los Angeles; you can start from New Orleans; you can start from France; you can start from the moon. But if you're all going to Iowa (and assuming you're all successful), you will all end up in Iowa, but you start in very different places and the journey will be very different from each place. You will travel a different countryside. Maybe one takes a plane, maybe one takes a car, maybe one takes a bicycle, and maybe one takes a rocket ship, but the process is the same for everyone, because you will all end up in Iowa. Once you get there, if you look back—once you get to the point where you can say, "Suffering has ended for me," you will look back—you will see how you got there. If you take ten people whose processes were all different, because it's ten entirely different people, once they have gotten to Iowa and you ask them to say how they got there, you get pretty much the same answer.

Even if one came from the moon, and one came from New York, you will get a surprisingly similar answer because what matters are those thresholds. What matters is what was passed through and passed beyond. That's what tends to stick in the mind. That's what tends to be noticed more than, "What was the scenery along the way?" or, "What did I have to figure out?" It's what actually *happens* that not only transforms you, but transfigures you. "Transfigures" is a stronger word—it means your cells change. It means something so essential changes in you that the word "transform," the word "transformation," isn't strong enough. For most people, actually to get to a point where you can say, legitimately and without hesitation, "The end of suffering has happened for me"—you will not be the same person.

Much has to transpire, much has to change. Much has to be dropped. That's half the equation. The other half is—you will be exactly the same person. Nothing elemental in you will change except for the insistence on suffering, but for that insistence to disappear, the factors have to line up differently from how they have up until now, and that's more like a transfiguration than a transformation. You'll say, "I'm a completely different person," but in many ways you will be exactly the same.

"Is the process the same for everyone?" The answer is really 'yes' and 'no.' It really is a real answer. Yes, you will end up in Iowa, the same as everybody else who is headed to Iowa and gets there. In that sense, it's the same. But it will be a completely different journey for you than for the next person, although you will cross the same milestones. But Joe crossing the milestone, and Jim crossing the milestone, will experience it differently; because Joe is not Jim, and Jim is not Joe.

"Are the stages predictable?" That's also 'yes' and 'no.' They are not predictable ahead of time, because you don't know for a fact what a person will have to pass through. But they are predictable in hindsight, predictable in the sense that once a person has passed through a stage, a point, a threshold, you can see it. It's visibly evident. You can predict that, "Now they are at this next point. Now this is possible; that wasn't possible before." So can the stages be predicted? In a loose way, yes. If you think of them as thresholds—that certain things have now happened.

The first thing that has to happen is the absolute, one hundred percent willingness to have an open mind. It sounds easy; it sounds like, "Well, I have an open mind. Or if I'm asked to have a more open mind, no biggie—I can do that." It's the hardest part of the journey, that first step, because what you will see if you bite into that hard, what you'll see is that you may be kidding yourself. You may not have anywhere near as open a mind as you might think you do or as you tell yourself you do or believe you do. An open mind means that there's no belief that you're unwilling to step out of. An open mind means that there's no idea or concept that you're not willing either to reject or accept, and most of all, explore. I could go on, but just those two—if you really consider them carefully—are mind-boggling. Are you ready and willing to drop *any* belief? The belief that you're a human being? The belief that you're a male or a female? The belief that you're on planet earth? Are you willing to consider dropping even those beliefs? Beliefs that are never questioned? Beliefs that the whole society signs off on in an unsaid, implicit agreement? The adjectives are important here. Are you willing to let go of *any* belief, if it's necessary, to get to the end of suffering? If you really examine that, the majority of the people on this planet will probably say, "No, I'm not willing to stop believing that I'm a man or a woman. I'm not willing to stop believing that I'm a human being. I'm not willing to stop believing that pigs can't fly." Whatever it takes. Are you actually willing to drop *any* belief, *any* limiting idea, *any* preconceived notion or concept, if that's what it takes? I'm not saying that's what it takes, but it takes that willingness. Are you willing—if that's what it takes to get to Iowa?—to the end of suffering? This is a tough question to chew on, because most of us would say a quick "yes," and then the more we examine, "Do we really mean that?" the more skittish we get. The more we will say, "Well, wait a minute—I'm not so sure." So an open mind usually translates for most of us human animals as, "Sure, I have an open mind," and more unconsciously, "as long as it vaguely, basically, agrees with what I mostly think." That's what we mean by an open mind. We don't really mean an open mind. We mean an open mind that's familiar to us, that jives with what we've come to accept as true.

A *really* open mind means we give up appointing ourselves as the final authority on all questions. We say, "I don't know for sure, and I'm willing to see if there really is an answer. I'm willing to see if there's something to be understood that's totally unimaginable to me now." Now, if you seriously go into that, it will scare the bejesus out of you. It should, if you're serious. Because it means that you're willing to drop all definitions that have sustained you thus far. "I'm this," "I'm that," "I'm Premodaya," "I'm fifty-eight years old," "I'm Caucasian," "I'm five foot six tall," "I'm a male."—whatever. If you're willing to set all that aside and consider other possibilities, *that's* an open mind. But most people can't conceive of that. Most people (and I don't mean people in this room, I mean *most* people) cling to those definitions as if their life depended on it. Their lives don't depend on it. Nobody's does. If you change your name tomorrow, your life will not change. If you change anything that you have been taught is essential, tomorrow, it won't make any big difference. You will still be you.

There's a price for the end of suffering. The price is that you have to be willing to have an *actually* open mind, and that's one of the beginning steps here. If you don't, it can't happen. It can't happen because a not completely open mind won't accept that suffering can end—because you've been taught so thoroughly, you've been conditioned so completely, that life includes suffering. You've been taught so powerfully that suffering can't end for you: It's just how it is. It's part of life. If you're breathing, then suffering is included.

There has to be enough willingness that that belief, that idea, can be permeated. It has to become porous enough that there's enough light shining in, that you can even begin to accept the idea that, "the end of suffering is possible for *me*." If you confront most people with that notion they will disagree. They will deny it, in my experience, vehemently. They will have every argument under the sun why suffering is absolutely guaranteed, necessary, unavoidable, and suffering cannot end for them, and it cannot end for you. It takes, oddly enough, an absolutely willing open mind even to take the first step of considering the possibility that it can end for you.

Now, even that requirement isn't in granite. None of these are, but it's the practical requirement for most people. It can happen differently. You can't have an open mind to that, and the process can still get jump-started if you can see the evidence for yourself and then get it, that it's possible for you. That's the harder way. That's what happens to more close-minded, stubborn people.

71

That's what happened to me. I got hit on the head with it so I had no choice but to accept it. You could not have talked me into it, so it could not happen that way. You can be smarter than I was and understand the benefit of a truly open mind. You can start from an easier place, which is simply opening the mind to all and any of the possibilities. I was not capable of that. That was too tough for me. I was too closed in my thinking, but you don't have to be like me—you can be smarter. I'm telling you the smart way, not the only way. There are probably six, or eight, or a dozen other ways that will work, depending on the proclivities of the individual. The universe is very forgiving. You can have all kinds of wacky stuff going on, and the universe will still provide a route for you. If you can't fit on ninety-nine percent of the other highways, there's still a secret back-path to Iowa—if you require that (some people require that). Some people insist on going the hard way: at night, on their hands and knees ... And even *they* get to go! I was not quite that bad, but I have seen those who *are* "quite that bad," and they are funny as hell. They'll fight you every step of the way.

Actually, I have heard that recently. A number of people have said to me recently, at these meetings, "Well, it's easy for you to say!" The person who says, "That's easy for you to say," thinks I'm somewhere or have something that they don't, like I have some special quality. I can tell you suffering ended for me. That's the truth. But if your assumption is that that's because (and this is an assumption many people would make) I have something you don't or I have some special knowledge, or special quality, or some different gift than you that allowed that to happen—you would be so wrong it's not even funny! Because I don't have anything you don't have. You probably have a few things I will never have.

So, when I say the end of suffering can happen for anyone, I really mean it! I'm the proof, because I'm a professional sufferer. If it can end for *me* ... I come from a long line of professional sufferers. I used to say, when I was very, very young, "My family can see the cloud on every silver lining." I remember saying that at twelve or thirteen years old. So if there's somebody whose name would be last on the list for suffering to end for them, then I would say that I would be a candidate for last on the list. I was good at it … ooooh! You think you're good at it? Ooooh, I got you *so beat*! I really was better than most. It's an art; it's an art to draw suffering out of anything—good or bad. Any questions about any or all of that?

Anna: Initially you mentioned criteria and thresholds. I would like to get the difference.

Premodaya: Thresholds are when you get to a certain point, and then something more is possible. Criteria are the things that need to happen to get to that point, to get to that threshold, the prerequisites. I gave the initial example that one prerequisite is to develop a willingness such that you're willing to have a completely open mind. So …

Anna: I thought that is the threshold, the first one?

Premodaya: No, that's the first criterion to get started so that you can get to the first threshold. Have you met that criterion? No? You shook your head no. "No" is the correct answer.

Anna: Sometimes I do, but not always. So, maybe no …

Premodaya: In your good moments you're close. In your bad moments, you get far away again.

Anna: Exactly. That's true.

Premodaya: That's part of the willingness issue, because willingness includes willingness not to be driven by whether it's "good moments" or "bad moments." The willingness to be so determined that your moods don't affect your results; your moods don't determine what and how you do. They're writing a lot of books about this now, "The Power of

Intention," but you can save your money. You don't need any of those books. Just be so determined that no mood shakes you from your purpose. It's as simple as that! You'll know you're there when no mood or event can deter you, can take your eyes off the goal. That's the criterion. That's the criterion for knowing that you have gotten to that point. If your mood can deter you, you'll never get there, because moods will always be there. If you're willing to let a mood be the excuse, it will always be excusable not to get there. There will always be some mood sooner or later that says, "Aah."

Riley: Would you include pain in that category?

Premodaya: Absolutely. You have to become single-minded. If there's one subject that, in all these years, I have talked about more than any other, it's probably willingness. Willingness is so all-encompassing a notion, so all-encompassing a word, that if you can think of something as a barrier, then willingness means including that. You can answer that question as well as I can—if you can think of it as a barrier, as something that can shift you, or stop you, or prevent you, or turn you back, or anything, then the answer is "yes." Willingness means: willingness for whatever comes. It doesn't matter; I'm going to Iowa!

That is the only way I got through graduate school. If I had not made that decision, I would have dropped out so many times!—like I did all the other schools. So that's when I learned something about determination and intention, because I made a decision, "For the first time in my life, I'm actually going to finish something. I'm going to finish graduate school. I'm not going to drop out, and go back five years later like I did for undergraduate. I'm not going to go to China for a year. I'm not going to go backpacking for six months. I'm not going to marry somebody and move to Florida. Whatever happens, I'm finishing this degree. Nothing will stop me." If I had not made that decision, there's no question I would not have made it. That's where I really learned about making up your mind and being single-minded, and then all kinds of things happened to prevent me.

My Master, my teacher, came into my life and turned everything upside down. Then I met a woman. She turned everything upside down three times over. All kinds of things happened, all of which in the past would have prevented me, except this time I had made up my mind that, "Nothing is going to prevent my finishing graduate school. Nothing! I don't care what it is: Chop off one of my arms—I'm finishing. Chop off the other one—I'm finishing." Because, it's really true. I had never (in sequence, the way you're supposed to) finished anything in my whole life until that. I always took the hard way—drop out and come back. I always took the less direct route. I always took the crazier way. Until I decided, "I'm finishing graduate school." And I finished it! I didn't even finish it at the school I started, because I was in school in Northern California and my Guru said, "All my people must leave California." The next day we left California, so I had to go through all the trouble of transferring everything, find another school, get everything transferred, start their program, make up some stuff they wanted you to do over again (because it doesn't transfer always the way you hope). It probably put me back about six months and many thousands of dollars, but it mattered! Whatever it took, I was going to finish that degree!

Willingness ... why does this come up? I'm not talking about the intention to have suffering end in your life—it may sound like I am, but that is not what's in my mind. I'm talking about the willingness to do whatever it takes, no matter what comes up. What comes up—every time, for everyone—is a fixed set of beliefs and ideas, all of which—individually or together—give a message that, "This cannot happen for you. There are reasons why maybe for somebody (if you're liberal-minded)—maybe for someone else, but not for me. Not most people; it can't happen for just anybody. Anybody who thinks it's happened for them, must be deluded—must have a screw loose." But then there are a few people like us here, who can accept the notion a little more readily and see that it's possible—or at least hope that it's possible, but then, along comes the issue of willingness. What are you willing to commit? What price are you willing to pay? Are you willing to pay the price of letting go of every belief you ever had? Are you willing to pay the price of accepting anything that happens and dealing with it? What is the depth and the breadth of your willingness?

Riley: I'd like to ask you, in terms of what you told in the way of your own process, your own trip, as you met your teacher you still kept this idea of graduate school? It seems like there might be a willingness to let go of graduate school to be with the teacher. That's what my mind went to.

Premodaya: Probably not. If he had told me, "Don't finish graduate school," I would've probably have said, "Screw you." I already made up my mind. That's my guess. I can't say for sure. My guess is that I would have finished no matter what.

Riley: But I also sense that you made up your mind that that was your teacher.

Premodaya: No, I never made up my mind.

Riley: That was not a choice?

Premodaya: Yes, that was not a choice. It was completely known from the first tenth of a second. Then I spent two years denying it, fighting it, and trying to say, "It can't be"—part of which I was in graduate school. Spiritual life didn't happen in my life because I was looking for something, and there are many like me, but we're not the majority. I wasn't looking for anything—it's what they call a "bolt out of the blue." So that is trustworthy. There was no way I could be fooling myself because I was not trying to get anywhere. I'm not saying that's a good way, but it's a trustworthy way. There's a certain luck in having it happen that way, because there's nothing to question, even though you could fight it like I did. But you can only fight what you absolutely know for so long, and then you just give up.

I didn't have to wrestle with these questions. My luck is that I didn't have to deal with willingness. I didn't have to deal with, "What beliefs am I willing to shed, or not shed?" There are all of these issues that happen for sincere people who are either trying to grow spiritually or trying to get to the end of suffering, or trying to evolve their consciousness—whatever it is that people struggle with. The schlemiels like me, that had it as a bolt out of the blue, the luck is that we don't have to go through all that. We go through it backwards. We fight those battles after we already know what's true and real, and then we're just fighting with ourselves. Then it's just a denial. It's trying to deny what you already know to be the case. It can't be much stupider than that, but so be it. Many people besides me are in that category, but we're not in the majority. I would say it's ten or twenty percent. I was not ever looking for the end of suffering, I was not looking for God, and I was not seeking Truth or any of all that good stuff. I was trying to get through life with as little responsibility as possible, basically. That didn't work out really well. I mean, look at what I do now.

That's how mysterious things are. There's no predicting and no explaining how these things happen. Are there stages? You could call them stages. I would rather call them thresholds. Certain things have to be in place. Is there a process? Yes. Are they the same for everyone? In one sense—yes, and in one sense—no. It is so much wider than that, in that in a sense anything is possible. That's the real answer. There are people for whom the process of the end of suffering happening from "point zero" to "it's all done" happens in literally fifteen minutes, and there are people who don't get there in seventy years. How do you explain that? There *is* an explanation: That's how vast the possibilities are; that's how diverse the possibilities are; you have that much freedom. This universe is *that* free that you can get there; you can not get there; you can go this way; you can go that way; halfway to Iowa, you can decide to go to Mars. You have no limits in what you can choose or decide.

That's the trouble. That's why most people don't get anywhere—because the possibilities are limitless. For most people, it's impossible to accept the real meaning of that. So people sequester themselves in a tiny, little lean-to of possibilities—generally referred to as beliefs and philosophies. And that's it—then that's all you've got. You limited yourself. It's like the man who sits in a little tent in the middle of the Grand Canyon; the whole sky is open, but he can't see beyond the top of the tent, and he says, "That's the whole universe—the top of the tent." Well, step out of the tent and it's a little bigger than that. Your beliefs and philosophies and fixed ideas are the tent. And that includes much more than most of us tend to recognize.

THAT WHICH MATTERS MOST

Premodaya: Most of us most of the time are concerning ourselves with anything and everything except the Ultimate, the Final, the Profound— what I like to simply refer to as "That which matters." That which matters has nothing to do with what we think about it.

Prof. Alex: Yeah, I get thrown off base very badly sometimes like this. I was tuned into these hearings of General Petraeus and I began to get angrier and angrier, and more involved. Afterwards I thought, "Hey, there have always been wars." I got very upset during the Vietnam War. It's very hard to handle, and I'm not really lucid for hours. It brings up stuff in me which I really didn't even know existed. If there's any way of short-circuiting this—

Premodaya: Why do you want to short-circuit it?

Prof. Alex: Because I feel it's a waste of time. I get very angry within myself. I get very emotional. I'm not a very outgoing, emotional guy, but internally, I get very emotional. A little part of me is saying, "This is so stupid, you know. None of this is real."

Premodaya: That's how, by listening to that part, by believing that part. You gave the answer, you often do. You gave the answer. By believing that part that says, "This isn't real. This doesn't matter."

Prof. Alex: Yeah, it's not real, but it seems very real, and everyone around me …

Premodaya: But you're saying something in you actually tells you, "It doesn't matter, it isn't real. There are always wars. This is ongoing, and any attention I give to it doesn't further anything." That's what you seem to be saying.

Prof. Alex: Yeah, that's a small voice. But the overwhelming loud-speaker is—

Premodaya: Ignore the loudspeaker and listen to the small voice. That's the method. Which one is right—the loudspeaker or the small voice?

Prof. Alex: The small voice is right—right down the line. I mean, I come from England. We had wars—the Boer War, the Zulu War—against harmless people. People like me were outraged, that we were doing that. It's always something going on. It has little logic because these wars …

Premodaya: Well, tell me any war that has logic.

Prof. Alex: Well, I think the one that ran over Hitler, that was a good one.

Premodaya: But is it logical? I'm not speaking for war or against war—I'm just responding to your comment that it's not logical. I don't see how you can look at any war and say, "It's logical." You're right in that sense—I agree with you—they're all the same. I don't even want to get into, "Is there a better war and a worse war?" You commented on it as, "It's not logical." That seems right to me. So, really, it's not about war. Your comment is really about everything. All the stuff in the newspaper, all the stuff in daily life that repeats itself endlessly and has always been going on and will always be going on. If some part of you, something in you, tells you that that's true, shows you that that's the fact of things, then why get all bent out of shape about something that is inevitable? We all do. Don't personalize it. You're speaking for every human being on the planet right now.

Prof. Alex: Just let it happen and hold on to that small voice?

Premodaya: You can't not "let it happen." How are you going to keep it from happening? It's not up to you to let it happen, because you don't have that power—to let it happen or not let it happen.

Prof. Alex: I know. I guess what I'm talking about is—I regret spending three or four hours and apparently there's no way out; just spend three or four hours.

Premodaya: No, the way out is to listen to your own wisdom and know what you know. Listen to that. Before you get upset, remember, listen to yourself. You said you heard a still voice, a small voice, telling you there's no point in getting upset. When did you hear it? Before you got upset? While you were upset? After you were upset?

Prof. Alex: After I was upset. Two hours later I said, "This is ridiculous."

Premodaya: Trust that voice and next time it will be one hour. Trust it some more and next time it will be towards the end. Sooner or later it will be in the middle. Sooner or later it will be in the beginning. Eventually it will be right before it starts and you'll know not to give yourself to what you can't do anything about, and what doesn't further anything. That's the process for everybody. This isn't about you—this is about every human being there is and really ever will be. Everybody's task is to learn better, to do better. To not get shoved down the wrong road by every loudspeaker we hear just because it's loud, just because it happens all the time, just because it seems to be so. You have to get smarter. The amazing thing is, here you are—the living proof that you already know. It's not like you don't know. It's not as if the wisdom isn't there. It's not as if the insight hasn't already happened.

This is the case for the majority of people. The insight is there, the wisdom is there, and it's not being listened to. It's not being followed. It's not being trusted. It's not being seen as the true wisdom it is, because the volume is down. So, what? Don't judge it based on the volume; judge it based on: do you know it to be true. This is everybody's dilemma—how to not be attached to every emotion that sweeps over us and every perception that seems to be valid. And everybody knows, absolutely, that the perspective changes an hour later; the perspective changes a day later; the perspective changes constantly. How can you be following the perspective of this moment, thinking that it's absolutely one hundred percent valid? Everybody knows this, but to live it is a whole different story.

To live it means being willing not to believe what goes on in your head, and even what goes on in your emotions. To recognize it for what it is—as things going on and nothing more. Not to give it the credence of absoluteness, of sureness, not to be one's own authority. To recognize that we have a limited perspective and not be so sure about everything. Most of us are very sure about most of our thoughts and most of our perceptions. That can't be accurate because they change an hour later. Everybody knows this, but not everybody lives the meaning of it, the lesson of it. The trick is to live it. The trick is to see, the task is to see, how in flux everything we think and feel really is. It's like saying, "I'm standing in the river right now, so my feeling of the river—this is the Truth, this is what's accurate." One second later the river is going to feel different, because it keeps moving. So, it's foolish to say, "Oh, now I know what the river is." It's trying to freeze a moment in time and cling to it.

That's why it's about attachment—we are attached to our own view of things and that's the entire problem. Literally, it's as simple as that. Be willing not to be attached to your own view of things and everything is revealed; everything takes on its proper perspective. Sounds so simple, but almost no one is willing to do it, because we believe ourselves to be the right authority. What we think, what we see, what we feel, what we perceive must be true and real and accurate and the basis for everything we do.

Prof. Alex: Feelings are very much like a river; I get swept away and then I get mad at myself for allowing this. That's part of it.

Premodaya: Well, the beauty of pursuing nonattachment is—there's nothing to get mad at. You just see the tendency we all have to attach and as much as you're able in that moment, you unattach yourself. It gets easier with practice, but the fundamental, essential base of it is the understanding. The understanding that any attachment is an attachment to a limited perspective. Therefore, by definition, one hundred percent of the time can't be accurate, can't be true—it's too limited.

That attachment is nothing more and nothing less than the barrier to what is true. There are two ways to attack it—become unattached through your own wisdom, through your own understanding—or the other way is the exact opposite—be so attached that you give yourself to it one hundred percent. Don't hold anything back in you towards that which moves you. If you go into it *completely*—lo and behold, strangely enough—you come out the other end and find nonattachment. It's a very amazing mechanism. The only way to reach nonattachment is to detach yourself or to attach yourself completely, and then you literally fall out. It's very strange, but it works every time. If you go all the way into it, you come out the other end into nonattachment, because you see somehow by going so deep, that it's not what you thought. It's very strange that both ends work.

It's a question of which one fits for you, which one is easier for you, more doable for you. It's amazing that it's actually nothing more and nothing less than the basic human tendency to become attached, and the thing we're most seriously and simply attached to is our own perception. It seems to us sacrosanct. It seems to us that to let go of that, to see through that—somehow, we lose ourselves; that's gotta be the outcome, but the fact of the matter is, that brings you more to yourself, oddly enough. It's a very strange set of processes, because it doesn't follow what we would expect.

Prof. Alex: I'm a loving person, and that's the way I end up. I guess I'm being resentful that it happened, but actually, I could be glad, "Hey, I'm so glad I came out of it."

Premodaya: Find a way to be as loving to yourself as you are to other people. Include yourself. Your thoughts aren't the problem. The attachment to those thoughts, the belief in those thoughts is the problem. Your feeling states aren't the problem—your belief in and following those feeling states creates the problem. It's all a matter of attaching, due to belief—believing it's real, believing that your perspective is the right one. We carry this idea unconsciously: We don't doubt ourselves. This is everybody's basic stance, because if we doubt ourselves, where are we? That's the feeling—the feeling behind it is, "If I start doubting myself, then I'll be lost." But the fact of the matter is, we're way on the far end of the pole on this. We don't think we are; we don't perceive it generally. We're way on the far end where we trust too much, believe too much (much more than we realize) our own perspective, our own limited, tiny perspective. One little human being in this grand universe and we take ourselves seriously.

Again—it's very important to understand this—we do this because we believe that if we didn't we would somehow lose ourselves; we somehow wouldn't be who we are. That's the mistaken idea, the mistaken feeling. You are who you are no matter what. But we limit our possibilities out of a false idea that we can gain some kind of security by doing that. We trade limitlessness and openness for safety and security, both of which are not possible. There is nothing safe or secure anywhere in this universe. Any feeling otherwise is a momentary delusion or long-term delusion. Right? Nobody disagrees with that?

Dylan: It's not that I disagree, but if we know that our perspective isn't the only perspective, and it's not our feelings, and not our thoughts that are the only perspective, what is the alternative?

Premodaya: The alternative is not to believe yourself, not to take yourself seriously. Very simple method, but very hard to climb on board, because we're so used to taking ourselves seriously. We are taught, we are trained to take ourselves seriously. Stop believing it. That's it—stop. Have the understanding and stop believing it. Think it through seriously enough, once and for all, so you finally see how ridiculous it is. From that under-standing, you automatically start not to grip so hard, believing yourself. It just has to be understood; it has to be seen in yourself—how invalid it is. Don't believe it; be willing. It's a question of willingness—be willing to be open to experiment with not believing what goes on in you; what you say to yourself; what you hear in your own thoughts; what you feel in your own feelings; what you perceive in your own perceptions. Be willing to stop believing it and see what happens.

Dylan: In terms of what Alex said, because I can certainly relate to that, where we get attached to something that upsets us, the idea would be lis-tening to the part that says, "You know."

Premodaya: Listening to what you already know. I'm saying it's very easy to change your mind about it, about anything, by simply being willing not to believe it anymore, as an experiment. Not as an adoption of a whole new lifestyle. See if it works. First, experiment. See what it's like not to believe yourself, not to take yourself so seriously, not to sit inside yourself as the one who has the right to judge and criticize and evaluate everything. That's what we're all doing all the time. Be willing to suspend that function of evaluating and then believing our own evaluation—analyzing and believing our own analysis, perceiving and trusting our own perception. To be willing to suspend that and see what it's like, to the degree that you actually can do it, will tell you volumes. You will see for yourself how it works. The hard part is being willing—trying it out to the point where you actually do it, because for a lifetime you have been practicing the exact opposite. It simply means moving from a position, from an attitude of "I know" to "I don't know," if you want to put it in a simpler dichotomy. Instead of "I know," assume "I don't know." If you do that, you'll be right one hundred percent of the time.

Prof. Alex: Yeah, I was sure I was right, "I'm *right* about this."

Premodaya: That's another—the methods are endless. They are little nuances of "how." Assume you're always not correct, and you'll be right, but that opens you up. That opens up the willingness not to sit as the authority. We're not even authorities on ourselves. Other people see us more clearly than we do. Any friend can list all your strengths and all your weaknesses much more accurately than you ever will be able to because you can't be objective. But anybody on the outside—easy. Yet we think our perspective is the best one for us to take. It's crazy. We're all crazy until you start not to believe yourself so steadfastly, so seriously, so assuredly. Just a little looser approach in that area, just a little less self-assurance about what we think and feel, and everything in you opens much wider to many more possibilities. You will see much more clearly. The less you know, the less you stand as a "knower," the more you will see and the more you will know. But when you see it and you know it more, don't assume you know anything, and even more you will know.

Priya: Recently I had an episode where I was very scared and then felt better, and when I got to the point where I was feeling, "Well things are really great," it occurred to me that I wanted to ride that feeling and be in it. But logically speaking, if I didn't want to identify with the terribly scared one, I probably had to—I don't mean not trust it, because I don't assume things are wrong when I feel good, but I should see that as just another feeling too. Is that right?

Premodaya: See the ever-changingness, instead of the thing that's changing. Your comment is correct—when we become in the beginning more of a not-knower, generally for most people, fear comes along, because a not-knower means you're standing more in the unknown and we are taught to avoid the unknown. We are taught to be knowledgeable—be a knower, so fear is almost inevitable. There are a few exceptions—a person here or there who isn't very particularly prone to fear—but that isn't the vast majority. That's one in a million. Fear will be inevitable in the beginning when you try to stand more in not-knowing than knowing, because you've dipped your toe into the unknown and when you dip your toe into the unknown, you can't see anything, including your toe. It's kind of dizzying, but it's worthwhile. If you experiment and keep going you'll see the value of that. You'll see the possibilities of that, but you have to tolerate the fear and the vertigo and the nausea that inevitably comes when it's not something you're used to.

Obviously, if you stand as a not-knower the ground isn't so solid under you, but that's your real situation; that's your real condition. You don't know what's going to happen one second from now; you have no way of knowing, one second from now, one hour from now, one day from now, one year from now, one decade from now, one century from now. You can't say one word about it. Well, we all say many words about it, but none of it holds any water because we don't know.

What I'm really advocating is: Be in the position that you're really in, instead of how we fool ourselves that we're not in that position. We're in a non-knowing position always. Unless you can tell me how you got here, how it was that you were born, how it is that you're alive, how it is that your heart keeps beating, how it is that thoughts happen for you, how it is that your hair grows, how it is that anything that has ever happened, happened—until you can explain that, you can't say you know, and no one will ever explain it, because we can't. It's a mystery.

You don't know how you got here. You don't know when you're leaving here. You've been told you're leaving; you accept it. You know you're going to die, but you can't say when. How can you say you know, when you can't say what that will mean with any absolute guarantee? This is a completely unguaranteed existence, so any idea of a guarantee is our hope for security, our desire for safety, but that doesn't make it so. How can you be safe if you can't know what's going to happen one second from now? One second from now I could have a heart attack; you could have a heart attack. You can't say with any assurance that won't happen. The roof could cave in. You can't say, "No, it won't." You don't know. I don't know and you don't know. That's the simple, inarguable truth of the position we're in. It doesn't take a lot of thought—if you're basically intelligent you can ponder that for minutes and see the truth of it.

But it's not enough; you have to take the next step. Once you see the truth of it, you have to start bringing that understanding into everything else so that you aren't continuing to further the delusion that somehow you know, somehow, you're secure, somehow you can feel OK and not experience yourself as a non-knower, you can feel knowledgeable, you can feel that you have some kind of control over the next moment. This is natural, this is what we all do, but to progress spiritually you have to get beyond that; you have to live more dangerously—which means accepting that you don't know. I don't know. You don't know. No human being knows. It's absolutely a mystery. And to start allowing that mystery to be present, instead of turning away and saying, "Well, I didn't have a heart attack, I didn't fall down dead all these minutes so far, so probably I won't in the next minute." Probably you won't, but a minute will come when you will, and then you'll be wrong.

You'll be right all those minutes, but what good did it do you? Because when you drop dead—you will be dead. That will negate all the minutes that you told yourself, "Not this minute. Not the next minute, not likely. I don't have to deal with what matters. I don't have to give myself to something more difficult, something more challenging. I'll just wait a few more minutes, a few more days, a few more weeks—not now, not today. Let's take it easy. I don't want to deal with it today. Hopefully I won't die tonight, so I have another day tomorrow." This goes on endlessly. We do this—this is what we do. And a minute becomes a day, becomes a year, becomes a lifetime. And you find yourself on your deathbed not having addressed that which matters. This is the basic human dilemma, and you tell yourself, "I'll get more serious when I'm older." Suddenly you're older and you're no more serious, no more willing to face what has to be faced—the existential dilemma, the basic question of life and death, of what's real, what isn't, what matters, what doesn't, what is the Ultimate.

We all live in postponement. All I'm saying is, be smart enough to listen to that little voice that says, "Hey, maybe I should stop postponing and give this some due consideration." Whatever that means. Maybe there's something that can be found out—not as a knowing—not, "Now I know," but, "Now I have a sense of the mystery of it. Now I can admit that I don't know. Now I can stop believing such a limited perspective called me." The odd thing—and I say it to you as a guarantee—you will lose nothing by doing that. The natural assumption is that you will lose something by doing that. I guarantee you—you can only gain. This isn't news to anybody in this room. Everybody has some sense of this. Everybody who would be at a meeting like this has some sense of this, so I'm not telling you what you don't know. I'm just trying to emphasize the importance of taking your own wisdom seriously. Not postponing any longer than you have to, that which has to be faced because you're here, because you're alive, because you're breathing. Not turning away one second longer than you have to, and you may have to. There may be some feeling of, "I can't," or, "Not now." I'm not saying, "Jump off a cliff," if that's the feeling. In your own time, in your own way—but at least recognize that that's the requirement. At least recognize how you're postponing. At least recognize how you've appointed yourself final authority and how it doesn't make sense if you really think about it—how we can be the final authority on anything? It's that authoritativeness that causes all the trouble. We believe ourselves.

There's not one human trouble that you can say to me or to anyone that you can't see readily that that's the source—believing yourself. Think of any trouble in the world, any trouble you have ever had, any trouble that you would like to not have to live, anything that's a problem, and I guarantee you—thirty seconds of thought and you'll see it. I guarantee you that you can trace it easily and quickly to the level of you believing in it. If you didn't believe in it, how would it be a problem?

Dylan: I certainly see that in thoughts, in judgments, but how are we doing that when we have a physical feeling? If you hit your finger with a hammer and it hurts, or you have a broken heart, what are we doing with those things that isn't the best thing we could be doing?

Premodaya: You believe yourselves to be a body. You believe yourselves to be the limited entity—no matter how you define it—instead of the living force, the living awareness. You believe yourself to be limited and finite instead of simply recognizing that at any moment, at every moment, you're standing in infinity and eternity. That the finite and the limited is just an inaccurate perception of the eternal and the infinite. That doesn't mean the hurt stops. That means you correctly see your condition, or accurately understand your situation.

Dylan: Because if our finger hurts our mind is going to, "This is the center of the universe, my pain"?

Premodaya: Well, your perception is your perception. What we've been saying all evening is: stop believing your perception. That doesn't mean there's no pain in the finger; that just means that isn't the be-all and end-all of what's going on in the universe right now. To respond as if it is, is just our foolishness. Knowing that, your finger won't hurt any less, and there's no problem in screaming and complaining, but don't believe it. It's just a question of, what's your understanding?—so that you're not promulgating a delusion to yourself. Nothing needs to change except your willingness to live in a mirage, to see the mirage as real.

Paula: What's the benefit of adopting that viewpoint? What's the benefit of not seeing the mirage as real, but realizing that you're always limitless, and yet, you're here in this body, on this earth to experience this lifetime?

Premodaya: The benefit depends on you. The benefit depends on what you want. If you want to be rich and famous there will be no benefit. If you want Truth, if you want Self, if you want God, or anything of that kind, then the benefit is: There's no other way to get there, except that. The trouble is you can't know it until you're actually experiencing it for yourself. You can't see the benefit until you get your toe in the water and felt whether it's hot or cold or lukewarm, whether it feels good or feels bad. Whichever one of those it is, dip a little more of your foot until enough has been dipped; then you can see the benefit for yourself. For eons, for countless time, we've all been told the benefit's incalculable. Everybody who speaks like I speak has said this. Everybody who we look at as "Maybe they know something," says the same thing. The problem is, you can take someone else's word for it, but until you see it for yourself with your own eyes, until you experience something of it yourself with your own heart, it's not going to make much difference. The value of accepting it from someone else is you can feel a little more ready, a little more willing to see for yourself. That's the only value. Until you see for yourself, it doesn't really mean much at all.

Paula: And once you do, what's the benefit of staying here?

Premodaya: Well, where else are you going to go?

Paula: Exactly. And yet you have both perceptions at once, and perhaps a hard time staying limited, at the same time limitless. Once I experienced what it was like to feel reality, I wanted to stay in that perception day after day, every moment of the day, but I had to drive a car and I had to deal with my kids and I had to think about the grocery list.

Premodaya: What was the perception? What was it, what did you perceive?

Paula: I perceived light, molecules, no separation. Light and pure joy.

Premodaya: OK, so there was a feeling that went with it. Is it possible to stay in that feeling endlessly?

Paula: Yes, on one level it is and to have that with you all the time. But I find my consciousness is drawn back, day after day, and into more mundane things. It's hard for me to take that feeling of joy into mundane things. Like Alex, I get dragged into the Iraq War and on a different part of the spectrum, I feel that rage. And at the same time, I know at the higher spectrum that it's absolute joy and absolute energy and there's really no differentiation and it's just God playing, energy playing. But it is painful to experience those fierce emotions.

Premodaya: Please don't be too angry with me if I suggest to you that the notion that you can hold on to the joy is a delusion—is a hope, rather than a true perception—because it's simply a feeling state and a feeling state by definition can't ever be permanent. Nobody has any trouble understanding why if immense joy is there, we would want to try to keep it, but the delusion, the mirage, is that we can. The most we can do, the most that's possible, is joy can have us, but we can't have joy. We don't have that control.

By some grace of God, you were lucky enough to experience the true and tremendous joy that's possible. I'm suggesting to you—don't take the leap, that that experience means somehow it should always be that feeling state: "Somehow I should be able to enter that and never leave." It's an understandable idea. We've all heard, we've all been told, that joy is the very base of everything. That we're made out of joy. That joy is what God is, what Truth is. That if we go to the very center of Truth, we will find only joy. Everybody has heard this. But the mind takes this and says, "Sounds good to me. I want that, so I must not be there. It must not be enough the real deal unless I can be there all the time. I should be able to do that." That's the slight error in understanding, because it isn't about any particular experience. It isn't about any particular feeling state. It's about being open to whatever is. The joy of this moment—might be the terror of the next moment. We don't know.

Going back to your original question, "What's the benefit?" One benefit is the more we are willing to recognize and truly "get it" that we don't control a thing, the more possible it is that the joy that is possible—the joy that is there—isn't being screened out by us. You're more likely to fall into joy, I would say, the more you recognize and actually are standing in, living, the non-knowing, non-sure attitude. The more you see that that's true, that that's one's real condition, everyone's real condition and particularly "my real condition," and personalize it—that you don't make a concept out of it by saying, "Yeah, it's true," but somehow you don't plug into it for yourself—the more that that's possible, the more you allow that, the more the joy that's in everything, including the worst things, can be apparent to you. Maybe you'll feel it to some degree, maybe you won't; but you will see it, whether you feel it or not. It will be apparent, whether you feel it in that moment or not. I think you're saying that that's your experience, that enough has become clear to you, enough has been experienced, that it is apparent to you. Now it's just a small matter of not clinging to the feeling state, because if that's apparent to you, then that puts you in a rare category of one of the few human beings who knows that out of the six and a half billion, who's seen it for themselves. Already you won't find much support for what you know, because most people don't know this. You have to be very, very strong in what you know so that you're supporting yourself, so that you're living what you know. You're listening to what you know, more than what your momentary experience is. More and more, when that becomes easier, when that's something you're more used to, more and more the confusion dissolves between this moment's experience and what's real, so that it's not felt to be two levels, not felt to be, "This is going on, and behind it, that's going on," so that you don't feel pulled.

It's really a matter of being willing not to evaluate it; just what we've been talking about. To let the experience be there, let the understanding be there, let the perception be there, without making a judgment about it. Without believing the words. Without believing our own take on it, but yet knowing deeper than words can give. You're saying that's your experience, so there isn't a big distance that has to be traversed. It's just a matter of believing what you know, trusting what you know, and knowing what you know, more than the momentary perception, the momentary experience, and, sorry, even the momentary joy. Even the joy is just this moment's perception, this moment's feeling perception.

Paula: You know, what was more important than that enlightenment or whatever, was the understanding of the energy. As you first spoke I understood that the joy wasn't as important as feeling the energy, and the energy can travel through each of the emotions. Thank you for that.

Premodaya: It isn't even feeling the energy—it's simply the one word you used: "understanding." Understanding is more important than any of it. Understanding supersedes any possible experience because any experience any of us have, one thing is guaranteed—it will change. So, what's the best you can do? The best you can do is: Can you take the right understanding out of it? Because *that* you can keep. The experience can't be kept, but the understanding can. The only thing that lasts is the understanding, so put your eggs in the understanding basket. What most of us are doing is we're putting our eggs—depending on our personality—we're putting our eggs in the feeling basket, we're putting our eggs in the knowledge basket, we're putting our eggs in the experience basket, whatever it is. But the only basket that takes you forward is the understanding basket. Put all your eggs in that and it becomes much easier—clears up many of the confusions that we naturally have, thinking "this" versus "that." "If I could only keep that!" Ultimately, you will keep nothing—only understanding. When all is said and done, only understanding will be there. What is awareness other than understanding?

When all is said and done, you won't keep a thing. You won't keep any of the emotions; you won't keep any thought processes; you won't keep the personality, the body—nothing. You will take one thing with you when you leave this life—*whatever understanding you have been able to garner.* That's what you will take with you. If you can see the truth of that, then sooner or later you have to recognize that the most precious commodity in this existence is understanding. There is nothing else.

Understanding doesn't mean you have figured it out. You will never figure it out. Understanding means you get it. You have allowed yourself the Truth. You have allowed yourself to not be fooling yourself out of a shared need that we all seem to have for some kind of feeling or notion of safety or security or knowledge or control. Everything you cling to—that we all cling to, some more, some less—will be ripped away from you sooner or later. The ancient wisdom is: give it up *now* voluntarily, so that it can't be ripped away from you. Give it up now, so that what remains is what can't be taken away from you. Ultimately the only word that comes close to expressing what that is, to giving some vague idea of what that might be, is "understanding."

All these words are synonymous: "Truth," "God," "love," "understanding," "joy." They are all synonyms. They are all synonymous because they all are inadequate attempts at expressing the essential nature of that which is, that which is the Profound, the Ultimate. Call it "Truth," call it "God," call it whatever. It's wordless. It's timeless. It can't be expressed but, you know, what are we going to do? Words is what we have, so we do the best we can. There's nothing that isn't best approached other than through understanding. There's nothing that can't be dealt with, except through understanding. If understanding can't deal with it, then nothing can. But understanding isn't of the mind. Understanding is of your total being, so don't be confused about the word "understanding." It doesn't mean you've figured something out. It doesn't mean your mind has mastered it. It means your total being gets it, whether you can express it or not. Whether it can be put into words or not. Whether you're even sure about what you get or not, but somehow you know that it's true. Somehow you know that you get it, even if you can't say to yourself for sure, but somehow you know.

Everybody in this room knows exactly what I'm talking about, even though it sounds so vague. Just live *that* more. I know it sounds really simple and trite, but it's the hardest thing in the world to do. Really do it—really live it more, just a little bit—and your life is completely transformed. Live it a little bit more, and "Oh my God!" Just that experiment, that seeing, that experience of it gives you the ability to give yourself to it finally even more, because you see that nothing gets lost; you see that you only gain when you do that. You get the courage; you get the willingness, seeing that again and again, to do it even more. Finally, you give up all notions once and for all that you know anything, you control anything, or that you're the authority on anything, and what's the benefit of that? You know.

When you can finally admit to yourself absolutely, once and for all without any hesitation or any misunderstanding or any lack of absolutely knowing it to be so, that God knows and you don't, and that God always will and you never will, then you can relax and let the bus drive itself. Then you get to breathe easy, laugh more, and not worry so much. Then you get to know better that whenever you mistake time and space for anything, it's still infinity and eternity. And at least you're not breaking your back building a big brick house in the middle of an empty mirage, thinking that you're somewhere.

No promises can be made about what all that will feel like, or give you, or be like. The promise is—you won't be in a delusion. You won't be drinking a mirage cup of tea thinking your thirst is being quenched, when you're dying of thirst. That's the most that you can be guaranteed from it. Nobody has ever, as far as I know, come out of that delusion, been willing to go closer to that, who hasn't said in one way or another, "It's all worth it beyond anything I ever imagined." Let that day come for you.

CHAPTER 4

THE STILL, SMALL VOICE WITHIN IS REAL

Premodaya: You always hear this phrase, "the still, small voice within." I heard it all my life that you should learn to listen to the still, small voice within. People say that's the voice of the Divine, that's your inner guide, that's your connection to the Ultimate, the Profound. That's your "guidance," as some people call it. It never meant much to me. I wasn't sure what they were talking about—"still, small voice." You hear it talked about and taught in groups like this, and people say, "Well, go into the forest and get quiet, and you'll hear the still, small voice." There's a wonderful teacher named Peace Pilgrim who says her whole spiritual path started that way—by taking walks in the forest, and getting quiet, and getting in touch with "God's will."

So, it never worked for me. If you're one of the lucky ones who has a sense of what people call the "still, small voice," and even more lucky, if you know how to hear it and know what to do about it, then you're quite, quite blessed. You're quite well-off. Then at least that part of things is done; you don't have to find the way to find out what that means and how to connect with it, how to hear what it's saying.

Everybody who is here has certainly heard, in some form, some kind of calling from the Beyond, some kind of message from way out there that says, "There's more than meets the eye." And for some people, quite clearly, a Divine presence, or God is, or Truth is available, or whatever—all the phrases, which are all true and basically synonymous—is available. But there's something quite unique about what they call the "still, small voice."

I would like to encourage you to understand better that that phrase is very, very limited. One of the reasons it never did much for me, is I never heard the voice—still or loud or small or large—so it confused me; and I don't want you to be confused.

It doesn't have to be a voice; it doesn't have to be still; it doesn't have to be small. It's just an inner urge, an inner sense, an inner knowing. It can be quite mundane; it can be quite matter of fact, all about everyday stuff. Don't think of it as, "It has to be grand and profound, and about something big and spiritual." It's very real.

I wondered about it for years and had no clue what it meant—now I know it's very, very real, and everybody's got it in there somewhere. And if you think you're the exception, you're not. But I would like you to recognize that it comes in many, many different forms.

For some people it's just an inner knowing. For some people it's a feeling, it rises up as a feeling. For other people it's a clarity of mind; it comes as a thought. It can come in any way, shape, or form. The real point about it is, that it's always crystal clear. Now that doesn't mean *we're* always crystal clear about it, or hear it, or know what it means—but from its side, it's crystal clear. It's really a matter of how much you're able to discern it, and then—oddly enough—able to respond to it, follow it, act on it.

Maybe why I'm speaking about it is because I was at a restaurant having breakfast. I got up and I left a two-dollar tip—breakfast was ten bucks (I don't eat expensively!). I started to go, and suddenly I had to turn around and leave another dollar. And I'm not the world's biggest tipper; I'm a fairly generous tipper, but the service wasn't that great, and two dollars seemed about right. But something made me turn around and put another dollar down. I don't know why—not because I'm so generous—but something did. And you know what? That's the "still, small voice."

I want you to understand what I didn't understand most of my life: that it doesn't have to be about Truth or God or something with a capital first letter. It can be about anything. If something that isn't *your* will, if it's something that doesn't necessarily seem like something *you* would think of, something *you* would feel, something *you* would decide—if that happens, even in a small way, can you get familiar enough with these little experiences to recognize that *that is* (literally) the "still, small voice"? *That is* the voice of God speaking to you—even if there's no voice.

I have never experienced it as a voice. Really, more than anything, as I've gotten more sensitive to it and understood it better, for me it comes very much as a feeling, and I've learned to trust it absolutely. That's why I didn't question; I just put that other dollar down—because you don't question that. Well, you do, and for much of my life I'm sure I did, or I just ignored it completely. But to not question it, that is the wisest thing you can do, if you ask me.

First, obviously, you have to know that that's what it is, because your mind can tell you all kinds of foolishness, and if you start following that, you'll get in all kinds of trouble. Your feelings can take you in all kinds of directions that have nothing to do with any "still, small voice," or any Divine connection, or any other thing other than our own foolishness.

I don't want to speak to you and give you suggestions, and then have you go out of here and start doing all kinds of wacky stuff. It's really up to you to find out what this means and to find out what it means in you—to find out what is the significance of these experiences that everybody has: where something moves you and you aren't necessarily quite sure what it is—but you may have some vague sense that it doesn't seem like "*you.*"

For me it has become much more a feeling. Even though it's mundane, even though it's everyday "nothing" kind of stuff—leave another dollar for the waitress, say "hi" to some stranger on the street—whatever it is, whenever that feeling comes, it is the sweetest, most glorious feeling that

I know. And the more I've gotten sensitive to it and the more I have been able to recognize what it is and what it means, the more that's the case.

The struggle for me was to follow it. To do what it says—that was a tough one. I'm good at it now, but I was not always good at it, even after I recognized what it was. But I'm a pretty stubborn person; probably you're less stubborn than I am. Whenever that feeling happens to me, there are a few things I know automatically, unquestioningly, at this point. First: that it's good, even if it seems bad. Second: that I should unquestioningly follow whatever it suggests or feels like it wants me to do, even if I disagree. Third: that it's definitely *not me*, that it's coming from something bigger, that the source isn't locatable in my mind or my heart or my feelings or my senses or my whatever (there's no *my* in it).

You hear this all the time, the "still, small voice" and people say, "Well, listen to your still, small voice." But I don't remember ever hearing anybody talk about the nature of it, that it's not necessarily a voice and it's not necessarily still or small, and it comes in many possible forms, and that it's really—I don't know if I would go as far as to say "necessary," but—absolutely beneficial in every way, to learn more about it in you. It absolutely can direct you.

People say, "I want to do God's will." Well, how are you going to figure that one out? This is one answer to that: by recognizing what this is and attuning yourself, learning enough, training yourself, investigating enough, exploring enough, that it's very clear to you—if you have this experience in any way—what exactly it is for you and what it means.

I'm not even vaguely suggesting you adopt my view of it; I'm sharing that with you, but that's just my view. You may have a whole different view. That's great, because it's not the same for me as for somebody else. Peace Pilgrim used to take walks in the woods and heard a "still, small voice" and felt God directing her. I've never had that experience. I probably never will. I'm not Peace Pilgrim; she's not me. I'm not you; you're not me. It's really about what that category of experience is for you.

But what I can say to you is, having attuned myself to it more, it's quite amazing. It never messes up. Apparently, it's not possible to take a wrong turn if you're clear about it and follow it. In fact, it's foolproof. Because even if something turns out wrong, you can just blame the voice! "I didn't do it; the voice said to do it."

My thought is: Don't think of it as a "still, small voice" only. I would encourage you to identify what it is for you—what form it comes in, for you—and is it possible for you to learn more about it, understand it better, and be more attuned to it, and more able to follow its message?

This is all under the heading of the biggest subject you can discuss, the biggest subject you can put on the table. This is one aspect, one small part, but the meta-subject is: *your will versus God's will; Truth versus personal preference.* This whole "still, small voice" thing is a beautiful way to enter that subject, is a beautiful road to explore the bigger geography. That's my "testimony" about the "still, small voice." I'd like to hear other folks' testimony or clarities or confusions or questions or comments or whatever.

Grant: For me, it depends on the situation. You know, if it's life or death it's not a "still, small voice"—it's more like it's yelling at me. A specific time that this happened, I was coming down the Ventura Freeway late at night and the exit was right there, and the "voice" yelled, "No you don't!—Keep going!"

Premodaya: The "still, screaming voice." [laughter]

Grant: It frightened me, it shocked me. I didn't know what to do, but I didn't take the exit. So, I took the next exit, and as I came around, I saw red and blue flashing lights. There had just been an accident right there— which I would have been a part of if the "voice" hadn't said, "No you don't, stupid." I had to laugh, because once I saw the accident I said, "I get it! I'm going to listen from now on." When you realize that the voice is talking or that feeling is there, there's a knowingness there for me. If I'm trying to find a parking place it will go very quietly, "Hey, it's over to the left." But if

I'm going to get killed, it's like it's *wailing*. It seems like it's so much a part of me that *it* wants to live too, and it lives through me.

Premodaya: But isn't it amazing? That this is?

Grant: It just is. I don't consider it to be amazing.

Premodaya: Well, I do. It's amazing to me. People want to trivialize it or explain it away or say there's no such thing or it's your own intuition and nothing more than that. Or there's the whole new-age mentality: "It's your inner wisdom." There are all these different attitudes toward it, and it astounds me. One of the things that astounds me is, it's very hard to find somebody who doesn't have some experience of it. Even if they don't believe it, even if they pooh-pooh it, they can still relate to you in their own experience. And you listen to it, and it's like, "Whoa!" It's amazing.

Dylan: I can relate to that small urge to go back and put the dollar. I'm one of those people that seek out God's will, but I hadn't thought in terms of that's doing God's will. But then, of course, that is the problem, walking around and not knowing what is my will and what is God's will, as you keep surrendering, more and more. I thought it was interesting you mentioned it was following God's will, it's one of those subtle things that I didn't think about—that wasn't brought up to my consciousness.

Premodaya: Good. Well, that's my job. We're glad to have you.

Prof. Alex: Something happened to me when I was very young. There's a famous temple in Penang with poisonous snakes and beautiful flowers. It's a beautiful place, and the word was to us children, "Don't touch anything." I walked off on my own, and I saw this beautiful flower. I looked around, there was no one watching, so I thought, "I'll take it; no one will know." But my right arm wouldn't move, I couldn't move to reach for it. For the first time in my life, I couldn't move. And then the flower moved—it was a snake's head, deadly poison. Something in me knew, "Don't move."

Premodaya: It's amazing.

Darshana: Grant was talking about the "voice" getting really loud. The last time I saw my father we had a very quick goodbye, and as I was driving away down the road, this voice came to me and said, "That wasn't a very good goodbye. What if this was the last time you saw him? Maybe you should turn around." And I didn't—and he died the next day. I have never regretted not listening to that voice as much as that particular time. But it is true how it gets really loud; it couldn't have been any louder without me probably thinking I was crazy.

Premodaya: Well, maybe the volume is an indicator. I mean, maybe one way to sort what that is—from all the other things we sense or feel or think that might be our foolishness—maybe one of the best indicators is, when it's very clear because it's very loud. I don't know; it sounds right. That's certainly suggested by your experience and Grant's. I love this subject; it's fascinating to me.

King: For me, it's not a voice; mine is much more visual and a seeing. What I find most amazing is how subtle it is and how always right-there it is. Maybe due to spirituality or spiritual circles there's almost a wanting to aggrandize it. We all have these grand stories and one of the most beautiful ones is the Peace Pilgrim story, how she walks through the meadow, and there's the moon, and then she just knew. But for me, there's a subtlety to it, and it's right there. Now, I never laugh more than when I miss it, and I realize after stumbling a couple of steps, "Wait, this was revealed to you a week ago or a few hours ago," or "Here it is—here it is." To me the amazing part is how it's always right there and how many times I've tricked myself into missing it.

Malik: I knew mine was not a voice, but I was thinking about all the times where I've gone with that pull and I think it's a pull of the heart. Sometimes it can be very gentle and a sweet kind of little feeling. And sometimes it can be more of a fast-beating heart when it's sometimes more intense. For me it's definitely in the heart, it's a feeling. I've questioned it a lot of times, but the more you trust it, it's taken me to some incredible places. A lot of times it feels like what you don't want to do, but it's a deeper feeling that you need to do it. Even though it can be really scary, the times when it's happened it's an incredible relief and an opening afterwards, after the fear or whatever it may be. It just is wide open.

James: There will be times for me, day-to-day situations, where I get the urge to do one thing and I think, "Oh, I want to do something else," and I either follow it or I don't. But there have been times in my life where it's like a light comes on—it's almost like heightened reality and it says, "This is for you." I've never not followed it. When the light comes on it's very strong, "This is for you." When that light came on, I changed careers. The various spiritual paths I have gone in, the light has come on. I came here six or seven months ago and sat in a chair and the light came on and it's like, "This is for you."

Vincent: It's possible that these voices or these urges, especially the ones that are alarming—are some kind of Divine interruption in a time/space thing, since in God or Divinity there's no time, but we're living through time. But on a spiritual side, we're probably not living through time; everything is happening simultaneously. Take one of these big events; for example, Darshana's father dying. These big events didn't really happen in time. They all happened at once. And somehow, there's some little blip, whether it's Divine or not, that says, "You know, you may never see your father again." It's one of those little blips in the system where, for some reason, it went out of sequence, because it was so powerful (or something) in your own physical life—so it comes out as a voice to some people.

Premodaya: That's a good point, and kind of what I'm saying, that there are really, as far as I can see, two possibilities. That's one of them; that goes under another broad category. There's the broad category of everything that isn't a Divine "message"—for want of a better way to say it—that isn't your connection with what's bigger in the ultimate sense. There's this whole other category that you're suggesting, that certainly has to be the case, which has to do with your intuition, has to do with a broader wisdom, has to do with a depth of understanding; different moments that happen in life—everybody has had these experiences, too. That's a clarification of what I'm trying to communicate, which is that both exist and my experience has been that it's wise to know the difference. It's wise and useful and beneficial to know when it's really Divine will asserting itself in you. Not that a greater wisdom or a deeper intuition isn't good and isn't valuable and isn't the right direction, but to know the difference, in my experience, makes all the difference. And the differentiating factor in what has happened for me, is that feeling part.

Ultimately, it's all the same thing. Ultimately you can differentiate all you want, and it's interesting and it's fun, and probably beneficial, and it probably leads to more understanding and more clarity, but ultimately what's the difference? Ultimately everything is a signal—*everything*. And I mean that very literally. There's not one second of your experience that isn't the Divine talking to you. There's not one second of anything that isn't a more or less discernible signal from existence to you.

It's all a message. In that sense we're just talking "apples and oranges" in the other conversation. But this is the whole nonsense of our time, that this has all been discounted. The scientific viewpoint, the kind of anti-metaphysical mindset, discounts all this stuff. And culture after culture, for eons, have talked about omens and portents and signs and symbols and this and that—cultures with great wisdom, cultures with great science, cultures clearly with deep knowledge. Then we come along—the last couple hundred years, Western-European societies—and say, "Oh, that's all nonsense," and certainly I used to think that. But now I'm very acutely aware that omens are everywhere. Believe me, I see omens I don't want to see.

On a less ominous-sounding note, there are signs and symbols everywhere, readily interpretable, if you become more sensitive and more open to simply recognizing that it is all a message. These aren't beyond the scope of us ordinary people to understand and interpret; you don't have to be an eighth-generation aboriginal shaman to read an omen. They are everywhere. It's our culture's loss that so much is just brushed aside as primitive or nonsensical or meaningless or insignificant.

Prof. Alex: When you live in a big city—highly organized—and you live an organized life, it's very hard to find and pick up on these subtle things.

Premodaya: I don't know, is it?

Grant: By being in the "more advanced culture," as things get speeded up, then we start to see that there's more meaninglessness in all the things we think there was supposed to be meaning in. We all have cars, get around, go see movies, eat the best food, do jobs and aspire to something, and then we start to find out that by acquiring them they have no meaning. The people that struggle to stay alive never get to discover that. In the East, the holiest men sit there, and their job is to sweep all day—or—we're told we find God in just washing the dishes all the time. To me, that's the real difficult part. I wish I could find God when I was just brushing my teeth. But these holy men that just sweep up all day seem to be able to find God in exactly that task, which holds out the possibility that we would find God in every single thing we do too. Maybe they are in some kind of bliss. Or maybe, they are just in a completely different embracing or belief that keeps them there, I can't say.

Prof. Alex: Well, it's a simple activity, sweeping. If they were high-pressure stockbrokers they might find it very difficult to let the mind relax and quiet the mind and *be* spiritual. But if I'm sweeping all day, I can be spiritual.

Priya: Sometimes, just for a second, you see a spark of light or you have a certain feeling and there's nothing wrong with it: It's just perfect, but it's not dependent on the nature of what activity is going on, or what kind of day is happening—there's no lack of perfection there. It wouldn't matter if you were sweeping or jumping up and down. It happens to everybody. In my view, you have a taste of that already—everybody does. I wanted to say that because it's beneficial, and I recently started to really appreciate it.

Grant: Are you able to appreciate it all the time? We all struggle with trying to find that.

Premodaya: What I want to say to you is [addressing Grant] the difference you imagine between you and the holy man isn't there.

Grant: Hence the frustration, I know that.

Premodaya: Do you really know it for a fact? I mean do you know it for real.

Grant: Well, I'm not living it, but that frustration—meaning, I know it, but I'm not living it—I'm not there. But, yeah, I know it's there.

Premodaya: That's a huge statement. Just the fact that you can make that statement is most of the proof that there isn't much difference between those holy sweepers and you; even to make that statement is phenomenal. How many people on this planet right now do you think could make that statement?

Let me suggest to you that the fact that you can make this huge statement is a doorway that you can take more advantage of, and there are ways to deepen that knowing so that the day comes when you don't have the knowing—the knowing has you. That's absolutely possible for you—and I don't mean you generically, I mean *you*. Be as frustrated as you want, but don't think it's not absolutely possible for you, and it doesn't have to involve going to the Himalayas or sweeping anything.

This is proof positive, a room full of people who can all attest to the same thing. If you went to the atheist convention and polled them, they would give you the same stories, unanimously. They would have a different interpretation; they would have a different explanation of what it means (and, of course, you would be right and they would be wrong), but the difference between you and the atheist is, the atheist just has a different interpretation of the same information, because they haven't been touched by something from the Beyond—keyword, "yet." But this is plenty of proof for intelligent minds: that you ask anybody, whatever they believe, whatever their mindset is, whatever their philosophy is, and they will all tell you these experiences. So, *very big* clue.

To surrender to the fact of that, is to open yourself more to the possibility of the Divine, the possibility of what you're saying, of it being more your life. There isn't a person in this room for whom that isn't quickly and imminently and truly possible. I don't know how you get here, but I know who brings you, which is the reason I show up every time.

LIVE WHAT YOUR HEART TRULY KNOWS

Premodaya: Really, only silence can speak, but since we're human beings and we have the power of speech, and words can help move things, we use them. There's nothing wrong with that, but don't misunderstand the reality, which is that it's not about the words. It's not about the ideas or the concepts that the words express. It's about what all that comes from. It's to get to the point where you hear the silence between the words louder than the words, more clearly than the words, where the Truth palpitates for you between the words, not in the words. Because the Truth is alive as you are. In fact, it's alive as you. It's alive as this world. It's alive as this universe and all the other universes. It's what this all sits in: this thing we call "me," this thing we call "life," this thing we call "the world," this thing we call "time." It's not just floating out there somewhere; it's *in* something. These meetings—any gathering in the name of Truth—is to try to connect with that. With that which everything sits in, comes from, is of.

All around the world there's this whole culture of satsang. It isn't just an Eastern thing; it isn't just an Indian thing or a Chinese thing. Now there's a whole world culture, people in every country, looking for what's deeper, what's beyond, what's true. So we're all part of the culture of satsang—a world community made up of very tiny numbers, because most of the world isn't looking for what's true. Most of the world is looking for comfort or pleasure or gain.

There's no gain in satsang. You won't get rich from the Truth. You won't have more money in the bank, although it's possible. Not likely to come directly from your commitment to Truth— although there are plenty of folks who want to sell you manifestation ideas and techniques—how to get rich through spiritual power. Real spiritual power has nothing to do with this world. It has to do with developing the ability to see beyond this world, and very strange things happen along the way that are not explainable.

Now, the strangest thing, certainly, that has ever happened to me is sitting in this chair. And the second strangest thing that ever happened to me was sitting in that [audience] chair. There's really no difference. In actuality, I'm sitting in that chair, and would be quite content to sit in that chair forever, and never sit in this chair. That's why it's so strange, because not even for a second did I ever want to sit in this chair. There are people who want to sit in this chair. I can't imagine, but there are. I don't know if you understand me, but there really is no benefit to sitting in this chair. To my personal experience, the benefit's sitting in *that* chair. I guess if you sit in that chair long enough, you're asked to sacrifice your body and sit up here. Don't ask me how that happened, because I can't explain it to you. But everybody has a part to play. And somehow, somewhere, it came about that I'm supposed to play the part of the guy in the red chair.

By the time that happened, I was old enough and clear enough that I didn't argue; I didn't fight with it. It didn't seem natural; it didn't seem possible; it didn't seem wise; it didn't even seem reasonable, but the message was very clear and I knew by then not to argue with the circumstances of the universe sending a clear message. That's where I would like you to be. We're all receiving messages all the time. I'm not talking about hocus-pocus; I'm talking about the inner hearing, the inner knowing, the inner sensing that's in everyone. Everyone, without exception. I don't think anybody would argue that. What I want to do is encourage you to listen to it. To not do what most of us typically do and either deny it, push it away, trivialize it, disbelieve it, ignore it, or decide that there are better things to do with our time and energy. Those inner messages, for want of a better way to say it, are straight from the Beyond. If you're in this room, you can afford to trust those messages. In fact, I'll be negative about it: You're a fool if you don't trust those messages. Be less foolish, and trust what your heart tells you. There are no bad hearts in this room.

In a room full of good-hearted people who are sincere, every heart can trust itself. Every heart should trust itself, because the world isn't going to come rushing in and say, "Hey, you're trying to plug in spiritually as much as you can; you're doing a great job; trust yourself more." No, the world's going to say, "Stop wasting your time and go out there"—at least the Western world—"Go out there and make some money, go out there and get a better job, go out there and finish your degree." Go out there and whatever. None of that is a problem. Nothing wrong with any of that. Unless it's saying it in a negation of that inner voice. Unless it's saying, "Don't listen to what's in your heart, and just do what the world expects you to do."

It's easy to say, "Listen to your heart," and it sounds like it's easy to do. It's not. It's the hardest thing to do. There's no support for it. In fact, you're likely to be criticized or attacked for it. You're likely to be called crazy. If you actually go out and follow your heart, not just think about it, not just implement one little tiny aspect of it, not just feel it and then do nothing, but actually do what your heart tells you to do—if you actually do it, it's highly likely to turn your life upside down. It's highly likely to revolutionize everything. It's highly likely to bring you to a place or a something that you never imagined for a second. When I say, "I encourage you to follow your heart," I'm not deluded that I'm speaking lightly. It's a very serious thing to say. There's every chance that if you listen to me and follow this suggestion that you'll pay a big price for it, whatever that may be.

But I want to suggest to you that if you do, and you pay that price, you won't regret it. The society, our society, teaches you that the head is the organ of knowing. They are wrong. The heart is the organ of knowing. Not the mind, not the brain. If you really want to know, you will have to listen to your heart. If you really want to plug in, then you have to plug in to what your heart tells you. And that really means feeling it; that includes actually letting yourself feel whatever needs to be felt, and that isn't always pleasant either. That isn't always easy either. The feelings may be difficult. The feelings may include feelings of loss, feelings of grief, feelings of shame. You'll feel more vulnerable. No question. Whether the feelings are thought to be good or thought to be bad, either way you'll feel much more vulnerable. You'll be much more vulnerable. You'll be much more permeable—things will affect you more. That isn't easy. That can become an ordeal. Staying open and listening to your heart can be the hardest ordeal you have ever gone through in your life.

When I say, "Follow your heart, listen to your heart," I'm not just saying a nice little phrase. I'm saying, let Truth move you, because there's nobody in this room who doesn't have a very well-developed capacity to hear the Truth within them. But do you trust it? Are you willing to actually allow it to make some decisions, to actually inform your actions, to actually change something from how it is now? Because if you allow it, that's what it will do, but it will be more the right decision than any decision your mind can make. It will be more in the proper direction for you than any direction your mind can choose. I'm not saying don't use your mind. I'm not saying don't consider and think about things. I'm saying listen to your heart first. Always bring in that aspect, because that's the bigger likelihood for clarity.

The real knowing is always heart knowing. Everybody knows this who's at least reached the age of twenty. But most of us don't trust it; we don't want to take the chance, it isn't safe. And it really isn't safe. You might do something you wouldn't ordinarily do. You might say something to someone you wouldn't ordinarily say. All I'm suggesting is that the risk is well worth it. That when you follow your heart more, when you follow that inner knowing more, something opens that can't open any other way. Something flows through you that wouldn't flow through you otherwise, that plugs you in, in a very direct way, more than anything else can that I'm familiar with. You start to develop the ability, a second sense, to recognize it in a subtler way. You start to feel subtle feelings that you may never have felt before.

Some people experience it as that famous phrase, "a still small voice." Some people actually hear a voice. It doesn't mean they are psychotic. It doesn't mean they have lost their mind. They actually hear it in the form of words. It comes to people in different ways. Or it's felt. It's simply a bath of feelings that washes over you. Either very powerfully or very subtly, far in the background. But you can key into it, and there are a hundred other ways that it gets experienced by different people and different personalities.

People in the sincerity of their seeking say, "I want God, I want Truth, I want clarity, I want to know what I'm supposed to do in this life." But they're ignoring the inner knowing that they already know. Somehow, they even know they know the answer, and they literally choose to stay obscure about it, to not be clear about it, to not tune in, because tuning in means you may have to do it. Tuning in means you may actually listen to the Truth, and it may change something. It may demand something. And who knows what that could be? Better to stay safe, and not get too risky about this inner knowing stuff. "Who knows? I could be deluding myself." "Who knows, I could fool myself; why take a chance?" Well, only if Truth is what you want.

If you're saying to yourself, "I'm looking for Truth, I'm looking for Reality, I'm seeking the Divine," then you're going to have to be as willing as you can possibly be to listen to your own heart. To trust and act on your own knowing, whatever form that knowing comes to you in. And whatever its felt-sense means. If you experiment with it, you'll see that it's not as dangerous as you might have thought. I'm not even saying that many of you, if not most of you, haven't even already done that—perhaps you have. I'm saying, do it more. Go further. Be riskier. Try harder to access what you already know and actually use it, actually live it. You're already living in it, whether you recognize it or not. It's not that the Truth is in you; it's that you're in the Truth; you're sitting in it. But it's known from inside. Just like you need ears to hear, the organ of recognizing the Truth is from the inside. It's your whole being, inside. It doesn't come from the outside. The hearing comes from the inside, just like hearing these words comes from the inside of your ears. That's not esoteric understanding; that's just common sense. Of course, it has to be that way.

But are we taking it seriously? Are you saying, "OK, let's see what I really know and what my heart really says," and then actually considering what to do about it? Most of us aren't doing that. Most of us are running around complaining, why we aren't clearer. "Why can't I get the answers? Why doesn't God speak to me?"

Priya: So often I feel a response is called for or some action is called for, but I have no idea what it is. There's been times when I felt very sure I was doing the right thing, and later I thought, "Jeez, what was I thinking? I was totally wrong." And times when I was totally unsure, it seemed later it worked out that it was actually the right place. It feels like being on a cliff that's totally windy where you don't know what's going on at all.

Premodaya: Are you willing to be a cliff dweller?

Priya: Whatever it takes, whatever it wants. Yes.

Premodaya: It's the perfect question because it pertains to everybody.

Nobody doesn't have this question. Nobody hasn't gotten to a point where exactly the conflicts you describe don't happen. Everybody comes to this point, sooner or later. Here is the answer; it's a three-part answer.

The first part of the three-part answer is: You actually do know. There is a way to measure. There is a way to gauge. The way you gauge is by getting quiet and literally letting your feeling tell you. You have to trust it. The hard part is trusting it. It will either clearly feel right or clearly feel wrong when you key in. By "clearly" I don't mean absolutely, and I don't mean once and for all and I don't mean so clear you can't miss it. You may have to tune in very subtly to get that piece of clarity. But you will feel it.

Most of us are in too much of a rush. We want the answer right away. We want it within eighteen seconds, usually. If you're willing to spend a little more time, whether that little more time is more seconds, more minutes, or hours—it's usually not more than hours—you will feel "Yes, this is more right than not" or "No, this is more wrong than not."

If you have the time to wait, the foolproof, corollary answer to part one, is just wait. If it doesn't need an immediate action or an immediate response, just wait. There's nobody who hasn't had the experience of sleeping on something and the next day it's, who knows how, more clear. But it's the same as we were saying a little bit earlier. You have to trust what your feeling tells you. Now, that's part one of a three-part answer.

Part two is you will never know the actual or full results. It is not part of this universe and it is not part of being a human being to know the eventual outcome. The outcome is always far further down the road than where we think the outcome is. What you said is accurate for every human being who has ever lived on this planet: "I did some things; I thought something was the right way to go; it was clear to me, and later events suggested to me I was wrong. And other times I was absolutely sure this was wrong, but for whatever reason I did it anyway and it turned out later events suggest it was right." But there are later events after that, and later events after that, and events when you're eighty, and events when you've been dead for a hundred years and events a thousand years later. You don't know the reverberation of what you did and its ultimate outcome, its ultimate results, its true meaning.

You have two choices. Follow your heart and do what you think best and do your best to know, and don't worry about the results. Don't make that interpretation at any point. And both are positive possibilities—that's one possibility you always have. The second possibility is, let the universe decide. How you do that is by giving up any notion of what's best for you or the one you care about, and what's best as an outcome. How you let the universe decide is by opening yourself to simply what's best for the entire world, and let that guide your choice.

Either way, you're making a positive choice. Either way, either method, takes you out of the dilemma of "What should I do?" and aligns you more fully with keying into what is—it's not about right and wrong. It's not that the right way leads to this and the wrong way leads to that, or the right decision or the wrong decision has such a huge impact, because in the grand scheme of things it's "Am I operating from what I *really* know and am I operating in concert with that which is greater than I?" That's the real question; that's the real crux of the matter. So that's part two of the answer.

Part three of the answer is to recognize as fully as you can that no dilemma is yours. That no dilemma is ever presented to you or to anyone that isn't a doorway to Truth. Part three of the answer really means, in my understanding, is don't be timid. Don't be so worried about the outcome. Don't be so concerned with how things turn out or whether I'm right or whether I'm wrong. If you're really listening to yourself and doing the best you know how, you don't need to tread so carefully.

Most of us simply don't trust ourselves enough. Most of us have been raised in a society that says, "Watch out; don't trust yourself; don't follow your heart" and "Better be careful; who do you think you are?" Most of us carry that tape. What I'm suggesting is that if you're as good-hearted a person and as spiritually sincere as everybody in this room is, everyone in this room can afford to trust themselves a whole lot more and forget about the result. Do what you have to do, make the decisions you have to make.

Most of us are far too cautious. That's really what I meant by "follow your heart." I meant, don't be so timid. Don't be so worried about what the result will be. Take a chance. What's the worst that happens? You were wrong, so you stop doing whatever it is. Or you do something else, or you go a different direction. Big deal. You bought the wrong car; it turned out to be a lemon, so what? You said the wrong thing to your husband or your wife, so what? Did they pull out a gun and threaten to shoot you? Most of us are imagining consequences to our actions that aren't there and aren't likely. We take ourselves much too seriously. Most of us agonize about every little thing that we have to decide or take an action on.

I'm saying there's another way to live that involves following your heart and it involves a lot less worrying, if you really get used to it, a lot less being concerned with comfort and safety, once you get comfortable with it and as you develop that ability to hear and to know that's already there. The organ is already functioning; you just have to key in more. Things start to fall into a more proper perspective. You start to be less egoistic about your own decisions. You recognize that you're part of something bigger. But that can't happen until you do the experiment. Until you try being riskier. "Riskier" means go with what you really know.

Most of us play a game in our head with what we really know. "Do I really know it; is it really true; should I really do it?" I'm saying, stop playing that game and try it. That's why it's a three-part answer. It's everything I said before. It's not even remotely easy in the beginning or any stage that we're at to go further with it, it demands a lot of us. It takes a real effort. It takes a real willingness. It takes a real adventurousness and willing to be even more vulnerable, even more chancy. It's living more dangerously. But bigger chances have bigger payoffs.

Now, you can hear this answer from many people. Many teachers, many people, many philosophers. But the trick isn't hearing this answer. The trick is actually doing it, actually living it, actually trying in a sincere way to take your own inner knowing much more seriously and trust it. To actually act on it and not to judge it based on results. Because you can always find a point in time where the results are "that was right" and another point in time where the results are "that was wrong," for the same thing. It just depends when you want to make the interpretation. What I'm saying is, don't put so much stock in the interpretation.

This is how we all drive ourselves nuts. We all second-guess ourselves constantly. But it's possible to not live that anymore. It's possible, not because you're more confident, not because you're surer of yourself, but because you just trust life more. It's possible to live another way. Where worries either disappear completely or get cut by ninety-nine point five percent. Where you don't spend hours on something that takes seconds, or years on something that should take an hour, because you're going round and round and round in your own non-self-trusting. You can do that for a lifetime; most of us do. But the people in this room can do better than that. And you're a worrier, Priya. Can you imagine a life without any significant worries?

Priya: That would be great—I can see that, despite the temptation to grab on to some other method of figuring things out. The other ways that I look at don't have any assurances anyway either, it's almost as if they are dry, like they're not part of life. It's like, "I read this in a book, so I will do it this way," but you don't know if it applies. No matter what the outcome, you still didn't really learn anything because it wasn't something you understood yourself or felt yourself. Although from what you're saying, it's not about, "OK, it turned out this way, next time I will do the same thing." It's true everything is always alive and changing and the same moment won't happen twice anyway.

Premodaya: What I'm saying is actually very, very simple in regard to that. I'm saying you can trust your inner knowing, and your feeling, your heart sense feeling, and the more you trust it, the more you develop the ability to hear it, interpret it, and follow it, and implement it. And as a human body-mind that's the best you can do, and it's pretty darn good once you're really clear. The only thing that beats that, is letting God decide.

That's a whole other topic.

What I'm really saying is that it's not the problem we tend to think it is. It's only that lack of self-trust, lack of own heart-trust that makes this a problem. If it turns out your decision was right or if it turns out your decision was wrong, or any combination thereof, what matters more is to trust yourself more. Either way things turn out. Either way you go, it should be about trusting your own heart more. That's what works. Not "Now I know how to do it right." The measure is: Are you trusting yourself more? Are you trusting your own heart more? In the long run, that's what matters. This decision was wrong; that decision was right—what matters more is how much are you trusting your own knowing, your own heart sense?

That's how the whole activity of worry evolved, from people not trusting their natural knowing, and it couldn't be any other way, it seems to me. There must have been somewhere in this world, a time and a place, where in the society people didn't really know how to worry. Because they enough trusted life, they enough trusted the Divine, they enough were plugged into this life. I will tell you quite happily that I spent most of my life as a worrier and that's one hundred percent over. That's possible for anybody. I'm not saying I don't have negative moments, and I'm not saying I don't have this thought or that thought. I'm saying the mechanism for automatic worry stopped operating. It's simply a mechanism. It can stop for you too. Believe me, if it stopped for me, it can stop for you. There are a lot of reasons why that mechanism should never stop for me. I may be the only Jew in history it ever stopped for. [laughter]

Priya: Sometimes when I'm waiting during an interaction, space opens up that I feel like is in front of me, instead of inside of me. But it seems fine; it doesn't matter—like you were saying, it comes different ways.

Premodaya: It doesn't matter where you locate it, because where you locate it is arbitrary. Most people feel it inside themselves. That's an illusion too, because it's not really inside you. But that's how most people experience it, so it's useful to put it that way in a conversation like this. But it's neither inside you or outside you. It just is. The Truth is neither inside you nor outside you. That's just our idea. Inside and outside is our idea. Reality recognizes no inside and no outside. Truth doesn't create any divisions. Our minds do—fine. But don't be fooled.

There's a certain utilitarian use to those divisions, but for a conversation like this it's better to understand that inner is just another aspect of outer, and outer is just another aspect of inner. They aren't two things like we generally think, and we generally think that, because that's what we are taught to think. But think smarter. We don't need to think about it for more than about twenty seconds to recognize it. Of course, inner is just another aspect of outer; of course, outer is just another aspect of inner; of course, they aren't two things. Obviously. There's no person in this room that can't readily, quickly, and almost instantly understand and accept that.

Don't ever be fooled again about higher or lower, inner and outer. That's mind. It's not what is. What is, what's real, what exists, doesn't have these characterizations. The characterizations are given by us. The less you characterize, the closer you are to Truth, to how it really *is*. You know I say—probably not a week goes by that I don't say—there's no such thing as a country. What's this idea "country"? It's an idea. Lines on a map. Show me where the United States ends and Mexico starts, by walking it. You can't show me. There's no line anywhere. These are our ideas.

Following your heart, following your own true knowing, is just smarter for intelligent people, and every person in this room is a highly intelligent person. That isn't true every time we have a meeting, but tonight it is.

Vivian: How would you know that everyone is intelligent here?

Premodaya: Because I can see it. It's visible. Do you see it? Look around, look around. Do you see anybody who doesn't look intelligent to you?

Vivian: I actually don't worry too much about intelligence. I worry about intuition.

Premodaya: Yes, intelligence means intuition.

Vivian: But the intelligence in the physical plane is a very limited thing, like you're saying. In the physical plane there are boundaries, there's in and out, there's hot and cold, that we put this in the physical plane, but the intuition goes beyond the physical plane. That's what I understood you were telling her.

Premodaya: Yes, that's the intelligence we were talking about.

Vivian: When we are in tuned to the cosmic will, meaning surrender to God, if you don't know what to do in a given situation, or simply listen to your inner voice that always tells you what's good, what's wrong, and what's good, or what was right. Like a six-year-old child has not much experience, but if he does something bad, he will go and hide; he is following his inner voice. But when people grow older, they are so busy in their minds, that they don't really listen to their inner voice. But when you relax, when you stop worrying, your intuition develops, and you can listen to your inner voice.

Premodaya: You're correct; "intuition" is a more accurate word than "intelligence." You have to be intelligent in that way, to really be intelligent. That's why I say everybody in here is intelligent, because everybody in here has that way of being smart. There's nobody in this room that would argue with what you just said. There are plenty of people out there that would.

You have to recognize who is in the room. In other words, if you don't see that not everyone would accept what we are saying, if you don't see that you have been, whether you know it or not, part of a special category, the ones that this is possible for, then you do need to see that. Because this isn't possible for anyone or everyone. It is, ultimately, but only once you're intelligent enough to recognize what this means. The majority of people haven't gotten there yet. You have. If you're part of the culture of satsang, if even once you go to satsang, it means the universe has graced you with that point of maturity, that point of intuitive knowing, that level of intelligence. No matter how intellectually smart or dumb you may be. It's not about intellectual smart, obviously. This is why you can afford to trust yourself. I would not say this to a random group. I don't want most people to trust themselves. Most people are dangerous and nuts. But you guys should absolutely trust yourselves.

You're the satsang-goers; you're the ones something is possible for. I don't waste my time on the people nothing is possible for. That's why ICODA exists. Because something is possible for you that isn't possible for just anybody randomly. You're closer to something truer. It's not something to be taken lightly. It's also not something to be all puffed up about.

I don't say that for your ego; I say that because, to my observation, most people who are in that position need to hear that. Most of us are needlessly and falsely humble. We don't recognize what we have been given. You have been given, by the Divine, the absolute possibility to know the Truth. Be glad. It doesn't make you better than Joe Schmo who isn't there yet. It just means you're further along. You have gotten further down the road, for whatever reason. I guarantee you the reason has nothing to do with you, so there's no reason to get egoistic about it. But absolutely recognize that you're in a special category. Something is possible for you that's the Divine. I say this at eighty percent of the meetings: If that was not true you would not be able to sit in this room. You would not be able to tolerate this conversation. You would run. Every once in a while, somebody wanders in here accidentally, and they don't last very long. But that's once in thirty meetings; it doesn't happen often, because most people who end up in this room belong in this room, know exactly that they belong in this room.

What are you going to do with that? You have to do something with it. It's not enough to just say, "Oh, isn't this great?" You have to live it.

You have to let that guide your life far more. You have to give your life to that. That's the Divine calling you. You really have to live that. Otherwise, what good is it to be in that category? Why was I put in this chair? That's exactly why. To get you to live it. There's no other purpose to this. To get you to live more what you already are, in any way that I can. And for no other reason than, you're the ones it's possible for. It's not possible for most folks. They are too busy with what doesn't matter. And they don't want to hear about it.

You have actually gotten to a point in life, for whatever reason, that you want to hear about it. You want to know, and it's possible to know. That's why you're here. That's why you're sitting in this room. But I can talk about it for the next fifty years, and if you don't start living it, it will make no difference. How you start living it is by starting to trust what you really know. Maybe it will turn out like Priya said; maybe it will turn out to be a wrong action, so what? How many wrong actions do you think you did today? Probably more than you are aware of. So what? You are among the tiny minority of people on this planet who have actually gotten to a point where it's no longer about "Am I right or am I wrong?" Most people are willing to kill and die for the *idea* of being right. You're the few among the few, interplanetary, who have actually gotten beyond that, who can see through that, who aren't living life just about whether they're right and wrong, or who's right and who is wrong. Who aren't living from a standpoint of "I'm right, God dammit!" Great! But now what?

If you've gotten to that point, you have a higher responsibility, a higher obligation and a higher potential. That has to be recognized; that has to be answered, responded to. The response is to trust yourself and give your life to it; give your heart to it. So what if you make a mistake along the way? There will never be a day in this lifetime you don't make a mistake. In one sense or another, one form or another. There will never be a single day. There's no such thing as a day without a mistake. Some of them you're aware of; some of them you're not. You will never know who you actually hurt, what creature you actually killed, what little action reverberated into a thousand other actions fifty years from now and changed everything. You will never know. So why be so minutely concerned with "Did I do the right thing?" Trust yourself and live. Trust your heart; you can afford to. Those other schmoes can't. You can. You have a richer potential. You can trust your heart much more. You can live a life where you're responding, rather than pre-evaluating everything. You're the only ones that's possible for.

Vivian: Also, what is right or wrong—for what? When I ask myself that, it seems there's already a plan that I'm protecting, so nothing is right or wrong, because I have an idea about how it should be.

Premodaya: There is a plan; it's the Divine plan, and you're part of it. It doesn't operate the way our minds operate when we hear the words "Divine plan"—either "Divine" or "plan." Our minds cannot grasp this. It's not about how it sounds. That's what I'm saying: For the people in this room, it's possible to recognize that the Divine plan is operating and you're part of it. It's not possible for most people. So why agonize about every little thing? Oddly enough, it really is taken care of, but only the kind of people who are in this room have the possibility of grasping that in this lifetime. If that hasn't fully crystallized for you, just get it that it's possible for that to fully crystallize for you. That's the good news. It's possible for you.

Lots of people, lots of teachers, say, "It's possible for you." And they mean it in the sense that it's possible for anybody. I don't mean it that way. It's not possible for most people, but it's possible for you because you've gotten to this point. That's what's important to me. I don't even want to talk to those other people. I don't even want to be in the same room with them; screw 'em. I want to be in a room with you. I love everybody, literally, but that doesn't mean I have to hang out with everybody. I would much rather hang out with you. You have much more potential.

EVERYONE KNOWS EVERYTHING

Premodaya: Almost everything we do that we experience as negative, that we tend to think of, maybe a little later, as, "that was wrong, or that was negative, or that was stupid of me, or that was a bad decision," it's usually, quite simply, us not going along with what we somehow already know. Somehow, we know deeper down; somehow, we know off to one side; somehow, we know out here somewhere; wherever it is, somehow we kind of know, and we tell ourselves we don't. We tell ourselves we have to figure it out, which is a very amazing game we all play with ourselves. We actually don't admit to ourselves how much we know (notice I'm saying "know" and not "control").

I would very much like to say to you *everyone knows everything*— which means, of course, *you* know everything. You may not be aware of it; you may not access what you know in a particular moment; you may be confused, or there may be some other overlay that prevents you from admitting to yourself or seeing clearly what you know, but if there's any truth in the statement, "everyone knows everything," the implications are phenomenal. Does that not have the ring of truth? Even just hearing it, "everyone knows everything," don't you just get a sense, thinking about yourself, that, "Yes, there's a bunch of stuff that I know."

I'm not talking about sets of knowledge, but when something has to happen, when a decision has to be made, when life is in the balance, when something important is going on, do we not usually have some kind of sense of what's right or what's good or what's in our best interest or what's in everyone's best interest or what's going to work?

But we tell ourselves we don't. We don't trust what some people call the "inner voice." We just simply don't trust it, which really isn't anything more or less than *we don't trust ourselves*. We don't trust ourselves as who we are; we don't trust our Divine nature; we don't trust our mind; we don't trust anything that isn't "the conventional." We tend not to trust anything that isn't the conventional way that we've come to think of how the mind works, and how people decide, and how people choose.

It's really all nonsense. When we actually come to the point where we make our choice, or make our decision, all that's happening (whether we realize it or not) is that we are finally letting ourselves key into what we already knew.

Everybody knows this, but we don't make it as important as it really is. That's all I'm saying to you, that it's wise to make that understanding far more important, to bring it higher on the priority list of what you pay attention to and what you bring into your consciousness—that it runs your life more.

You already know, yet you live day-to-day telling yourself that you don't know. But here, we've been talking now twenty minutes, and everyone's nodding their head when I say, "You know this." I'm saying: Now *really* know it—absolutely, once and for all—accept that this is true, that this is how it works for people, and let that inform how you view your own ability to decide and to choose. Accept that you already know everything, not in an egoistic puffed-up, crazy way, "Oh, I know everything," not a know-it-all, but that somehow, the miracle of life includes that you came here with enough inner "whatever," that you have a certain inner knowledge and inner knowing that is there when you need it—is *certainly there* when you need it most—and that, if you're anything over the age of twenty-two, you've relied on it much of your life.

See that. Admit that. Factor that into how you view how things work, is all I'm saying. But really get it, once and for all! Because if you get it—which means give it some thought after you leave here tonight—and get it once and for all, it will change everything. You will start to automatically trust that which you could not trust before. You will automatically start to feel good about that which was causing you fear before. You will automatically and involuntarily start to relax about what it means to be alive. I promise.

Anna: Sometimes I'm confused; I start listening to my inner voice and sometimes it's very clear and sometimes I was trapped by myself because it was sort of wishful thinking or something; I thought this was my inner voice. Can you help more?

Premodaya: Yes, that's an excellent question.

It's the perfect question because this is exactly the dilemma that happens for so many people. We are so good, so adept at this whole "false security" thing, that we can actually fake our own inner voice. We actually can, without a whole lot of trouble, or a whole lot of effort, immediately fool ourselves in a thousand different ways—so, instead of keying into what you really, truly know, you're keying into what you really, truly would like, what you'd like to hear. This is no different from when the wife says to the husband, "Honey, look at these travel brochures ...," you know, she wants a certain answer. The answer is really stupidly simple. You've got to be smart enough, alert enough to that possibility that you're actually watching out to make sure you're not fooling yourself. You have to be skeptical enough to develop the discernment of what is real knowing, what is the real inner voice, if you will, versus, "What is my mind fooling me, what is my ego trapping me into ... yet another false idea that does not benefit me in the long run?" You just have to get good at telling when there's a lie going on.

To my experience and to my observation that's partly a function of time and practice. You have to get good at catching yourself in a self-lie. The way you stated your question already gives clues about the answer, because you really have to listen to yourself, to what you're saying to yourself, and if you can ask the question, "Is this what I *want* or is this what I *know*?" that's a clue. If you sit with that, it will usually get clear. My experience is, for most people, it will usually get clear when it's just a desire, because the trap here is desire. This is tricky ground because when you really key into what you know, it may or may not be close or related to what you want. You have got to be able to read yourself well enough to have some sense of, "How much of this is about my own desire, and how much is this me letting go and listening to what I know, or keying into what I know?"

If you remain confused about this, if you have trouble with this, there is a true test. The test is: are you willing to completely let go of it and not have it at all? Are you willing to not get it?

Anna: Let go of your desire.

Premodaya: Whatever it is. If it's real knowing, it will be very easy to say, "It's fine if I don't get it." It won't be a struggle to say, "I can let go of that." If it's coming from a place mostly, or all, of just desire, ego, false mind, self-trickery, you will have a very difficult time saying, "And if it doesn't happen, fine, I can let go of it." You will feel a strengthening of the desire, instead of a willingness to let go of the desire. That's a huge clue; that's really the final test, "Is this desire tricking me? Is this my mind parading as inner knowing, mimicking the voice of inner knowing, or is it the real voice of inner knowing?" If you're willing to let it all go, that's the test. That's the final test when all else remains confused. And it's amazing how clear it is. It works; it's the litmus test … the litmus test works. The paper really does change color, and you will feel—right away—a lightness, "Yeah, I'm willing to let that go," or, "No way, I've got to have it!" Try it, you'll see.

YOUR WISDOM MIND

Morgan: How do you know it is your ego's voice speaking to you?

Premodaya: If it isn't your ego, what would it be? I'm asking personally for you.

Morgan: That wisdom that you were speaking of earlier.

Premodaya: In that sense it's not a problem. Because if it's the wisdom you tend to know it. If you're really not sure, you will be right ninety-nine percent of the time if you assume it's your ego. Because when it's not your ego, we tend to know it; we tend to have a clear sense, or at least clear-enough sense, that this is not my ordinary ego giving me a dialogue; something else, something different, something yet again altogether different is going on. If you're not sure, assume it's the ego because if it isn't, you will tend to be fairly sure it isn't. The question is extremely valid for everybody, because the ego is fantastic, excellent, at disguising itself into the voice of wisdom.

Morgan y: Exactly, that's the issue.

Premodaya: Yes, so assume it's the ego unless you have a very good sense that it's the voice of wisdom, a sense that tells you pretty much without a lot of doubt that this isn't my ego. But if it sounds wise and you aren't sure, assume it's the ego. You will be right most of the time.

Morgan: Is there a certain part of your body where you can have greater access to the Buddha's wisdom? You have heard of the chakras, right?

Premodaya: It has nothing to do with any part of your body. It has much more to do with the whole of you than any part, and it has next to nothing to do with anything physical, whether it's esoterically physical like chakras or energy patterns, or whether it's grossly physical like your head or your heart or your legs or your hands. If you want to give it a physical dimension, if it's helpful to you to give it a physical dimension, then in the general sense one could say it's much closer, has more to do with your heart than with your head, but beyond that you're pigeonholing it more than is useful.

The wisdom mind is about universal wisdom, so there's no individual component that helps you or gives you a map to access it more readily. It's not about finding it somewhere; it's about knowing it's there and being willing to hear it. It has much more to do with attitude than anything else.

The willingness to hear it, the willingness to let it be heard more clearly, to develop the ears to hear it. What do you think? Because you're tremendously sincere and you're asking very sincerely and seriously, and I take you seriously, so I want to know what you think.

Morgan: I think it's a valid point that ninety-nine percent of the time, it's your ego speaking; I agree with you. I've been on this path for a while now, and it's been so amazing, because I thought that psychology was the answer for everything. Whatever psychology said was the answer, but that's not the answer.

Premodaya: Good, so the only problem is the "for everything."

Morgan: Really what's healed me, is just finding it within myself; it's been an arduous journey but it's been so valuable.

Premodaya: The word you're looking for is "rewarding," it was so rewarding. That's what you're describing.

Morgan: It showed me; it proved to me how valuable I am. Even the turmoil that you go through is so beautiful. I see every heartache as such; I see the beauty in everybody's heartache.

Premodaya: So, is that your ego talking?

Morgan: No, I don't think so; I don't think there's any reason to fight against anything.

Premodaya: Yes, so there's your wisdom mind talking; there's your Buddha mind talking right now, when you say you can see the beauty in everything, even people's struggles and sufferings. Isn't that statement not your wisdom mind speaking? See if you can get that even a little more, right now; everything you just said, you were speaking from your wisdom mind; you were completely, absolutely accessing your wisdom mind.

Morgan: That's beautiful. I could be with it all day; if I could do nothing else but be with it, I would.

Premodaya: It's not necessary, if you can access it like you just did for two and a half minutes, that's good enough, because the understanding that comes from it is with you every second, every day. You may not be sitting in it; you may not be implementing it; you may not be living it necessarily, but it's there. It's given you an understanding that few people who ever live get.

How many people who are born and die on the planet earth ever are able to, anytime in their lifetime including at the end of it, say, "I can see the beauty in everything and in everyone. I can see that people's sufferings and struggles and pains and anguishes have a certain beauty—take them to a certain truth or a certain knowing. I can see the beauty even in all that other people would call terrible"? How many people do you think ever get to that piece of wisdom that's obviously true? Very few. That's your wisdom mind. To be able to make that statement, so much had to have happened first; so much wisdom had to be accessed, acknowledged and known first to be able just to say that. Your question originally was, "How do I know when it's my ego versus when it's my wisdom mind?" That question doesn't matter anymore. What matters is that you have been enough able to live the wisdom mind that you can make that statement that you made, that most people never get to in their entire lifetime: the beauty in everything.

Whether you know it or not, whether you're aware of it or live it in a particular moment—three o'clock on Tuesday, sitting at work, watching TV—whether you know it or not in any given moment, the understanding is there in you, and has to affect everything else whether you know it or not, because it's the wisdom mind understanding. You couldn't make the statement otherwise.

Morgan: My intention and my prayer for myself is that I take that to the next level and apply it every day, because I notice I can turn that on and off.

Premodaya: Well, that's good, and if you actually can turn it on and off and if you can actually apply it more, nothing wrong with it. But what I'm trying to impart to you, what I'm trying to encourage you to do, is see more the significance of what has already happened, the fact that you know what you know, just the fact that you've seen what you've seen. Having that already happen matters more than anything. Even if you can't apply it one iota more than you have so far, it doesn't change the importance of what's already happened. Good for you. My only advice to you is be a little less worried about applying it and a little more aware of how much it's already yours.

Morgan: How's that going to work? What will doing that do for me, what will that create, if I sit on that thought longer, in your opinion?

Premodaya: It will allow it to flower more in you without any effort on your part, other than recognizing the significance more of what has already happened. And if you're really lucky, as a result, your heart will open even more. Good enough?

Morgan: You don't think it will feed my ego?

Premodaya: I'm not worried about that for you. I'm not worried about that.

Morgan: Really? Can you look into my future of something? Where does that come from?

Premodaya: I can look into your heart. So I trust your heart. A person who asks, "Will it feed my ego? How can I know it isn't my ego talking?" I don't worry about their ego. It's the people who don't ask that, that I worry about their ego. See the point?

Morgan: That's pretty profound.

Premodaya: Just remember, the wisdom mind is not some faraway attainment: You got it when you were born; you have it every second, and it's always trying to get you to listen a little closer. See if you can't be a little more willing, a little more patient, a little more trusting that it's as much available to you as anybody else—and by anybody else I mean *anybody* else—and that the concern doesn't need to be so much "How will I recognize it?" or "How can I keep it?" or "How can I make it more so?" The concern should simply be, "Am I willing to listen to it and believe it when I hear it?"

CHAPTER 5

FREEDOM FROM JUDGMENT

Miles: I'm looking for a practice.

Premodaya: You're looking for a practice, because …?

Miles: Because I feel I'm about ten years ripe for one. Something I can sink my teeth into and dig one hole rather than a hundred different holes.

Premodaya: And once that hole is dug, what do you expect? What do you want from that hole?

Miles: To stop judging so much.

Premodaya: Don't add the "so much." The only way to stop judging so much is to stop judging. Then "so much" takes care of itself. One last question: What do you want from not judging?

Miles: I want to know what it feels like. I actually know what it feels like, but I haven't felt it in a while. It feels good.

Premodaya: It's freer. If we could stop judging and did nothing else, if that was the practice, just all judgment ceases—I don't mean discrimination or making important decisions or knowing the difference between this and that ceases—but if all judging would cease, *that's it.* That would take you as far as it's humanly possible to go. Ram Dass tells a story that for forty-five years now, he has carried a note in his wallet; it's all tattered, frayed. It's his own reminder and all it says is, "cease judging." He says he is still trying to achieve it.

Let me say a few words about not judging. It isn't what you think it is. Unless you've had a profound shift where there's not a lot of judging going on, and maybe many of you have had that, it probably isn't what you may think it is. It doesn't mean judgment stops—because we are so conditioned, so trained almost from birth, so "messaged" by the society and by the people around us, and by friends and enemies alike, to judge. There's a constant push to be judging, "This is better than that, Coke or Pepsi. This is better than that; that is not as good as this."

Judgment ceasing doesn't mean you will never again feel or experience a judgment. It really means you will never again be fooled by it. You will never believe in it the way you used to believe in it. It won't have the hold over you. You can choose whether to listen to it or not, follow it or not, put any stock in it or not put any stock in it. When judgment has really ceased, the interesting and unexpected thing is you choose almost never to follow it.

The mind is a judging machine—it comes up. When judgment ceases, sure, a lot less of it comes up. But don't think the ceasing of judging, being beyond judgment or having transcended judgment means no judgment ever comes up. They come up now and again. More than anything, you laugh at them because you see how ridiculous these judgments are, how absolutely meaningless, without any real value. It's funny they are called "value" judgments, because they are without any value at all. They should be called "no-value" judgments.

Judgments are the way your mind keeps you from being right here, right now, fully satisfied, fully happy. How can you be happy if you're judging something as not the way it should be? There's no judgment any of us can have that doesn't, at its base say, "Things should not be the way they are right now." It's another way of saying, "I'm not happy. It's not OK."

This is a group of smart people. Everybody in the room raises their hand when I say, "Who is interested in being less judgmental or ceasing judgment?" Because everybody knows deep down that judging is the road to hell. That's the people in this room. There are about six and a half billion people who aren't in this room. Many of them are completely snowed, completely fooled by judging. They think it's good stuff. They think the more they judge the better off they'll be, the clearer things will get, the more they'll define their territory or what's important.

The people who come to a meeting like this have had the tremendously good fortune and the true grace of having realized that judgment only leads to more judgment. It doesn't bring you anything. It doesn't add to life; in fact, it detracts. It's a self-contained poison system; it just goes round and round. You have to first and foremost, before anything else, be glad. Be glad that you are among the rare few people on the planet who have figured that out, who have somehow come to that wisdom. It is wisdom, it's absolute wisdom. Remember that most people do not realize this. Most people think it's good to judge; the more judgments the better. They have a strong opinion—that's what makes you who you are. No, that's what guarantees you unhappiness.

Good for you that you're already ninety percent of the way down the road, to have actually recognized that judgments don't serve you. I would much rather be in a room with you guys than those other six and a half billion, because that belief in judgment leads to all kinds of craziness, all kinds of hostility, misunderstanding and hurt, nonsense, craziness, conflicts. Already every person in this room is a helper for the planet, being that there's one more individual who's not caught in the judgment trap. I'm confirming to you that you may not be as caught as you think. If you already know that that's one of the ways out, if you already know that judgments don't take you anywhere, then probably, without realizing it, you're already doing a great deal that serves everything, and everyone, because you're not a full participant in all the nonsense. There are probably things you say "no" to without even really realizing it. You don't choose to engage in what the rest of the world is busily doing, usually involving some kind of conflict or negativity; good for you. First realize that. Give yourself credit for that. You may not even realize how significant that is. That's on my job description to tell you. It's something you may not see about yourself.

CHAPTER 6

SPIRITUAL ADVANCEMENT IS NOTHING OTHER THAN BECOMING MATURE

OUR WORLDLY RESPONSIBILITY

John: For me it's a tendency to indulge in escapism, to not deal with my basic human responsibilities—relationships, jobs, money—and excuse it by saying, "Well, none of that's real." That's number one of the ways that I con myself.

Premodaya: You've already said everything that can be said when you said, "Ways that I con myself." You already know that this is conning yourself. Ninety percent of the work is done. If you didn't know that, we would have a lot of things to talk about and a lot of work to do and a lot of things that have to happen, but because you know that, not much has to happen. So, keep going. Talk about what it's like to con yourself.

John: The way it works is I come up against an uncomfortable situation in life and not want to confront the pain of it. Fear of confrontation, of feeling emotions too intensely, and I would spiritualize that. I would say, "I really would rather just be in the world and not of it."

Premodaya: That isn't in the world and not of it; that's avoiding the world entirely. This is a fantastic example for other people of how you can be aware—he's totally aware—that you're conning yourself, and still be stuck. It's amazing, and that's the humility, when you say, "That's why I come to these satsangs." That's saying, "I can't do it by myself. I'll trick myself even though I'm aware of it, even though I know I'm conning myself, even though I know the mechanics of it, how I con myself—it's in this situation; it's in that situation; it has to do with money; it has to do with intimacy. I actually know it when it's happening; I know when I'm conning myself—and I still do it. And if I leave it all to my own devices, if I just tell myself I'll deal with it, I know it's a lie; I know that I'll trick myself somehow." This is how wacky it gets.

John: It's actually the mind and the ego, the subtlety of the mind, that cons me, that also has all this stuff figured out. So, you can't resolve it on its own level. You can't resolve problems with mind and ego and self-deception on the level of mind which is the level you're deceiving yourself at. That's why you have to just bow; put yourself at the feet of somebody you can trust, because you can't trust yourself. That's my experience of it.

Premodaya: You can trust yourself. But you have to keep a sharp eye out, and you have to assume that there's a trick going on and then look for it. I say that because I don't want you to fall into the trap of not trusting yourself, because that's throwing out the baby with the bathwater. That's saying, "I know my ego fools me, I know I con myself, I know I trick myself, so that means I can't trust myself." It doesn't mean that. It means you know yourself well enough and you're aware enough to know that you fool yourself. The antidote isn't "I have got to stop trusting myself." But it is part of the solution; it's part of the antidote—what you said, that you have to go outside yourself.

You have to go to someone or something that can call you on the con. That can say, "Yes, that's it" and "Stop that," because you won't say it to yourself. The ego can never tell itself to stop. It has that much licentious-ness. So little responsibility, so little real self-love, that it can't corral itself; it can't bring itself in; it will always take the easy tricky road.

How is it, sitting in a room full of good folks and admitting all this? I've never heard you say this before. I've always known it, because you can see it; anyone who knows you sees it; even you know you when you see it; that's the proof. This is a tremendous opportunity, a tremendous moving forward. I have heard you in many satsangs with other teachers, other Masters and never heard you talk like this.

John: It's pretty extraordinary, actually. I mean I rarely get up and talk, period. I'm the guy sitting in the back or sitting in the front silently. The only time I've ever gone up to talk to Gangaji, she was like, "How does it feel to not have an instrument tied behind you?" I couldn't say a word. I tend to implode, not be able to articulate.

Premodaya: You're articulating fine tonight, so you had better be careful because you might actually become mature.

John: Yeah, there's a certain hiding that happens, a hiding from oneself and it can take on a spiritual style or fashion such as, "Oh, I'm being silent."

Premodaya: Do you want the good news or the bad news?

John: I want the bad news first.

Premodaya: The bad news is that the actual solution to this is the hardest thing in the world, and the simplest: You actually have to do it. We can talk about it the rest of the night, doesn't matter. All other possible solu-tions lead to this—the only solution is you simply and absolutely have to do it. If the question is intimacy, you have to experience and go into the intimacy. If the issue is money, you have to go out and make the money.

If the issue is showing up in the world and taking care of some business, you have to actually go and take care of the business. There's no other end point. You can analyze it; you can spiritualize it; you can do everything and anything with it and in the end you still have to do it. That's the bad news, because the only reason this ever occurs for anyone is because they don't want to do it for one reason or another. Reasons may vary: fear, laziness, self-loathing, anything and everything, who knows? But whatever it is, in the end, you just have to do it. The Nike commercial is probably the most accurate spiritual statement that can be made: "Just do it."

That's the bad news, because it's hard if the life has included avoiding doing it, and we're talking about everybody; this is everybody, all of us, because everybody avoids something for their whole life. This is not unique in any way, shape or form. Everybody has something that they aren't doing to which the only answer, in the end, is going to be, "You know what, I'm sorry, you just have to do it." No matter how you talk to yourself about it, no matter what you understand or don't understand about it, no matter what it means or doesn't mean, no matter how it got there, where it came from. Anything that can be said or understood about it, no matter any of it; in the end you still just have to do it. Then people get into "Well, how do I do it?" and you can spend ten, twelve years figuring that out.

John: Yeah, I've done that, and it didn't work.

Premodaya: It's really about biting the bullet and doing it. It really, truly is. This isn't talked about a lot in these kind of spiritual circles, in meetings like this, because this is not what spiritual seekers want to hear.

John: It's not such a bitter pill as one would think.

Premodaya: Oh, it will be when you go to do it. Hearing the bad news isn't going to be that bad because I'm not telling you anything you probably don't already know, but let's see you go do it.

The good news is it's all done except for the doing. The awareness is there; the understanding is there; the ability to express it to a room full of strangers is there. There's no lack of clarity; there's no lack of insight or analysis. It's all clear. There's nothing to figure out. That's the good news: ninety-nine percent of the work has been done. That's the good news. The one percent that's left is doing, which is a thousand times harder than the ninety-nine percent that's already done. So the good news is in a way actually bad news.

John: That's what I was going to say. That is not incredibly good news. It's kind of mediocre news.

Premodaya: The other mediocre news is if you don't do it—and it's perfectly possible to live the rest of your life and never do it, never do it—

John: Live my life in mediocrity—that's a big fear of mine.

Premodaya: Valid fear. It's perfectly possible for that to happen if you end up not doing it. If you do it, it means that you finally accept that you have to grow up, because on some level this can only be a refusal to grow up. Are you aware of that? Acutely aware of that?

John: I'm more acutely now, yes—it rings true.

Premodaya: It's a refusal to accept the basic adult responsibilities of life, which are all very unspiritual but all have to be done. They aren't really *unspiritual* because how can you devote yourself to anything spiritually if the basics aren't taken care of, if you don't know how the rent is going to be paid? Then you're going to be spending your time and your energy worrying about that instead of finding your depth.

But this is fantastic; to me this is fantastic. I didn't know if you would ever take this seriously. It's funny because I don't think I've met with any group in the last month without it coming up, this issue. And again and again I found myself quoting Jesus: "Render unto Caesar what is Caesar's." They asked him, "Well, what about taxes? How come we have to pay taxes? You know, you talk about the kingdom of heaven. If that's really all there is, if it's all about finding God, what do we have to do all these lousy things for, and pay taxes to Caesar and the Romans and all this?" And apparently without batting an eye he said, "Render unto Caesar what is Caesar's." In other words, pay the taxes; don't spend your life arguing about whether it's fair or not that you have to pay the rent. I take that message; I interpret that message, just me personally, as: Don't waste time on it. Don't struggle with the things that you can't have much control over. Caesar's going to send his guys and they are going to mess with you—they got those helmets and spears. You don't want to mess with that.

That's how I look at that statement, "Render unto Caesar." It's not just, "Fine, pay the taxes." It's really "and don't spend a lot of time going around talking about how unfair it is that you've got to pay these taxes and how much of your time has to go into going to your job and doing what you don't like to do just so you can eat. Sorry folks, that's how it is on this planet." I think that's what he was saying—that's how it is on this planet. Just do it. Nike's right again. Some of the greatest quotes in history are from Jesus and Nike.

Growing up means rendering unto Caesar what is Caesar's and not complaining about it. Not trying to find the way out, trying to be the exception. You're ninety-nine percent of the way there. So what do you think is going to happen now?

John: I really have no idea. There are no thoughts about it right now. There's a lot of feeling. What's happening in my body is a tremendous amount of what feels like excitement.

Premodaya: Aliveness.

John: Aliveness. It's coming from the belly; it's like a fire in the belly.

Premodaya: Yes, because that whole refusal to grow up is, in a sense, a refusal to live. A refusal to grow, to evolve.

John: Yeah, it's really a stagnation—it's deep suffering.

Premodaya: It's insisting on staying stuck. Not just being stuck, insisting on it. If we want not to spiritualize this but really understand it spiritually, it means coming alive. It means being willing to allow yourself to come alive. The really good news is now that possibility is there, to *really* come alive. The other good news is it hasn't apparently done anything to retard, hold back or diminish your connection with music.

John: Yes, I'm very blessed with a karmic momentum in that area. Gigs come; even if I don't practice I can still express myself. There's some grace there.

Premodaya: I have said this to you before; in my view some people are born into music. If a person is lucky enough to be born to music, they have to really recognize that; they have to admit that to themselves that the music is what matters, but there's no way you can now allow the aliveness without it—no way you can do that—without it enriching the music, without that feeding the music. You really don't even have to let me know how it's going. I'll hear it in the music. What a leap.

John: Yes, what a leap. It's funny; there was a very strong movement today to come here.

YOU ARE MEANT TO GROW

Diego: When I first came here *nothing* was going the way I wanted; I was absolutely miserable; here it was mirrored back to me how I am so stuck on having certain results in my life and how it was completely running my life. We're on the fourth week of ICODA's 'Beyond Self' Training program, and we have come down to what I really want: I definitely want to be happy and fulfilled. At the same time, I don't want to give up all the material stuff. I am honestly focused on that, having things the way I want. But the feelings behind all the things I want are coming up really strong. This weekend was so lonely. I haven't felt this lonely—Why are you smiling?

Premodaya: I never really expected you to go this far. I couldn't be happier with you and your progress. And you don't have a single clue what you're on the edge of. You are on the edge of real possibilities. Now it's going to get really hard and really painful and really challenging. Not just standing on the edge of the cliff, but with like the wind blowing in your face; your back is up against the wall. It couldn't be better. My worry for you was that you wouldn't take it seriously enough, that you wouldn't take *me* seriously enough. And by God, you did; you came through. I kept saying to you, "Get serious," and you did! That's why this is happening, because you got serious.

Now you're beginning to experience the things that happen when people let what needs to happen, happen; when people get serious. If I had to bet, I would have bet you wouldn't get serious, and I love to be proven wrong. For you, as far as I'm concerned, it's all good news. Now the trick is to stay serious. You got serious; now you have to stay serious. If you can sit here and say, "All the feelings behind all my stuff are now coming up," that's huge. What a progress! What a precipice of awareness you're standing on. You're going to become aware of stuff that you have no clue about yet. It's suddenly going to get clear, *if* you can stay serious and withstand the wind. You're at a fantastic point. A point that I really didn't dare hope you would be able to get to. But here you are, fantastic.

Diego: I just actually got the awareness sitting in that chair, because of what I was feeling last night. I was thinking, you know, "It's the same old stuff again," and then I realized it felt differently than before. It was more of a vibrant feeling—and I even had the highs too, starting to feel more, getting frustrated easily, getting annoyed. And just allowing; to look at it, "OK, I'm annoyed right now," and be OK with it versus "Well, I'm supposed to feel good. I'm supposed to feel happy."

Premodaya: So, are you willing to feel worse?

Diego: Yes, I have gone this far.

Premodaya: You can turn back. There is a point at which you can't turn back. You haven't gotten to that point yet. You *can* turn back—so you have to be very careful about that statement, "Sure, I've come this far," because you actually still have the choice to turn back. There will be a point where you don't have the choice anymore—where you actually still have the choice but it's really not possible, where you have come so far there's no way to turn back. The example I always give is puberty. When you're sixteen you can try to be like you were when you were nine, but once you have gone through puberty there's no way to go back to *not* puberty.

There comes a point of awareness where you can't fall back anymore and say, "I don't want to know." This is what happens, that there comes a point inevitably where emotionally you pay the piper, psychologically you pay the piper. That's the beginning of real spirituality. You experience, with the one difference that this time you allow it—whatever is your agony, whatever is your anguish—with the one difference that this time you're not fighting it. This time you say, "I can't keep fighting; I can't do it anymore." You give up. This is the part people don't want to hear, generally, that there's this painful, difficult part to spiritual growth, to finding yourself, to getting closer to Truth, to finding God. There's this unavoidable part that's painful. It simply means whatever pain in your life you've been avoiding, whatever fear has been closing the door, whatever is just too much to bear, finally gets borne. Finally, isn't being fought against anymore, finally is just allowed to be there, no matter how much it hurts, no matter how frightening it is, no matter how much it feels like it's going to tear you apart. You just say, "OK, I can't keep fighting it." Everybody who really goes forward gets to that point.

Now, that's not the good news—nobody wants to hear that—but it's in a way the good news because it speaks to the possibilities, it speaks to if you're willing to bear what you feel you really can't bear, then everything becomes possible that was not possible before. But the truth is, you can bear it; there just has to be the willingness. The piece that's missing—why people feel they can't bear it—is the willingness isn't there. They're just too afraid, or it just hurts too much, but people are far more capable than they give themselves credit. It's literally a matter of developing the willingness, literally nothing other than that—the willingness to bear it. That's really growing up. That's really "rendering unto Caesar what is Caesar's." Bear your burden; don't try to find a place to throw it, and a miraculous thing happens—and I'm saying to you it is a miracle—once you're willing to bear your burden; somehow it changes, and it's not a burden. That's the real good news, but you won't know that until you actually are willing to bear the burden. You actually do have to carry the cross, and it actually is heavy and hurts. It doesn't change until you're willing to carry the cross. What I have seen in you, in that course, is every week more and more willing, every week more and more willing. I'm not worried about you.

THE WILLINGNESS TO FACE WHAT HURTS

Melanie: I have come into some sort of realization that for almost as long as I can remember, I have completely shut off things that just hurt too much.

Premodaya: And now you're completely ready to do different, right?

Melanie: I don't know about completely.

Premodaya: Yes, I'm telling you, completely. You know you're ready. The only part I'm adding is, you're completely ready.

Melanie: I've spent so long covering it up, that the prospect of feeling it frightened me so much; I don't think it's something I can take.

Premodaya: You were here once or twice, maybe six months ago.

Melanie: Yes. I was too busy then letting other people decide for me who I was—that I didn't want to hear anything.

Premodaya: A lot has happened in the last six months.

Melanie: Yes. I moved here from New York with my boyfriend. Things weren't going well; when we moved here it was to see if the change would do good, and it didn't. That was the thing I let define me for the past seven years of my life, and now that's no more. It scares me the way that it feels. I still don't know how to let go of something that I used to gauge my happiness in.

Premodaya: You can't let go of it; it will let go of you. But what you can do, and that will make it let go of you quicker, is truly being willing to recognize where you truly are.

Melanie: My problem is I have no idea who I really am anymore. I'm ready to find out who I am, but the thought of it terrifies me because I've spent so long trying to cover up and push away who I am, that I'm not sure which way is up anymore.

Premodaya: And you have been pushing away who you are because?

Melanie: Because I think I was more concerned with who other people wanted me to be? And the way I thought I should be? I thought that that was going to make me happy, as stupid as that sounds.

Premodaya: It's what millions and tens of millions and hundreds of millions of people choose.

Melanie: I'd been doing it so long that when it finally all came to a head, it really scared me because it was ugly, and it's ugly, and frightening, when it all comes to the surface and finally feeling things. It's so overwhelming, because it has been so bottled up for so long.

Premodaya: When what all comes to the surface? What's "it"?

Melanie: It, as far as I know, is a lot of anger and a lot of being hurt, and it came out in such a force that it scared me because of how powerful both the anger and the hurt really were. I have the feeling if I keep doing it, that the next time everything decides to bubble over, I won't be able to handle it anymore.

Premodaya: If you keep doing what?

Melanie: If I keep hiding what I'm actually feeling and trying to change that into something it isn't.

Premodaya: Were you amazed by the anger?

Melanie: I was amazed by the anger, and for a long time I didn't even realize it. Looking back on it, I don't know how I didn't, and that scares me as well, because it was obvious to everybody around me except for me.

Premodaya: Well, if you're busy trying to be what you think other people want you to be, one thing other people never want you to be is angry, so you wouldn't be aware of it. Everybody else would and you wouldn't. That makes sense.

Melanie: Now it's crystal clear and a lot of the anger has already gone, just realizing it was there. But it's still there. I can feel it and I don't know what to do with it.

Premodaya: Recognize it as life force. Recognize it as aliveness, coming out in the form of anger because anger is what has been denied. But it's just life force. It means you have more life force, more aliveness, than you've been willing to admit. Are you willing to admit it?

Melanie: I think so.

Premodaya: That's the good news. The bad news is now you can't stop, because the genie is out of the bottle. You can't put the cork back in; it will be too uncomfortable. That's truly the good news, but let's call it the bad news.

Melanie: I can't pretend I don't know anymore.

Premodaya: Yes, you can't go back. You've gotten to where you can't go back. On this, you can't go back.

Melanie: I wouldn't really want to.

Premodaya: Good, that's more mature. Now—this will sound funny— you have to tolerate finding out who you are. Now you have to tolerate actually what are going to turn out to be good things, but they haven't been tolerated before. It's not really bad things you're afraid of; it's good things—good things about you, good things in you. Good or bad really doesn't matter in this case, because if it's you, then it's you. I mean it's whatever is there; it's whatever is. It's not like, "Well, I don't like that, so I'm going to be her now."

Melanie: That's what it has been.

Premodaya: Now you've matured, or life has thrown you around enough, to the point where you just can't live that falsity anymore. Now it's a matter of "good or bad, at least it's me. Right or wrong, easy or hard, at least it's real, at least it's true; at least it's what I am." Now that has to be tolerated. It's been seen, but I don't get the sense the decision has been made one hundred percent to tolerate it, to be willing to really allow it—ninety-nine percent, but now go a hundred percent. The insight is there; the wisdom is there; the growing maturity is there to say, "OK, I will," but now why waste time? Go one hundred percent: "Whatever it turns out to be that I am, I am. I'm one hundred percent willing to find out." Are you one hundred percent willing to find out?

Melanie: Yes. Not knowing is too much, too difficult, so I can't imagine knowing is going to be harder.

Premodaya: When you really, ultimately know who you are and what you are, it will turn out you're nothing. I don't mean "nothing" in the negative; I mean your emptiness, your silence. In the meantime, it's fine to believe you're this or that, but in the end, you will find out you're not any of the things you think you are or experience yourself to be. Do you have the sense of that?

Melanie: I think so.

Premodaya: That's amazing. I certainly didn't have a sense of it at your age, so you're that much ahead. But until then, you can find yourself, because you can't find that unless you pass through finding yourself first. I was wondering how you were doing. I'm glad you came and told us. I said many months ago that I wasn't worried about you, that you'll find your way, because the intelligence and the wisdom is there. I said: She will get to where she needs to get to, whether she comes here or not.

Melanie: It's so odd now to see it, because at the time it should have been so obvious to me, like it is now, that there's probably a benefit. I just didn't see it at all.

I always sort of saw the things I was doing, bottling it up, and even kind of knew for a long time that I bottled things because I didn't want to feel them, but even realizing it didn't do anything, didn't change anything, didn't make me stop doing it. It got worse, if anything.

Premodaya: This is the amazing thing about human beings. You're obviously more intelligent than the average, have more insight than the average; you obviously have a lot going for you, and we still play the same crazy games with ourselves. It doesn't matter how smart you are, it doesn't matter how wonderful your life or how terrible your life experience has been. It doesn't matter if you're rich or poor. It doesn't matter what happened or didn't happen—intelligent, good-hearted people still playing amazing, crazy games with themselves. This is what we are all doing.

That's why I'm for the spiritual, because that's the only thing I know that offers the possibility to just stop the dumb games. Nothing else that I know offers that. And for every person who has any gifts at all, any intelligence at all, any willingness to face themselves at all, it's completely possible to stop all these crazy games, completely possible for anybody, anybody who is simply willing to face the truth. The interesting thing is most of the world will say no, they are not willing to face the truth, "Give me my thirty-six-inch TV, my beer and my Cadillac."

They're truly not willing to face the truth, but every person who spoke tonight basically said, "I'm willing to face the truth"—every single person. Think about everybody who sat in that chair. Every person said, in one way or another, "I admit it publicly; I'm willing to face the truth." That's what you're saying now. That's it, that's the whole ball of wax: Are you willing to face the truth? Again—I'll say it again; the vast majority of the world will answer that question "No." That's the amazing part.

This is why I love being here. It isn't because I love my job so much—I really don't love it that much. It's because there's nothing richer and more joyful to me than being with people who are willing to say, "Yes, I'm willing to face the truth." That to me feels great. I don't want to be hanging out with people who aren't willing to face the truth. They are no fun—they're overly serious, they're self-deluded, their values are nuts, they care about nonsense. It may surprise you to hear it, because I'm sitting in the big chair, but I admire each and every one of you, each and every one of you. If you don't think that that's the truth, think again. I have so much admiration and respect for every person in this room. That you are the rare few who are willing to face the truth. You're who I want to spend my time with, not those yahoos out there. That's why I like it. If it wasn't for you I would probably never leave the house.

Because for me I will tell you quite frankly, for me it's over. The world has nothing to offer me, nothing—it's just *crap*. The only thing the world offers me is you. You're the only thing that isn't crap. The world can give me more money, great, I'll take it, but it's just more crap. I don't need a bigger house, I don't need a better car, I don't need better clothes, and I don't need any of the glitzy stuff the world holds up in front of you as a carrot and says, "Ah, run after this"—they can't make me run. But I will run to be with you. So at the end of the evening when I thank you for coming, and tell you what a joy it is to be with you, I mean it, that is not social niceties. So, Thank you.

CHAPTER 7

DEATH: EMBRACING THE ULTIMATE FEAR

FEAR OF NON-EXISTENCE

Sebastian: I've been having this insomnia, and the other night I became conscious of almost an energetic structure in my chest, which was the fear of doing things wrong. I asked it to leave, and I physically felt it leave my body. And then I became conscious of the fear of all unknowns and the fear of impermanence and death.

Premodaya: That's the only fear there is. All fears are traceable to *that*.

Sebastian: Yeah, that I might not even be real, and nothing is.

Premodaya: I guarantee you you're not real. You can drop that fear, because I'm confirming for you your fear is true. You're absolutely not real. What leads you to suspect you're not real?

Sebastian: Understanding that everything is a fabrication, and that concepts of memory and experience are also a fabrication, or at the very least, an interpretation through filters.

Premodaya: Interpretation is a good word for that. It sounds like fear is keeping you awake, so it means you have to face it. If it's making you not sleep, then it means you're not fully facing it. It means it's creeping in and saying, "Hey! Here I am. You need to really meet me." Is that something you would be willing to do right now?

Sebastian: Sure, let's go for it.

Premodaya: Let yourself relax and let your eyes close; just drop inside and find it. See what you can find. See if right now, right here, you can contact that fear. That fear that is based on, "Maybe I'm not real. Maybe it's all an illusion. Maybe everything that I think and feel and sense is a mind game I'm playing with myself." And the notion of that is very frightening. The notion of that is disorienting. What you're saying is: "Somehow, I have a sense, at least in some ways—it might be so—but it's very, very overwhelming and very, very frightening to consider facing that. Really checking that out, really seeing if that's the truth." So, relax. Just be. And let me remind you that, if it's the truth, if it really is so, then it's always been so. That facing it, meeting it, knowing it, changes nothing. If it's so, it has always been so and it will always be so. Whether you want it to be or not. What I'm saying to you is, there's really no danger in meeting it. It's just seeing what is. And seeing it doesn't change what is. See if you can meet that fear right now, just like a stranger on the road that you come across. See if that fear can be met. And then staying relaxed, staying with eyes closed, tell us what happens.

Sebastian: I can sense this turbulent energy towards the base of my torso. And a pulsation that accompanies it.

Premodaya: Is the fear there? Are you meeting the fear?

Sebastian: Well, it's meeting me. There's actually welcoming to it, in a sense. But the body wants to fight it.

Premodaya: See if you can welcome it one hundred percent. Because again, there's no danger in it. It won't harm you. It may feel overwhelming, but ultimately, it's just fear. Take a few deep breaths. What's happening?

Sebastian: There's no separation between myself and the fear. It's kind of like flying into turbulence. Once you get past the choppiness, there's actually solidity, or resonance to it.

Premodaya: But a chaotic resonance.

Sebastian: A frenetic one.

Premodaya: That's the natural resistance that fear carries. See if you can relax even more, and literally, let the fear have you. Even it feels more overwhelming. Even if the fear intensifies, see if you can let it be there. Because it's not really coming to harm you. It's a natural psychophysical response. It's all very natural. Nothing is happening to you that isn't organic. And that opportunity that I talked about—you can use this moment to see what's really there.

What are you experiencing?

Sebastian: Now I'm sensing the fear outside of me, and it is almost the same shape and size that I am, but no discernable appendages. And the lightening, or the perception of the lightening, that I had on the outside of it, is now on the inside of it. And it's paralleling me.

Premodaya: It's not so amorphous. It's not so overwhelming. It's taking on a certain shape.

Sebastian: Yes. It's less compressed and dense so it's actually easier to work with—but the feeling on outside my body there's coldness that's related to it.

Premodaya: Don't work with it. Just let it be. There's nothing to work with. There's only a meeting. Meeting isn't working. Meeting is: Walking down the road and somebody's coming the other way and you meet. And when you meet, you see who is there. Who are you seeing now?

Sebastian: I'm getting a sense of a face, but I'm not sure. The sensation is that the energy is actually pulling things out of my body.

Premodaya: Is that good, bad, or doesn't matter?

Sebastian: Neutral. Buoyant. I imagine it's a good thing. It's almost like taking things out of me, which I hold to be positive.

Premodaya: Taking out things—for instance, like things you don't need, in other words?

Sebastian: Yes. Maybe hidden fears, or fears that have attached themselves to me.

Premodaya: Does that mean you're getting lighter?

Sebastian: Possibly. The coolness is still the persistent sensation, almost like someone left the fridge open. I feel like it's cleaning me in a sense or taking back all the fears that I've held in my body over these years.

Premodaya: Good. If you allow the experience even more, if you allow it to continue into happening even more, what happens?

Sebastian: There's a softening. And the color of the light is changing from a white to more of an amber. And it's getting calmer.

Premodaya: You can relax into it. So far, you've met the fear and you've seen it's not this gigantic monster. It's actually meetable and doesn't obliterate you. Is there more than that that can be said?

Sebastian: It feels that now it's external but overlapping with me slightly, and there's a sense of manageability that it won't destroy me. And perhaps even a sense that it's here to help.

Premodaya: Actually, it's just energy, and it manifests as fear. We experience it as fear, but it's always energy. The energy that is there, and it gets experienced as fear. The experiencing of it as fear is simply a signal that something is asking to be explored. Something is asking to be faced that isn't fully being faced. What do you need to fully face right now?

Sebastian: The only word that comes to mind is action. It feels like it parallels the other side of the fear of doing things wrong; it's important just to be doing.

Premodaya: Rather than be inactive.

Sebastian: Right, out of the fear that I'm doing this wrong, or it's inappropriate, or there's something that isn't quite right. That just doing it—

Premodaya: That's exactly right. The only mistake is not doing. The only mistake is being passive. Because the opportunity is to move forward. The key word there isn't "forward," believe it or not, the key word is "move." Do *anything*, because anything you do leads you to what's next. Doing nothing is what makes you stale. Doing nothing is what keeps you stuck. Doing nothing is what kills your growth. Doing nothing prevents you from knowing the truth. What you're really explaining is, that you had a little bit of a paralysis. A little bit of a fear of doing.

Both the fear and the urge to "do" is a natural energy. If you quash that energy you might have trouble sleeping, because that energy wants to move. That's just life energy. Now, I'm not in the "cure insomnia" business, but if I was going to give you a prescription, it would be: to do. To not hesitate, because even doing something wrong is better than doing nothing.

In that light, it doesn't matter whether you're real or not. If you're doing, the question of, "Am I real or am I not real?" is irrelevant. It's the doing. For you—for you at this point in your life—it's the doing that matters, not the answer to the question, "Am I real or not?" The doing will lead you to the answer. You won't figure out the answer. "Doing" in life will bring you to the answer. So yes, let yourself get more active. Let yourself—whether fear is there or not, whether the feeling of, "I'm doing it wrong," is there or not—let yourself *do*. Don't sit on your life energy. And then see if you start sleeping better. If you're not doing anything, you aren't going to be very tired.

So, what's your best guess? Forget what I say—do you think you're real or do you think you're not real?

Sebastian: Does it matter? If I'm doing, then it's immaterial.

Premodaya: Well, if you're doing, then eventually you'll have a clearer sense of what's real and what isn't, including you. For you, doing leads more to reality than thinking. It's not true for everybody, so everybody shouldn't take what I say to Sebastian and say, "Oh, that's true for me." Because that isn't true for everybody. But it's true for you.

In "doing" you will be more in touch with yourself. You will be less self-conscious, self-concerned. You will find yourself more on the outside. The more you're on the outside (doing leads you to the outside), the more you—Sebastian—are on the outside, the more you'll know yourself. For you, knowing yourself isn't going inside—it's going outside. That's just a certain personality structure. It's not complicated, but it's good to know that about yourself. It's good to know that *you* reach the inside by reaching out, outside. If you forget everything else, just remember that. That you find your inside by going outside. That's a key for you. Got it?

Sebastian: Got it. Thank you.

FEAR OF LOVE

Darshana: I have moments of intense fear. I had a moment when I was dancing with somebody, and it's like my mind completely forgot about everything before, everything in the future—and it scared the shit out of me.

Premodaya: That is the true purpose, believe it or not; that is why dancing was invented. That's the true purpose of dancing, to lose yourself. When there's no division between the dancer and the dance. That was a moment of reality. But everybody can easily understand how fearsome that can feel. How overwhelmingly frightening it could be to suddenly not be there. Only the dance is there. The dancer is gone. The fear won't harm you; it will just feel overwhelming. Fear isn't the enemy. But the fear is significant. I don't want to trivialize it by saying, "It's not the enemy." I'm not trivializing it, because the fear is really a key for you. If you had to guess what that fear really is, if you traced it—I'm asking about the fear in general that's there, not just what happened during the dance. You have some sense of what the fear in general is about? The fear that makes you stay in the fan seat, and not on the field?

Darshana: The first thing that comes to mind is aloneness. How to relate, how to be in the world. The next word that comes up is "functioning."

Premodaya: Yes, you are on the right track—but it is simpler than that. This is big. It is *fear of love*. It is fear of love in every sense. But in the most basic sense, the love that is life. The love that is existence. But its mani-festation for you is fear of love, acknowledging the love that is. In every sense, the love that is available. The love that is in you. The love that is for you. Fear of love.

That's how far you have come. Even a month ago I couldn't have said this to you. You wouldn't have got it. You have come so far that now you have come to the base issue, the core issue, which is the fear of love. The absolute core issue. Everything else has been dealt with one way or an-other, more or less. What's left is facing fear of love. From this point on, would you be willing to face that? Because you do have a choice. It can be moved away from. Nobody, including me, is going to stand over you with a whip saying, "You have to face this fear of love!" It has to be you deciding that you want to do that. You want to see all the aspects of what's in this and how it works for you.

I'm really saying to you—this is all that's left. There's not much more that's left. Once you face this you have reached the end of any meaningful questions. Then you can't call yourself a seeker anymore, whatsoever. Then you have to start calling yourself a finder. But first, find out why there's this fear of love, how that works. How you're in a hundred different ways keeping love at bay. Inside and out. Speaking about it, it sounds sad, but it's really not. It's wonderful to be at the core issue. It's not easy to get—it's the top of Mount Everest. You have been climbing and you have reached the top. Hold it that way, see it that way.

Darshana: And just watch it.

Premodaya: No, you have to do much more than watch it. You have to really go into this. You have to really figure out, "What's this all about?" But you have to know that this is the top of the mountain. That you have reached that far. You have to give yourself, or I'm encouraging you to give yourself, the credit for that. This—you don't get to this without effort. You don't get to this without having done a lot already. All the searching has been to get to this. It's good news—now you're there, but don't stop there. Now find out what this means. I will help you. You aren't on your own.

Darshana: OK. Good. Thank you.

ALL FEAR IS FEAR OF DEATH

Premodaya: See, fear is just fear. Really, usually, when fear pulls us back or stops us, it's usually not fear. It's usually fear *of* fear. If you can get beyond the fear of the fear—and just have the fear—it is a little easier to go.

Deborah: Is there one best way of getting past that fear? Meditating? Diving into it?

Premodaya: The first thing is: Understand what fear is. There's only one fear. All fears are traceable to one fear. The simple way to say it is, the fear of death. Fear of death is actually fear of the unknown. If you take any fear you have, or anybody has, and trace it all the way to what's at the root of it, I guarantee you, it's the fear of death. See if you can plug into the understanding, in your own understanding, of how all fears stem from fear of death. Whatever it is, its original form, where it comes from, is fear of death. That's the first thing. I have two answers to your question. The first answer is, understand—even just as a concept—that all fear is fear of death. Fear of the unknown. But it's easier to grasp if you think of it as fear of death, because we all plug into that.

The second part of my answer to the question is, the best way I know is to meet it. Like a stranger coming down the road in the other direction. That has to be explained a little bit—which really means: letting go of the idea of overcoming it. Meeting it doesn't mean overcoming it. If you meet a stranger on the road, and you really meet them, you're not going to overcome them. You're going to meet them. You say, "Let's see who you are. Let's see what you are. Let's see what you're about. Let's see who you are in relation to me. Let's see what happens between us together, alive, organic meeting."

Deborah: So it comes back to the surrender part.

Premodaya: It could be understood as a kind of surrender, sure. That's the more esoteric understanding. That's the correct understanding.

King: I'd like to share a trap and pitfall that happens a lot in my own experience. In overcoming fear, oftentimes, there's a clause that goes with that, which is, "In order to overcome fear, I have to not be afraid." And I find that to be exactly not the truth. Meeting the fear, you could easily still be afraid.

Premodaya: Or you could even get more afraid.

King: If you have the idea that, "When you meet the fear I'm no longer going to be afraid," to me, that was the first pitfall.

Premodaya: Then it's not a meeting.

King: Exactly. It doesn't necessarily mean you won't be afraid; you could easily be more afraid.

Premodaya: Whatever you're meeting, it may kill you. I'm saying, for real, that it could be small, it could be big. It could be nothing; it could be lethal. I don't know. I'm giving you the generic answer, which is to the best of my knowledge the real answer. Which is: If you meet it, then whatever it has for you can happen. What typically happens—as somebody who works with people, what I see again and again—is that it quickly becomes something else. But there's no guarantee. And I'm very practical—and I've seen the best and the worst, so I always add stuff like, "It can kill you, too."

I want people to have their eyes open, because a lot of times people have the idea when talking about these things, that it's all bliss and light and beautiful. Things happen and you meet it, and rainbows appear. That's not my experience. Now, that is some people's experience. And I'm not denying that there isn't bliss out there, and that you can be ecstatic. But I'm saying you can also be killed. You can also physically die. You can also lose your mind. All kind of things can happen, and you have to know that these energies, these phenomena that we're talking about are real and real things can happen. So I'm not an advocate of, "Just throw yourself to the winds and whatever happens, happens." I've seen people die from spiritual opening.

Just know that these things are real. That's why it's a significant question, "What about my fear? How do I deal with fear? Do I need courage?" Going into the unknown can kill you.

THE TWO MOST IMPORTANT FACTS OF LIFE

Premodaya: There are really only two important facts of life, in the following order of priority: first, you're going to die; second is, here you are. That's the whole story in a nutshell. If you think about it, anything that happens to you, any thought you have, any feeling you have, any event that occurs, any experience of any kind, any non-experience of any kind, can be categorized under those two understandings. Those are the two things that matter in terms of a human life. A: you're going to die; you will not be here endlessly, as you are now. And, B: you're here, you exist. You don't really know how you really got here; you don't really know what it means to leave here; nobody does. But those are the two facts of life. The facts of life aren't the birds and the bees; that's the facts of procreation. The facts of life are, life is short and then it ends; you die; and here you are existing with no idea of how all this happened and maybe even no idea of who you really are, or maybe vaguely some idea that something eternal is going on, something infinite is happening, but maybe or maybe not beyond that.

Those facts of life when considered seriously are sobering. It means time is limited and is running out. And it means there's something to understand; there's something to figure out; there's something to know. Otherwise, what's the point of that you already exist? What's the point of that you are here? Common sense, innate knowing of any minimally intelligent adult tells us that there's some drive, some need to understand what this is all about to the best of our ability. "Why am I here?"

How did you get here? You will never figure out; that's a mystery. Nobody ever has, nobody ever will. It's what I refer to as an "unknowable"—there's the unknown and then there's the unknowable. At least as long as you're in this body, you will never know how you got here. You might have some idea; you might even have come to some clear sense, but it will be broad; it will be part of a pattern; it won't be specifically all the details.

And, in fact, it all works in patterns; the mistake we make is to think that it's about "me," or it's about some specific thing that we can get our mind around. In some ways with some things we can, but generally if you really delve into it, it's hard not to come to the conclusion that everything that works, works through patterns; everything that happens, happens through a pattern. And one of those patterns you call "you." But that pattern is going to die, and that pattern is here now. So it calls up endless questions.

What I'm suggesting to you is all those endless questions are the trick, the mind game of avoiding facing what has to be faced, what's essential, what's the nub of what's real. I'm suggesting that those two questions are the important ones, those two considerations, that death is coming and that here you are existing. Those are the considerations that deserve your attention, that can take you into something, forward toward something, that can answer some of those peripheral questions that may or may not be answerable, but they aren't as much the nub as those two facts of life. The mind seizes this stuff and goes in all kinds of directions: "Well, are there angels?" and "Is there a creator?" The list is endless; I don't have to list off all the eighty thousand possible questions that people have. I'm not saying there isn't value to some of those questions. I am saying there's not a whole lot to learn from them. But we get caught up in them—"What's time?" "What's space?" It goes on and on and on and the mind can occupy itself with these questions for a lifetime, preventing you from facing the simple facts that you're going to die and that here you are.

When a statement is made, "You're going to die," I always feel the need to add the word "soon." Because when you're twelve you think it's forever, you your life is endless; when you're thirty you don't really see your own mortality, but once you're in your mid to late forties, once you pass the fifty mark, it's staring you in the face. Usually, you're very aware of the sand running out, and before you know it, always too soon, always as if it happened in a moment, life is over.

The trick is to not be facing these facts on your deathbed; it's too late. It can't be faced when only moments are left. They can, but your chances of getting anywhere with these are not good in the last few minutes. What I'm urging you to recognize, no matter what your age, whether you're twenty-eight or eighty-eight, is that that last moment is literally just around the corner. When it comes it will feel like it came instantly. It will feel like you were just graduating high school and here you are dying. It will feel like, "How could it be this fast? How could it be here already?" The smart money accepts that "that's how it is" and tries to deal with it, tries to face it when, hopefully, there's still time. And none of us know when there's still time and when there's not. You can be dead a minute from now, for no foreseeable reason. The roof could crash in; we could all be gone in a second. 9/11, people were sitting at their desks at work; five seconds later they were dead. A plane came through the wall! Whenever you die, whenever that moment comes for you, it will be like a plane came through the wall. It will be instant; Even if it's a long, slow death it will be as if, "This isn't possible that it could be now already, so soon!"

Most of our current society is geared toward forgetting all about this, distracting ourselves in any way we can—more, maybe, than in the past. But that's a mistake, because how can you know life if you don't really face death? The biggest single topic, the biggest section in the 'Beyond Self' Training program, is about death and how to face death *now*. That is not for no reason. This is what, in one way or another, most of us are more or less avoiding, for any of a number of reasons, because it's hard, because it's frightening, because it's anxiety-provoking, because it's mind-boggling. There are ten thousand and one reasons to avoid it, all of which don't matter, all of which keep you poor because you're not concerning yourself with the most essential concerns. Now, when I talk like this people accuse me of being morbid. That's another societal trick—whenever you start talking about death in blunt terms people tend to experience it as morbid; they don't want to have to think about it and they don't necessarily want to talk about it, and they don't necessarily want to hear about it.

Certainly, that's less true of the people in this room than somebody randomly off the street. Nevertheless, don't let yourself off the hook; don't say to yourself, "Well, I'm a sincere spiritual seeker so I'm willing to face it. I don't run from it like some people I know." Maybe that's true but don't rationalize to yourself. If you haven't faced it one hundred percent, if you haven't gone into death as something that involves all of you, as something that's going to happen to you, as something that involves every aspect of what you think of as you and every aspect of this life, then my suggestion to you is that you can only gain by doing that, no matter how frightened you get, no matter how weird the experience becomes.

This is a weird universe. Facing death more directly, more truly, brings you closer to the *weird* aspect, because then things get shaky. Then you don't have quick or easy answers for everything; then all the interpretations and the assumptions don't have such a hold on you, because you're looking at something that has the tendency, the power, to cut away some of the delusions, cut away some of the rationalizations, cut away the self-deceptions. You can't really lie to yourself very effectively when you're dealing with your own death. Something in a human being doesn't let them self-deceive like we do so easily during the day, during our actions and our distractions.

Ask yourself: Do you ever really think about death? Do you really think about it non-abstractly, not as something that you know happens to everyone and everything, but absolutely personally as, "I'm going to die." Most of us don't; most of us never go terribly far into it. There's more chance we do if we are close to death, if someone close to us has already died, if we have witnessed death personally. And for some people that makes them run away even more.

That's a shame, because if you ever have the opportunity, the privilege to be with someone who is dying, my suggestion is you absolutely avail yourself of that chance to go more deeply into death while you're fully alive and fully cognizant and have all your faculties. To watch someone die is a great, great privilege and a great, great lesson. And it's so strange that the society that we are in now has no conception of that. Death is something to be avoided; it's something to be stepped away from, hidden. This is not how it has been in most cultures in most times. Death isn't something far away that happens to someone in some hospital with a bunch of strangers. In most cultures, in most times, death is in your living room. Death is next to you; death is this one and that one close to you, and you're not removed from it. But nowadays, in this society, we're about as removed as we can be. That doesn't help to face what has to be faced and to delve into what should be delved into, which is one of the reasons it's useful to have a conversation like this, just to remind people that death is not the enemy, and death is not unnatural.

There's nothing more natural. There's nothing that doesn't die, nothing on this planet that doesn't die—how can you be more natural and organic than that? If everything goes through it, how can there be anything more natural? We develop these morbid fears of death, and the society supports it, reinforces it. But it's the natural question—if you're already here, if you exist and you accept the fact that you're going to die, that's the natural next place to go: "Well, here I am, I already exist, so what's this death thing all about?"

I would like to encourage you to take that subject more seriously, to take that subject as the core subject of the spiritual search. "What does it mean that I'm going to die? What does it suggest about how things work? What does it suggest about who and what I am?" I'm not interested in sitting here and giving you pat answers to those questions. I'm much more interested in you delving into it and seeing what you find, because any time you do, you'll find something more real. You will find something more than you may imagine.

Consider that there's much to understand about death that doesn't even occur to us. Whether we think of death as the cessation of everything or whether we think of death as a continuation, we rarely think about the details of what it means that can be assumed. What I would like to say to you, from my own knowing, is that death does mean your eyes don't see anymore, but it doesn't mean you can't see, because eyes aren't needed to see. Death does mean your ears will never hear again, but it doesn't mean you can't hear. Ears aren't needed to hear. Your brain will stop functioning, but it doesn't mean you won't know anything, because you don't need a brain to know.

It's disturbing to me that when I say these things, they're probably hopeful or soothing to some people, because it's not my intention to soothe you or to give you any hope whatsoever. I would like to take all hope away. Hope is the idea that things will get better in the future. "When I die, I'll go to a better land, a better realm, a sweeter place." Well, that's kind of a childish conception; you don't know that; there's no guarantee of that. I'm not saying you won't, but I'm saying, how do you know? If it's wishful thinking, then that can't take you to anything real. For most people, it's my sense that that notion is wishful thinking.

There's also this idea, which I think is very common, that death is a release, that, "I'll be released and I will be freer—this body, this physical entity is a kind of a prison; it's a limitation, and death liberates you." I think most of us have some idea like that. But death isn't just your legs die and your feet die and you can't go somewhere. Death is the death of all movement, all notion of movement. Imagine never moving. If there's some idea you have picked up from what you have been taught or what you have been told or prior training or just because it's in the air with most people that death is some kind of a tremendous release and final liberation, I would encourage you to consider what you know for sure and what you know factually that would suggest that. My guess is probably not much, because death isn't any more 'liberation' than this life is a 'liberation.' You *will* be liberated in death, but only if you can say you're liberated right now. If you can't say that right now, death is not going to be a magic solution. You won't be catapulted into some miraculous condition that didn't exist before. In fact, what I'd really like you to chew on and consider if it sounds true, is that whatever you feel yourself to be, in truth, essentially—that if you got woken up in the middle of the night suddenly, *the you* that would wake up—*that's* the real you. Whatever that is, isn't going to be any different in death than it is right now. Whatever that is, is the essence of what you are, the essence of what exists. If anything persists at all, it's that what does persist. You won't be magically turned into some better being; you will be the being you are now.

From my understanding, my experiences, and my knowing, this is the great after-death shock—that it's still *you*. You're hoping that somehow you would be like a caterpillar and come out in a better form, brighter and better like some butterfly that got released from its cocoon. But life is not a cocoon. That's what I mean by "here you are; you already exist." You're not in the larva stage; this isn't the larva stage preparing you for some greater world after death. This is it. What you are—you are right now, and what you are *here*—is what you will be five seconds after you're not here.

The meta-message that I'm trying to get to is that whatever can be done, and whatever has to be done, has to be done here. It can't be done there. You won't be in a better condition after you die, a more liberated condition to grow spiritually, to mature somehow, to evolve into some kind of higher being, because somehow "death is the magic door and allows you to be something you couldn't be here." Whatever you are here is what you are there. So this is the place—this is, for real, where you make yourself. This is where you evolve; this is where you grow. Not like a school to graduate to different realms and pass a certain test and then you get to go to a brighter, better place, but simply for the fact that here you are; you already exist; you're already fully formed. If you want to make something better out of it, if you want to be closer to Truth, if you want it to be real, *this* is the opportunity, because here you can move. I am completely against this idea that the body is a prison, even though people I respect and love greatly will say that to you.

This body is the liberation because with this body, with these senses, with these eyes, with these ears, with these legs—you can move. A certain kind of growth is possible because you can change things; you have a control mechanism. The body is a control mechanism. You have control over where you go, what you do, what you give yourself to perceive and where you put your attention, and that's incalculably valuable. That is your mechanism, your apparatus for growth, for evolution, for spiritual advancing. When you're dead, you're not going anywhere. You can't just pick up, and go here, go there. You don't have that apparatus; it's not as localized as it is now, in this body on this planet.

I'm really saying to you with all my heart, this is the golden opportunity, being in this body, being alive on this planet, being here as you. This is your divine gift, your golden opportunity to develop yourself, to go as far into what's true and real as you possibly can. This is the time and the place and the way—not some other state, before birth, after death on some other planet, in some other universe, in some completely different dimension. These are the kind of things that go through our heads and they seem valid. We've heard things all our lives, esoteric things, "Oh, there's other dimensions, and there's billions of planets and billions of civilizations." Probably there are, I have no doubt about it actually, but what makes you think you're going to end up in one of those places? This is here and now, your best chance, your best vehicle and your best opportunity to get to where you want to go and to be where you want to be. If that includes coming truly to Truth, you have the best method for doing it while you're alive, not after you're dead. Because you have a brain; you have senses; you have a body that is able to move; you are able to take action.

After death you may not be able to determine your action. If you can determine it here with absolute consciousness, then there's a good chance after death you'll have some level of determination. But if you're not in control of your own mind, if you're not able to carry out your own discipline while in this body, you won't be able to do it after death. The after-death state will take you wherever it wants to take you. You won't get a vote. And let me tell you, eternity is long and infinity is big, so where it can take you is beyond measure. And you may or may not want to go.

It's a question of Truth; it's a question of Reality; it's a question of getting to Truth and getting to Reality here and now in this body, in this place, at this time, as you. This is very hard to hold as a focus because every conditioning we have and every societal teaching and every natural mind tendency wants to move away from this basic condition, because it's uncomfortable; it's a tremendous responsibility; it's a tremendous challenge and it can be felt as a tremendous pressure in the beginning. It's natural to want to turn away from it, "Well, what do you mean I have to do it in this life? I thought life was eternal; I thought I could do it whenever." But you don't know what eternity means and you don't know what whenever might mean. You do know, without any doubt whatsoever, that here you are now and the opportunity exists now. All I'm really saying is, you have to see that one hundred percent. You have to see one hundred percent with your full self, with all your senses, including your second senses, your spiritual senses, that this is the golden opportunity, this life, you—you as you are right now. No special condition has to be met; it's already been met—you're alive. You exist; you've met the condition for ultimate spiritual growth. If you're breathing, you meet all necessary conditions.

I'm going against all the ideas and all the traditions that say that there are different levels and different realms and different states and different universes. I'm not saying there aren't, but I'm saying that none of that matters. All of that will distract you; all of that will prevent you from putting everything into this life, this you, this existence—here. Why does every true teacher talk about here, now? Here, now—this is why—because *now* is the only moment and because *here* is the only place, and because this is the maximum opportunity.

That's the right phrase—"the maximum opportunity." We all have this vague idea from a million sources that after death is probably a better opportunity. I'm going against all that and telling you no way; this is the best opportunity. This is where you have to grow. This is where you have to become everything that you already are; truly, this is where you have to reach your potential—in this body, on this planet, in this lifetime. I wouldn't say that to a room full of Hindus because they'd throw things at me, but I could say it to you. Because the Hindu idea is that there's countless lifetimes and what's the rush? You'd get there sooner or later. But do we know that for sure? What we know for sure is here you are now, already existing with all the mechanisms to get to all the potential that you are. But it means you have to pull out all the stops; it means you have to use everything that's in you and delve into everything that can be delved into as deeply as possible. It means you have to burn the candle at both ends. It means you have to hold nothing of yourself back, and we are taught, literally, to hold ourselves back, to save ourselves. For what? For some idea, some future challenge, but it never comes. There's nothing to save yourself for—there's every reason, in fact, to spend yourself, to burn as bright as you can burn.

This is how death takes you into the very deepest core of life. This is the gift of death, that it gives you urgency, that you don't have forever, and that this life and this lifetime is limited, and there's a best use you can make of it. Whatever your phrase for that is—finding Truth, finding God, finding Reality, finding Realization, finding yourself, and about one hundred and fifty other phrases, whatever one is right for you—it has to be done here in this lifetime. Any idea to the contrary, no matter how valid it seems, is more than likely a mind trick to postpone, whether it's due to fear, whether it's due to some philosophy, whether it's due to some doubt or some conflict or some confusion; whatever the reason, it becomes a postponement.

Whatever you call it—Truth, God—the only way to Truth is here now. The only way to God is here now; there is no other way. It can't be in the next moment, because that's the trick of postponement. It seems like, "I'll be more ready tomorrow. I'm not with it enough today, I can't tap into all my resources, but I'll gather myself and tomorrow I'll really be ready to be in this moment!" That's the trick of postponement. Whether you're ready or not it has to be now; whether you feel ready or not, it has to be now, just as you are. You won't gather any extra resource by waiting. It won't be any better or easier or more conducive tomorrow than it is today. In fact, it won't be any more conducive one second from now than it is this second. Throw your whole self into *this second* and you're eons closer.

Casey: I was wondering if you have an opinion if any human being really does know, or even *can* know about what it is after this brain stops functioning and the body stops functioning. I tended to believe with my best shot, with my intelligence, that it could all be speculation. You hear Buddhist masters talk about stuff; I don't know myself. Can man know anything about after death?

Premodaya: You said the most significant and important thing that can be said, "From your intelligence," which is simply that you can never absolutely, positively know for sure unless you know for yourself. That's the most important point, that there's always this doubt piece unless you know it from your own knowing, unless you have delved into it yourself and gone somewhere with it yourself, anything from even a higher authority still has a tinge of doubt at the edges no matter how much you revere that authority. So that has to be taken very seriously; that's the challenge—you have to know for yourself as much as you can know.

Now, that being said, there's a very interesting aspect to this whole question, which is kind of the "agnostic viewpoint," and many people get stuck in this: "I'm not really sure, I don't really have a clear idea for myself. And either there is no authority I trust to take a cue from or there is an authority I trust, but how can I believe someone else's statement about it?" All of that is the doubt track, simply because of the urgency. My real answer to your question, is delve into it as deeply as you can, know as much as you can know yourself, and if you're feeling is that you don't know enough, that you can't come to a definitive conclusion regarding whether death means cessation or continuation, don't fall into the trap of spending the rest of your life chewing on this question, and then you're gone. Take the word of an authority that you recognize or trust or feel may know something more than you. That's wiser than spending fifty years trying to have a certain experience or trying to get the answer, and then it's too late.

It's a very important point because I believe the majority do that. The majority have an egoistic problem accepting an outside authority, no matter how much they respect that source, and spend their lives—when it comes to this question—going round and round, and then life is over. I'm really saying if you can't come to a final answer for yourself, then take the answer of someone you feel you can take it from, so that you don't go round and round, needlessly, forever with no answer. Because even if you're having that edge of doubt, it's better than the big piece of doubt, better than simply being in doubt about this question, because whichever answer you go with, the implications touch everything. To be in doubt about it is to run around in circles, and I'm saying better not to run around in circles; better to place your bet and then go deeply into that.

IT'S POSSIBLE RIGHT NOW TO ENTER THE MYSTERY

Prof. Alex: I have been so great. I'm a radiant being! We have talked about the God within. I have contacted it. I was feeling it. A week ago, everything sort of fizzled—I began to get a tremendous emptiness, feeling like I have nothing to give. And then I look within, the God within, at all the wonderful feelings I had—gone—and it was terrible emptiness.

Premodaya: What's there now? You say it disappeared and it's just an emptiness. What's in that emptiness?

Prof. Alex: An emptiness like something's bad inside me. When it disappeared, it's a terrible shock. I'm reminded of Jesus on the cross just before he died; he said, "Oh, God, why have you deserted me?" He looked around and there isn't any God. There isn't any sunset. There isn't any radiance. No voices. He's just dying. He must have had the same feeling.

It's gone, just gone. For about the last four or five days, I've been looking within and seeing nothing. Where did the radiance all go?

Premodaya: Can you be in that emptiness now?

Prof. Alex: Well, I don't feel the emptiness right now. But when I'm alone—

Premodaya: Well, is it possible to just get into that mindset and enter that emptiness, even though you're not alone? To kind of act as if you were alone? Because if you're lucky, you get to a point where emptiness is all there is.

Prof. Alex: That doesn't sound good.

Premodaya: If you're lucky and you have been sensitive enough and aware enough to find the radiance that existence demonstrates everywhere, and if you have felt the presence all your life of something greater than you, then if you're really lucky, sooner or later the deeper level comes up. And that has something to do with emptiness. Something to do with nothing being there. Something to do with facing existence more nakedly, where the radiance doesn't act as a protection, where you aren't insulated from the hard realities of Truth, which has something to do with what the mind can't comprehend. Something to do with beyond this life. Can you in any way imagine that this emptiness could be a doorway to something even deeper than that radiance?

When a person starts experiencing that emptiness, maybe for the first time, the typical first reaction is absolute terror. Absolute horror. It seems so cold. It seems so dark. It seems so foreboding. It means you have fallen deeper. Deeper inside of yourself to that point where things disappear.

Radiance means *things*. There's a point (this is what the Buddhists are always talking about)—there's a point at which there are no more things. It's about the intersection of Eternity, Infinity—right now. "God, why have you deserted me? Why hast thou forsaken me?" That's the natural response, because it feels like everything is gone. It feels like everything has been taken away. It feels like the rug has been pulled out.

Prof. Alex: That's right, that's what it feels like. And looking around, there's not the slightest sign that gives me any kind of good feeling.

Premodaya: Are you willing to live, at least for a time, without a good feeling and not try to escape it by finding a good feeling? Because falling to a greater depth, falling to this depth, the depth that is about the emptiness at the core of things, never feels good. It isn't about being pleasant or feeling good or including certain kinds of feelings or experiences. It's about facing the vastness of Eternity and the hugeness of Infinity. Whether it's good news or bad news—it's about facing death, finally. Do you sense that?

Prof. Alex: Not death, but—the dark night of the soul.

Premodaya: Yes, the dark night of the soul is about facing death, finally. Facing death doesn't mean dying. It means facing it. It means really, once and for all, maybe for the first time, maybe more than ever, accepting the reality that death is coming. Which is everyone's condition. All of us.

Prof. Alex: You talked about once when you found Gangaji, there was a time when you became helpless and there was nothing to hold on to. Then what happens?

Premodaya: Then you face death.

Prof. Alex: I mentioned to you once I was in the Air Force—and it looked like we were going to be killed, we were all certain of it, but then something happened—and we all lived. And I thought afterward "boy, that's no big deal at all!" So, death itself has no fear for me, no terror for me at all.

Premodaya: What about the idea of no "you?"

Prof. Alex: That's it. The radiant me. See, I come into a room—I like people—I feel radiant. I just want to know him, I would like to know her, I would like to talk—

Premodaya: So death means they're all gone. That's death. No "you." What you're saying is you experience yourself by connecting with others, so death—in the way we're talking about it—means no others to connect with. Not you die—*they* disappear. Let's un-abstract the word "death" and say that, at least for the purpose of this conversation, death means: no them, no you.

Prof. Alex: That's right—no me. Absolutely—they're gone, I'm gone.

Premodaya: That's what has to be faced. Can you face that?

Prof. Alex: I will, because I know anything I do now will just be to cover it up. Calling friends, go to a party—whatever.

Premodaya: That's spiritual maturity—that understanding. And the willingness not to run for cover. What I want to say to you is that emptiness isn't the end. There's something deeper than that. I'm not saying that to comfort you. And I'm not saying that to soothe you. I'm saying that to fortify you, that this dark night of the soul, this facing emptiness directly, this accepting the dissolution of that which you experience as "you," has to be faced. Has to be met directly. And there's plenty of support for meeting it. What I'm really saying to you is the call has come to you to face the Absolute Reality at this point, before your physical death.

It seems like a horrible event, but it's a great opportunity. It is a falling to a deeper level. And it's terrifying and it's horrifying and it feels like it's going to tear you to pieces and it feels like the dissolution of everything. That is the dark night of the soul. But it's a calling; it's an opportunity to go to that which is beyond even that. That's the process; that's how it works.

Prof. Alex: I can see that. It's something I don't know about.

Premodaya: Exactly. It's something none of us know about. Because it's the willingness to enter the unknown here and now. It's the willingness to enter the unknown before physical death takes you. Does that seem like something you would be willing to do?

Prof. Alex: It looks like that's what I'm going to do and that's what I am doing. I can see it all happening. I will be in the apartment alone and I can see this happening.

Premodaya: Well, possibility is to fall into the emotional and psychological edge of it, which is depression, which is bad feelings, which is self-pity, which is fear, which is terror, but that acts as a diversion. It's a Divine call to face life and face death once and for all. Before the physical body ends. It's not a psychological process. It's a spiritual process. It's becoming the prey of the unknown and saying, "Yes, take me. I give up." Not, "I give up," with a sense of resentment and a sense of anger and a sense of, "It was all a bust," but with a sense of, "I'm willing to meet that which has to be met. I'm willing to face that which has to be faced. I'm willing to dissolve into existence and see what that means. I'm willing to experience directly what's really going on, before the physical death comes." This is everybody's situation. Everybody is going to die and everybody has the challenge of dying before the physical death. Of falling into the Reality that can't be spoken in words. And, yes, a moment, a day, a year, a period comes that can rightly be called within that "a dark night of the soul." If yours has come, then what I say to you is: Lucky you, that you didn't physically die without that coming to you. Terrifying as it is, nauseating, sickening, horrible, experientially not to be desired as it is, nevertheless, it's a call to face that which hasn't yet been faced.

To give it up now and see what that means, is the opportunity to go beyond all of it. Everyone has this possibility. Not everyone is lucky enough to have it grab them by the throat like has happened to you.

Prof. Alex: As you're talking about it, it doesn't seem that bad.

Premodaya: It will when you face it.

Prof. Alex: I think I already have; there have been some pretty dark moments.

Premodaya: It's not about the dark moments. It's about really allowing that emptiness to take you wherever it's going to take you and with no guarantee that it's taking you somewhere good or somewhere bad.

Prof. Alex: I got an idea it's going to be good.

Premodaya: Then I suggest you drop that idea. My intention is to help you and encourage you to face that which existence is calling you to face, and it always means that which hasn't fully yet been faced, fully yet been met, fully been allowed to simply take you. It's very much actually being the prey, actually being swallowed. Not just caught—swallowed. It's the belly of the beast. To soothe yourself with the idea that it leads to heaven is unrealistic. You don't know. It may lead to hell.

Let's sum it up by saying it's a mystery. And if you're willing, it's possible *right now* to enter the mystery. To face what now needs to be faced, all ideas have to be left behind. And just see what's in that emptiness.

Let's end with a little meditative consideration. I will ask you to get comfortable and let yourself relax into the chair, let your eyes fall closed without any effort on your part. Just letting yourself fall into yourself. Letting yourself be with yourself. Because you have heard tonight some very self-exposing, honest, truthful, and profound sharing. Profound witnessing to the struggle, to the search, to the finding, which takes endless forms. As many forms as there are people. No two exactly the same.

So consider your own uniqueness. Consider that in all the eons of time and all the countless numbers who've been born and have died and will be born and will die, just like no two snowflakes are exactly alike, you are absolutely unique. Existence, the Divine, never repeats itself. In all of time, in all eternity, there's only been one you. And there will never be another one. Absolutely one you, and no other. Absolutely unique. Absolutely singular. And that uniqueness, that singularity, occurs at the intersection of what's experienced as the meeting of what's inside you and what's outside you. But the truth is, there's no such division. It's just how we experience it. One way "the dark night of the soul" comes, and why it tends to be so terrifying, is when that experience starts to dissolve, which really is the dissolution of what you think of as you, it's absolutely death. It's absolutely the disappearance of the story, of the set of circumstances, of the history, of the characteristics that you identify with and call "me." "This" is me.

Well, what if none of those things are you? What if you're not your story? What if you're not all the things that have happened to you? What if you're not this body? What if you're not even this mind? What if you're something that is so mysterious, so huge, that no mind can comprehend it? No words can suggest it? No experience can capture it? Tasting *that* directly can be the dark night of the soul.

Much like the first moments of when prey is caught. It must be horribly terrifying, staring death in the face. "I'm captured! This is the end—who knows what comes now?" It feels horrible. It feels black, dark, forbidding, cold, empty—forsaken. This is the sense of death that every living person has to face. Becoming a finder, really includes the willingness to face whatever existence brings to you. And that unknowing, the "unknowability" of it, the unknowability of what is coming next, gets experienced as absolute emptiness. Terrifying, horrifying, emptiness. Deserted by all that is. Deserted by every idea and every object and everything that has ever given us any comfort and any happiness.

Can you face the reality that this is what death takes away? The physical death takes away, not just the world around you, not just your friends and loved ones, it takes away everything you have ever clung to even for a second. It takes away your name. It takes away more than your body; it takes away your identity. It takes away the future. It takes away time. It takes away space. It's unimaginable. It's literally unimaginable—the loss of everything. But it's terrifying only because we have sought our comfort in that which can be clung to. We have sought our comfort in our name, in our identity, in our role, in our friends, in our body, in our present existence as we experience it. In life as it seems to us.

The call from the Beyond ultimately is saying that all that exists is contained in an unspeakable, an unknowable, a mysterious "something" far greater—far more permanent—Eternal, Infinite. And it's suggesting that you can step out of the illusion that you're in a particular place, with a particular body, with a particular identity, that all the things you have been taught to cling to will somehow satisfy and somehow comfort you.

They won't. Ultimately, they won't. So why not end the clinging before death, physical death, takes them all away? Why not see what all of that is sitting in? Why not taste the Eternal and the Infinite and the Divine before the physical death comes? Why not be willing to be the prey and let the Divine, the All-And-The-Everything, come crashing into you? Capture you? So that you, just as you are, can know something of that which is absolutely real, absolutely true, eternal, infinite and already your true condition?

This takes great courage. This takes absolute willingness for the truth. This takes the bravery to endure whatever terror that includes, whatever horrible feelings it brings up. But it means that after, "Why hast thou forsaken me?" comes, "Thy will be done." "Thy will be done," means: Something much greater than anything I can know about myself is at play in what I call me. And I'm willing to say, "Thy will be done, not mine." I'm willing to be, and identify with that, instead of with this limited body, this limited lifetime, this limited set of circumstances. I'm willing to recognize that it's all occurring within something far greater, and that that is the reality I've always been in.

I'm willing to see it for myself. I'm willing to surrender to it. I'm willing to let it have me. If for no other reason than it already has me. Otherwise, I wouldn't be here. It amounts to facing the truth with the attitude of, "Whatever that means, I'm willing to go." And that willingness, that willingness without conditions, is the absolute merging with the Divine.

The mind can't comprehend it or grab it. And finding simply means, "I'm willing to go there. I'm willing to be gotten. I'm willing for the Truth, for the Divine to be all there is. Because that's already the case." If you can even entertain the possibility of what that implies, if you can even consider what's being said, then the Mystery, the Divine, has already taken you deeply. Has already got you in its sights, in a very serious way.

This is grace. This is the luck of this lifetime. That you're able to open, to respond to the call of something this vast, this mysterious. Don't look for false comforts and soothing but be very glad this is the case for you. All the seeking in the world is simply to get to this possibility and it's already the case for you. It's already under your nose. All that's left is recognizing that more. Good for you. Grace is stalking you. Good for you. Don't take comfort in it. Just be glad.

CHAPTER 8

YOU ARE NOT THE DOER

Premodaya: Some people are morning people. They wake up in the morning very fresh, ready to go. Some people aren't. They're evening people—they wake up as the day progresses. But it doesn't matter if you're a morning person or an evening person because, for most people, waking up is the same phenomenon. You just wake up. Now, 'you' didn't wake up. To say, "I woke up" is misleading, because really, 'you' didn't wake up. Waking up happened to you. You didn't do anything to wake up. You didn't make yourself wake up.

You didn't say to yourself in some dream, "It's time to wake up now; I have to go to work." Without your participation—in any way, shape, or form, you just wake up, and you happen to be breathing. You didn't control that. You didn't wake up and say, "OK. I can breathe now. It's time to be alive!" You wake up, and it turns out you're still breathing. You're able to move your fingers. You're able to move your legs and get out of bed. You didn't do that. You didn't say, "Legs, let's see if you can move now." You see that your legs work. You can get out of bed, you can go into the kitchen, you can put your clothes on. None of that did you do. You wake up, and there are still hairs on your head. There are still fingernails on your fingers. You didn't make sure during the night that they didn't drop off. There are still teeth in your mouth. You didn't put a guard in to make sure they don't fall out in the night.

All this happens without you doing a thing. You don't have to think about it. You don't have to control it. You don't have to make anything happen. It just is. It's just what happens. But a funny thing happens in waking up in the morning, or in the evening, or whenever you wake up: That first gap, that first second, that first moment of waking up, nobody is really there. If you really think about it, if you really pay attention when you wake up, you will see no thought is there. It may be a tenth of a second, it may be five seconds, but for however long it lasts, when you first go from sleep to wake, *you're not there*. There's no idea, "I'm a man," "I'm a woman," "I'm the human species," "I'm in a bed," "I'm not in a bed." Last night, tonight, there's no measurement. You just *are*. In reality, that's the spiritual state. Everybody for a split second every day, when they wake up, experiences the spiritual state—the more pure, unconfused, spiritual state.

Then suddenly, the mind kicks in. Suddenly, you're a man, you're a woman, you're young, you're old, you're tired, you're refreshed. You have to do this, you have to do that. "I have to go here—I have to go there." Now, nothing wrong with that, except, in that split-second gap, when the mind kicks in, that's when the illusion begins.

When you first woke up there was no illusion. You weren't anything. You were just consciousness waking up. It happened by itself. You didn't control it. You didn't try to control it. You didn't do a thing. Then, every morning, the idea kicks in that you're doing something. You went from, "I don't control a hair on my head, and all this is happening," to, "I have to go do this. And now I have to do that. And now I'm going to do this. And then, this is going to happen."

Somehow the idea creeps in every day, for most of us, that you're doing something, that you're controlling something, that you're making something happen—that you have a certain power over life. That's the illusion. You have no more power when you're thinking that, than the second you woke up, when you were empty, when you were nobody. But now you have the idea that "I'm doing something." That's all that has changed. Everybody can experience that for themselves. The beauty of it is you can explore that every morning and see more clearly what's real.

What's real is: You don't do any of it. Even after the mind kicks in and you think you're getting up, and you think you're making breakfast, and you think you're going to work, and you think you're driving the car, it's no different from when you were lying there that first second of waking up, happening by itself. Not making yourself breathe, not making sure you're alive. It took care of itself. The rest of the day, believe it or not, actually takes care of itself too. Except, you have the idea that you did it, that you're doing it, that you're making it happen. You're not. I'm saying to you, you're not making it happen any more than that first second, making yourself breathe. You didn't make yourself breathe.

If you can be one of the lucky few that in this lifetime starts to see that, then you're in the wonderful position of being able to start to let go and relax more and more about everything. Start to see more and more in everything how you're not living your life—*life is living you*. You don't have a life—*life has you*. You're the expression of life. You're the expression of life sitting in that chair right now. It's not the other way around, "You're sitting in the chair." Life is sitting in the chair as 'you.'

That's the beginning of the letting go of the illusion that you're doing something. And it's not easy, because it seems like you're doing something. It feels real. That's the way things are wired. It feels real. It's hard to fully, in the kinesthetic sense—in every sense, with all the senses, with all the powers within you—"get it" that you don't do a thing. *It does you.*

It's hard to get because you can get it the way I explained it, or other ways, too, that you can get it, but then you come to a point where it really seems like it doesn't go any further than that. "Well, this I absolutely do control," whatever that may be for you. Usually when people examine this, and explore this very deeply, they get to that point, "Well, it's true up to a point, but there's a point at which I do make a decision. I decided to live in Los Angeles. I could be in Vancouver. I could be in China. Obviously, that's my exerting a certain control—the decision-making. That's where I have an effect. That's where there is a difference, depending what I decide."

No. If you trace it back as far as it can be traced, you didn't decide to live in China, assuming you live in China. Somehow, China happened to you. Really getting it, is seeing how things happen, not how 'you' make them happen. Seeing that you're an actor in the play. You aren't the producer; you aren't the director; you aren't the scriptwriter; you aren't even the wardrobe girl's assistant's assistant. God is the producer. Existence is the director. But you're in the play—no question. That's the inner experience. Even that—to say it bluntly—is an illusion, but we won't go there. It's enough to start to know that 'you' aren't doing it.

That's actually good news. For some people, when they really accept that that's a possibility, they go into a bit of a panic. "I don't have any power! I can't do anything! I'm lost! I'm adrift on the sea here. What's going to happen? I'm going to float down the sewage tank! Anything can happen if I don't get to decide. What will become of me?" People actually do experience that. Especially very controlling types, when they first glimpse that this might be true, they panic a little bit. Doesn't matter. It is what it is. It's always been what it is. It will always be what it is. So, if anybody is panicking a little bit—relax, because nothing has changed. If you start to see it, if you start to know it, nothing has changed from how it's always been. It's good news, because it really, truly means you can relax.

People get into this whole conceptual thing of: "Is there free will?" "Is there not free will?" "Is there a destiny?" "What's my purpose in life?" All kinds of what you could call "philosophical questions," and they're interesting, and some of them actually are growth promoting, to find your position in all that. But the simple truth is: It all is what it is. No matter what you think about it. No matter how you characterize it or philosophize about it.

I encourage you, I invite you, to see in your own life, more and more, as much as you can, how much existence lives you, and how little you live it. How little is really up to you. How much happens to you, and how much you're given! Without anything from your side. Not being asked to give anything, to do anything. No price of admission. If you're breathing, you have been given unfathomable gifts already. I don't care what condition you're in. I don't care if you're in a wheelchair and you have no arms and you're blind. As long as you're breathing, you're one of the lucky ones. You have tremendous—I don't even have a strong enough word—tremendous, tremendous, tremendous, opportunity to come to full consciousness, to recognize what really is, to know who and what you are and what you're part of.

This is more doable, more possible, while you're breathing. When you're not breathing, before you were breathing, after you're not breathing, it's very difficult. Growth is easiest when you can move—when you have legs. This is the opportunity—while you're alive, while you're in a body. A lot of times people who come to spiritual meetings like this, kind of live with the idea, "It'll be great when I don't have a body. The body is so limiting. It is a confinement." We all feel that there's something about physicality that's a confinement. I don't think anybody would argue it. But that's an illusion too, because the real confinement is when you can't move—when you don't have a body. When all there is, is mind, because, ultimately, what you are is mind. If you didn't know that before, consider that now. If you're only mind, and there's no body to locomote, you're restricted. You're limited in what's possible for you—for you as a mind. That's why you have a body. Because it actually, rather than limiting your possibilities, expands them. So be glad you have a body. Be glad you're breathing and make use of every moment of breathing, while the opportunity is there, because you won't be breathing forever.

We live pretending that we will be here forever, that the opportunity doesn't end, because we don't want to deal with facing that reality.

LIFE IS LIVING YOU

Premodaya: You don't make decisions. Decisions are being made in the sense that things are happening. Movement is occurring, actions are occurring, thoughts are occurring; but the idea, the experience we all have that, "I'm deciding," is our interpretation of what's happening, and it's wrong. It's wrong for no other reason than it's our interpretation. We don't have the ability as human beings to interpret anything correctly about reality. We can experience it correctly, but as soon as the mind starts to interpret we are on false ground.

Anna: Where I'm still struggling is the part where there is responsibility.

Premodaya: It doesn't mean you don't have to decide. It means that you aren't lying to yourself that after you have decided, 'you' did something. It means your ego doesn't get to be puffed up, "I decided."

Anna: If I'm acting against my inner knowing—denial, running away, not doing something. Who is deciding then, or is this also not me, but my ego?

Premodaya: It's all you.

Anna: I don't get it at that point.

Premodaya: You don't need to get it. All you need to do is get more clear, get more in tune with being able to discern in yourself what's really what you're calling "an inner voice," and what's every other voice. Because there are a thousand other voices in you that are all from mind or ego, or however you want to characterize it, that are all vying to get you to go here, do that, decide this, and those all come under the heading, I said before, that's desire pulling you.

Anna: Or the opposite, wanting or not wanting, "I don't want something."

Premodaya: Same thing. Not wanting is, wanting not. It's either a push or a pull. Only the direction is different; it's the same thing. Wanting to pull something in, wanting to push something away; the same mechanism is operating. It doesn't matter if it's positive or negative. "Yes, I want it, no, I don't want it"—it's you, believing that you get to decide; it's you, thinking that somehow you control the events of this universe where you live. And not only do you not control the events of this universe, you don't even control the ones where you live.

Anna: If I don't do something I think I should do, then I'm beating myself up, because I thought I made the decision that I didn't do it, even though my deeper sense tells me I should have done this.

Premodaya: Learn from that to follow your deeper sense next time. Learn from how things didn't work out right, to try to trust a little more next time. Be smart enough to learn from your mistakes. What you're talking about is the mistake of disregarding the inner knowing. It doesn't mean you have to beat yourself up and retrace your steps; it means the next time you're in that situation be a little more open to listening to your inner knowing and see how it works out. Experiment with it; trust it a little more; follow it and see what happens. Maybe a disaster will happen and you'll come back and throw eggs at me. But it isn't about accepting these ideas; it's about seeing how it works in your actual life, in your actual everything. It's simply about recognizing—do you really already know? And what I'm saying is, most of the time you do; you just don't trust it; you don't believe, "I can actually know something. My inner voice can actually be the voice of Truth." Most of us are not ready to accept that. The only reason I'm in this chair is somewhere along the line I must have accepted it. I must have said, "Why not, if he can be the voice of Truth, if she can be the voice of Truth, why can't this voice also? What's so wrong with me that

I'm not as good as this one or that one?" But it's not about me; it's about recognizing that I'm not doing any of this.

Anna: It's also surrender, when you say "accepting." Not only seeing it but knowing it.

Premodaya: If you want to call it surrender, that's fine. You're certainly correct, but a simpler view of it is, "There's much I already know if I access that inner knowing. Not in my mind, not as my ego, 'I'm so smart, I'm so knowledgeable,' but simply, 'There is already divine knowledge in me or else I wouldn't be here. There must be, because how did I get here? It wasn't through me. What's keeping it going, it isn't me.'"

I'm not making my heart beat; you're not making your heart beat. You're not making yourself breathe; that's all being done for you—but what you *know* is already done for you. This vessel knows what it knows, but you have to trust it; you have to start experimenting with it to see if it's real and true. When you see even just a little bit that it guides you rightly, you will start to trust, very quickly, a lot more.

YOU HAVE NEVER MADE A DECISION

Premodaya: I never know what I will be talking about any time at ICODA. That's really what I would like for you. That you, also, don't know, and live with a sense of not knowing what's going to come out of your mouth. That would be closer to how life really works, because we tell ourselves that we know what we're going to say, we tell ourselves, "We know our own thought process," but that's a self-delusion.

If you really think about it, if you're minimally intelligent, if you think about it reasonably and honestly, you will realize very quickly, within minutes, that you have no idea what you're going to say, ever, or what the next moment is going to be. It's a false, self-generated—you could say, delusional sense of security—that prompts you to tell yourself 'you know.'

Otherwise, you have to experience, at least in the beginning, some uncomfortable feelings, some insecure feelings, but that actually doesn't last long. You start to accept how much you don't know and, particularly, that it involves every next moment. Actually, every "this" moment.

That's closer to the truth, closer to what's really, truly going on. This need for security is absolutely not our friend. This need for security is what prevents you from living life more fully. We all have it; it's not like somebody has it and somebody doesn't. It's part and parcel of being a human being, so there's no reason for us to get down on ourselves that we have this automatic, conditioned need to feel secure somehow and section ourselves off with the idea that we are in control of something, and we're living our life, instead of life is living us. Life is living us, so why delude ourselves? Why paint ourselves a picture that's false just for the sake of false comfort? If it's for real comfort—fine, but it's false comfort, because it's not true.

The willingness has to be there to actually consider the truth, to actually allow the unsettling reality to be recognized. For some people that's very scary and for other people, that's very anxiety-provoking, and for some people it's downright terrifying, horrifying. The good news is that that terrified feeling, that anxiety, that horror, that fear, whatever it is for any particular person, is not long-lasting. It doesn't take tremendous effort, or years of trying to get your sea legs, in the midst of realizing that you don't control what you think you control. And you certainly don't dominate your own life; you certainly don't run your own show.

This is the first hurdle for many people in spiritual understanding. Many very good-hearted, sincere people come to spirituality, come to seek some kind of spiritual path—and they're not really anywhere solid, anywhere real, until the understanding starts to dawn that you're not living this life; this isn't your life; this life was given to you. You didn't go to the store and buy it; you didn't dial up and order it; you didn't ask for it. When people get really upset, they say, "Well, I didn't ask to be born." Just that understanding alone, if you take it seriously—let that permeate a little bit—immediately shows that you didn't do *anything* to get here. You didn't create this life, and you didn't even create it after you got here, although, most of us think we do. So it's valuable to get shaken up a little. It's necessary in any sincere spiritual search, in looking for true answers to real questions, to get, at the very minimum, to the point of recognition that you're not in charge.

That's a major dissolution, right there, of ego. Just to admit that is not possible for most of the people on the planet. They will fight you on that one. Nobody in this room will probably fight about it, but if we were in some other room most people would say, "That's crazy!" Most people would say, "I don't agree with that." Most people would say, "Of course I'm in charge of my life!" But they could never prove it, because it isn't true. If you asked them "Prove it," it would be very mean; it would be unfair, because they would come up with all kinds of things that are nonsense. "Well, I decided this, and I went there; I married so and so, and I got this job, and I got my degree in advanced physics …" whatever. Well, that doesn't prove anything; that's just what happened and what keeps happening. The first big hurdle for all real truth finding, the one that is unavoidable, that has to be surmounted (I'm repeating it because it's that important), is to recognize that you aren't in charge, even of your own life.

You don't know when this life is over; you don't know if it's going to be thirty years from now, ten years from now, or ten minutes from now. Even if you knew, even if you had some disease and the doctor told you that you've got two years left, roughly—so what? Everybody you know could be dead before you. We don't know anything about the next moment, ever. For most of us the first recognition, the first realization of the truth of that is very unsettling and even very shocking, because we have spent our whole lives building up, propping up, strengthening this false sense of security based on, "I'm in control of things. I make the decisions, at least about my life."

Let me invite you right now to relax for a minute and think about your own life and every one of the super-major decisions of your life:

career, marriage, love, geography, moving from New York to L.A. Think about the two or three most major decisions you have ever made. Do you not, without thinking about it for more than thirty seconds, come to a sense that, somehow, that was not really a decision? It wasn't just some mental process that you sat down and decided, "OK, what makes sense for my life is I'm going to move from here to that part of the country and I'm going to get a job doing this or that." Do you not quickly see that— and really think about it right now while you listen to this—isn't it very obvious, very quickly, that there's a bigger sense of it just happening? Of it, kind of just all, coming about? That if you hadn't thought about it at all even, the same things might have happened? You would have somehow decided that in some other way, or come to that in some other way?

The thing that is so interesting is that it doesn't take intelligent people a long time to figure this stuff out—it's just we never think about it; nobody tells us to look at it this way. In fact, the culture is telling us most of the time, "You're in control—make decisions." That's called "advertising," but it's also propaganda. It's also promulgating a certain view of life that, for one reason or another, the government has a vested interest in; the culture has a vested interest in; certain parts of society have a vested interest in us thinking a certain way. It's not a conspiracy; it's not nefarious, but it fools us into having all kinds of ideas that aren't necessarily reality. They usually are in some form about how we control something, which if you really look into, give it some serious thought for ten or fifteen minutes— which most of us have rarely done, you see it's not true. It's really quite amazing!

The more you look at it, the more you talk to people, other people, it's very interesting. I have actually asked many people to do this little invitation I have given you, to think about your own life, and if you ask them, "Think about the two or three biggest decisions you have made and share that," they end up telling you, universally, "Yeah you're right; when I really think about how that all happened, the sense I have of it, it wasn't like it was a decision; it all just kind of lined up." I'm sure somewhere I've asked that of someone who is a more argumentative type, has to say no just for the sake of no, but I forget that quickly.

It's amazing; everybody reports pretty much the same experience, and yet, we keep going along with the idea that we're in charge; we decided; we made it happen. But when we really look into it and start to see that it happened and we were there, if you're lucky, things shift a little bit; a different kind of perspective starts to enter into your understanding. Things start to open up a little bit and you start to see more about more. It's really about more related to what you really control, and what you don't. I'm saying to you that all we really control is our degree of cooperativeness with what's happening. We can cooperate; we can cooperate one hundred percent; we can resist; we can say no; we can run away; we can take a trip to Borneo; we can do anything we want really, but it all amounts to: Are you cooperating with what's true and what's real? Or are you somehow battling it, somehow in an antagonism with what's true and what's real? Most of us are often in some more or less form of antagonism, and we give it a thousand different names: denial … and you can really list them off for yourself.

Lucas: It seems delightful to me, to think, "I don't know what's going to happen next." Because I tend to be very compulsive before I speak, I rehearse what I'm going to say.

Premodaya: That's what I said right at the beginning of tonight's talk, I said, "My hope for you is you come to the point where you never rehearse again, where you let whatever is going to come out, come out, and *you* get out of the way."

Lucas: That takes a lot of security.

Premodaya: No, it doesn't take any security because it's the most insecure thing you can do. It takes a lot of understanding, that every time you open your mouth it isn't *you* talking. Talking is happening; words are being said; ideas are being promulgated; something is going on, but if you claim responsibility for it, you've already gotten yourself in trouble. It's a matter of being willing to relax; it's a matter of being willing to let go and recognize that you aren't in charge, even of the words that come out of your mouth, although we really have a hard time recognizing that if that's a new idea, because it feels very much like we're saying it. But when I'm sitting up here, I'm very aware that I'm not saying a word. Something is being said by something, someone, but it ain't me, Jack!

That's my hope for you; that's my hope for everybody. That you come to that point in life where you experience the words that come out of your mouth and the actions that come out of your consciousness as not emanating from you, because that's the truth.

Lucas: Is it a kind of letting go?

Premodaya: Absolutely, but you have to experiment with it to experience it. What I was saying earlier is a very important point. In the beginning it's shaky ground. In the beginning it's very anxiety-provoking. Or very fearsome. Or very whatever it is. But usually, people are reticent to do that because it's not just letting go of your ego; it's actually standing on softer ground because you're putting yourself more in a position where anything can happen. Imagine every time I sit in this chair. I don't know what's going to happen; I could say something; you guys could all rush me and beat me to a pulp; I don't know. Who knows what I'm going to say? You could all throw eggs at me; I don't know.

I'm not talking as a practice, although in the beginning, you may need to practice it. I'm talking about recognizing that that's what's really going on. Hopefully, I said that clearly a little earlier. When you look into it, when you consider it, when you ponder it, when you really give it honest thought: You never control any word that ever comes out of your mouth. You don't know how it forms. Do you understand how the human mind works? How *you* work, as an organism, as a totality that forms ideas and words? Certain emotions are there, and certain conditions are there; you feel not sick; you're able to talk, and your mouth moves a certain way because of certain muscles and bone structure; the ears can have certain structures that hear things. And sound waves; you form these entities that are sounds, and they actually represent words, which are actually ideas; and this all comes out of you instantly. And you think *you're doing this?* Come on! If you had to do that, your head would blow up.

Sebastian: It's very anxiety-provoking; it really is. It makes sense, but I still can't find my inner voice.

Premodaya: Don't worry about finding your inner voice. Don't give it one second's attention.

Sebastian: How do I make decisions then?

Premodaya: No, no, all that's needed is: Are you willing to recognize that when you make a decision, 'you' didn't do it?

Sebastian: Boy, I've made some bad decisions, but I guess I didn't do it.

Premodaya: This is good news! You're off the hook. You know, this is really interesting, because this is what happens for some people—they really *are* off the hook if they really see the truth of this, and there's a need to blame oneself. There's a need to say, "I made the stupidest decision, and back in 1984 if I hadn't done that my whole life would be good now." Make sure there isn't a need to beat yourself up behind that statement. Because I am really saying, you aren't to blame. I am really saying you aren't responsible. I am absolutely, truly saying, that you've never decided anything, so how can you be responsible? How can you say, "I've made a bad decision"? A decision got made; maybe it didn't work out the way you would have liked it to work out, but you can't legitimately—in this universe—say as a human that you made a bad decision, because my position is, you've never made any decision. You think you have; it feels like you have; the experience is, "I made a decision," but that's a self-delusion. It didn't really happen. Something happened, and the mind turned it into, "I decided and this is how it turned out." That's all one hundred percent interpretation. What I'm saying is very radical; I'm saying, if it's interpretation, by definition, it's wrong.

We have no ability to interpret because we are only interpreting through our filters. When we interpret, we are operating through our desires. Through our assumptions. Through our philosophies. Through our beliefs. Through our preferences. And all of that is multilayers of smoke screens. It's just our own ideas. It's just a puff of smoke. It has no validity; it has no actual validity in the actual universe. Now, in the mind's universe, where we think we are in control and we get to decide, it seems perfectly valid, perfectly legitimate, and absolutely real. What I'm saying is, it *ain't*. This is good news!

CHAPTER 9

YOU ARE FULL OF EMPTINESS

THE WATCHER

Prof. Alex: This morning, for no reason I could think of life seemed grim, like I was under a cloud, and I said, "Osho says don't try to do anything, just watch, just watch it."

Premodaya: OK. But you didn't just watch it, right?

Prof. Alex: Something has happened in the last couple of days; what is it?

Premodaya: But you didn't just watch it.

Prof. Alex: OK. But then it didn't go away, didn't go away, and then I'm watching it, and watching it.

Premodaya: Watching it doesn't mean watch it with the idea that that will make it go away. "Watch it" means watch it objectively with no intention. Otherwise, it's not watching; otherwise, it's actively trying to make something happen, even if it's very subtle. Really watching means not having a goal, not having an intention. Then something can be seen. Until then the intention blinds you, even if there's just the tiniest bit of it. If there's the tiniest bit of feeling to make it go away, you're caught in it. It can't be watched; you can't be objective; you can't see what's actually happening because you're too involved, even if it's the tiniest bit.

"Watch" means have no intention other than to see what can be seen. Otherwise your vision is clouded; otherwise your watching isn't a real watching. It's a profound advice from Osho to watch, because he doesn't mean watch to make the good feeling stay or watch to make the bad feeling go. He means just watch. To develop the ability to be a watcher, to develop the ability to not be pulled in or pushed away, is huge.

Prof. Alex: Don't see it as good or bad.

Premodaya: You can't be a watcher until you step out of good and bad, until you step out of having an intention one way or the other. This is Osho's trick, he's very tricky; he gives you a simple instruction, "watch it," but to really carry out his instruction you have to change and transform completely; you have to become completely objective, and most of us have spent our entire lives not even in one minute of objectivity. Not in one minute of truly watching, always with some intention, always with some goal, always with some preference, some desire—which is normal. We're taught that this is the way we are supposed to be, moving toward something, having a goal. We live in a goal-oriented society. There's no question; nobody would argue that. But if you seek the spiritual path, then you have to learn the opposite of goal orientation. You have to learn how to watch with no goal in mind. You have to learn how to stand in the middle and not lean either direction. This is very, very difficult, because it goes against our whole life training.

It's a very tricky instruction that he gives, because if you take it seriously and you really learn how to watch, many things will change in your life. But he doesn't tell you that, because if he told you, you wouldn't do it. You would say, "I don't want to take any chances; this sounds dangerous; this sounds too big. Why don't we do something a little less ambitious?" He doesn't tell you the whole story. He just says "watch." But if you try to practice it, automatically—just by trial and error—you will start to find the right road; you will start to see what it is to be objective, to really watch; then when you get down the road a little bit, it's too late. Then he has got you.

Prof. Alex: The "watcher" can be a happy guy.

Premodaya: No, the watcher has no stance; the watcher is just watching; he's not happy; he's not unhappy. This is how the mind works, exactly how you're saying, "Well, if I achieve that, then I will be a happy guy." But that desire to be a happy guy absolutely guarantees that you will keep moving between happy and unhappy, because you can't be happy and not fall into unhappy. It's impossible. There's a price for every happiness; it's called unhappiness. The only thing that's guaranteed about happiness is it will end in unhappiness, and the only thing guaranteed in unhappiness is that it will change to happiness, sooner or later. It's so simple, nobody figures it out. It's so basic and so true, nobody sees it, because it's just so plainly obvious.

Being a "watcher" means you aren't limiting your repertoire to that one movement between those two. You're finding a different dimension to stand in; otherwise, you're locked in; otherwise, you're stuck with a very limited repertoire, like most of us, where we get angry over nothing, where we get inflamed over nothing, where we become flat and bored quickly, all these ups and downs that we think are the bane of existence. But we don't see how one creates the other and that we're constantly putting ourselves here and there, and then blaming life when we don't like it.

Every true teacher has to be very tricky, has to fool you—Osho was a master of masters at fooling people—has to seduce you into trying something different, because if they told you the ins and outs of it ahead of time, you wouldn't go. It's like telling someone that the road is dark and cold and dangerous and there's every chance that you will stub your toe and fall in a ditch. If you're given too much information, it's like those drug warnings; if you read all the drug warning, you would never take the drug. The telling of it is more dire sounding than the actuality of it. If it was complete disclosure—like what the drug companies are trying to do so they don't get sued—every true Guru would tell you there's this chance, and this chance, and this chance of going wrong, and these bad things can happen. But in reality, it doesn't happen; in reality your chances are very good, but it sounds dire if you listed it all out, so you have to be tricked. You can't be told everything because your mind will trick you into saying, "It's not worth it; I'll just stay safe. I won't shoot for something higher, something better."

So never read or listen to or study any teacher with the idea that it's at face value. You're always being tricked, but it's you that requires that. You're being tricked out of compassion because the teacher knows you won't go any other way, that if you get all the information ahead of time, which is what the mind wants, you'll say, "See you later. Not for me, I'm going to go have me a mocha," because much has to be given up; much has to be let go of. That's the spiritual path.

The spiritual path is not the accumulation of anything; it's the letting go of everything. The spiritual path is nothing more and nothing less than renunciation. It's the one word that's the definition of the spiritual journey: renunciation. Renunciation isn't negative; it sounds negative to our ears, giving something up, renouncing something, letting go of something, stepping away from something. It sounds extremely negative. Most of us shy away, even from the word, once we hear it, but it's not negative at all. This is why you have to be tricked, because words don't convey the reality; words are limited. Even though renunciation is the exact, correct, accurate, perfect word, it has connotations that people don't like. You get fooled by the word itself, so you have to be counter-fooled so that you won't reject that which is in your best interest. It's like when they make the cough medicine cherry flavored. But you're all adults; there's no reason you can't understand that renunciation is all it's about and nothing else.

Renunciation means you become willing to let go of what isn't true, what isn't real and what isn't you. And it turns out that most of what we are carrying is that: the untrue, the unreal, and the not-us. Because we've been trained, we've been programmed, we've been habituated, we have been filled from birth and even before birth, with all kinds of programs and ideas and leanings, and we think this is us. We experience ourselves as our preferences, but these preferences are preprogrammed; they aren't yours. They aren't you, but they are so deep, so ingrained, so taught from the very beginning in so many ways, verbal and nonverbal, culturally instilled, familially instilled—that we don't recognize it. It feels to us like us. It feels like, "That's who I am," but it's not. It doesn't take a lot of thinking for intelligent people to quickly get it that that can't be who you really are. There has to be something that's before that, that's more the essential you, and you can't get to it without getting rid of that other stuff. That's renunciation. Getting rid of the false you, being willing to let go of what feels safe and secure, because we hide out in it—and being willing to step into a different light. In that sense, that's what I mean by it's not negative; it's only getting rid of extra baggage. It's only getting rid of what isn't yours in the first place. It's getting rid of all the garbage that's been piled on top that keeps us confused, that keeps us in suffering, keeps us away from what's real. It's everybody's dilemma, but only a rare few are willing to renounce, get to the point in a lifetime where the willingness is there to say, "OK, I don't want to settle for the false; I don't want to settle for what isn't real. I don't care what you call it; Truth, God, Self-Realization—whatever it is, I want what's real; I don't want the fake life." Very few people in every generation come to that point.

If that has any meaning for you, and it probably has tremendous meaning for every person in the room, it doesn't make you special in the sense that you're better than someone, but it does make you very special in the sense that you're a tiny minority on the entire planet who have come to a point of maturity, of spiritual awareness, that you're able to recognize what matters. You may not have every answer; you may not be clear about it. It doesn't matter; you're on the tip of unspeakable possibilities. This is your great good fortune—this is grace itself. So be glad! You have much reason to be glad whether you are aware of it or not; I'm just trying to get you to be more aware of it.

Darshana: Well, I feel like I struggle a certain amount in relationships. When I'm here and I'm surrounded by the like-minded, it's definitely comfortable. It's hard to commune with the others, including people that are very close to me in my life. My ego wants to go crazy places with that and that's painful. I'm not really sure how to find peace around all that.

Premodaya: Are you willing to be a watcher and wait? I could give you a flashier answer but if I wanted to give you good advice, that's the answer; be a watcher and wait. See where that goes, and don't worry about it. Remember what I said about being a watcher; it doesn't involve worrying; it doesn't involve being concerned with what gets seen. It doesn't involve trying to reach a certain goal. Just objectively wait and objectively watch.

Anna: But then how do you deal with the pain that comes with it?

Premodaya: By watching it, and waiting.

Anna: By watching it you have pain—because you're just sitting there watching it.

Premodaya: Yes, whatever comes, just watch, but don't take my advice to her personally, because I'm giving her specific advice, for her. You may or may not benefit by trying to apply it to your situation. But be careful with that, because when I give somebody specific advice, I'm really giving them something tailored for them specifically. It may not be appropriate for you.

When somebody asks me a specific question and I answer them, "Do this," I'm only talking to them, although you may decide it applies to you. That's why I'm saying be careful, because it may or may not apply to you. It may or may not be the best route for you, but for what she is talking about, first wait and watch is the best method because it has to sort out first. There's nothing to be done at this stage. Let it become clearer what's going on. If there's a problem, then waiting and watching will clarify what the problem is, in this case. If there is no problem, waiting and watching will clearly show that there's no problem. Sometimes we think there's a problem when there isn't. I'm not suggesting there's no problem here, but I'm suggesting wait and watch for real, and see if there is not or is a problem. It will be clear, if you actually wait as a true watcher.

EMPTY AS A FLUTE

Premodaya: You have to be as hollow and empty as the inside of a flute, so that existence can play its music through you. Anything less than that complete hollowness, that complete emptiness, and even the slightest little bit of anything there, and you're in the way of the music. You won't produce the same notes as if you're empty. So, your job, your challenge, is to be as empty as that flute. Now, people come to meetings like this for all kinds of reasons, but it boils down to a few simple searches, a few simple longings—happiness, Truth, Self-Realization, God. Maybe you could put a few more items on the list, but that's about it. People are coming to find something.

It can be found when you become as empty as a flute. Not until then. You can find pieces of it; you can get closer to it, but you can't really get there until you're empty, until you find the emptiness that's in you. Otherwise, *you* are in the way. Otherwise, happiness can't find you; Truth can't find you; God can't reach you, because you are in the way. It's really a very simple understanding that has to happen. Just that you are in the way. And when you are out of the way, something can happen more like what you're looking for.

Now, that's not how we are taught and that isn't generally how we look at things. We look at things as, "We have to find it. We have to get there. We have to find the way. We have to make it happen." I'm not against goals and planning, or any of it, but ultimately, only emptiness can bring you what you really want.

For some people, hearing that, they get it, but it's a scary notion. They get the idea that somehow, they disappear. It's like a death. They lose something. "Well, then I won't be me, if there is any truth in that. If I follow that, I won't be *me* anymore. It doesn't sound like a great idea." The funny part of is, it's only scary as *a thought*. When you actually move toward it, when you actually taste it, it's not really so fearsome.

In fact, if you think about it, every moment of ecstatic joy (and everybody has had a moment here and a moment there, if not many, of ecstatic joy), every moment of real happiness in your life, were you there? Or wasn't it really that—for a minute—you weren't there?—you weren't concerned with anything—you were truly relaxed; you were truly caught up in something outside of you, and suddenly, you felt this great happiness, this great joy. That's more what it's like.

So there's nothing to lose. Really, all I'm saying to you is: there's nothing to lose in becoming the hollow flute. Just the opposite—there's everything to gain. Because then existence can play you. And beautiful music comes out.

That's why we do a silent meditation. It's the same thing, to fall into the silence. To fall into the emptiness. The deeper you go inside yourself—and that's why you're here, to go deeper inside yourself, to find something—the deeper you go, the emptier it gets. The more silent, the quieter it gets. Now, even if that's a scary-sounding notion, it's the same thing. Once you're going deeper, it's not scary. The silence feels good. Feels like a relief. Feels naturally refreshing.

THE WHOLE SITUATION IS: YOU ARE MUSIC

Premodaya: Music isn't quite like anything else. The whole situation is: you are music. The only problem is when you don't realize that. When you forget, you think you're different from music. It comes up; it's around for a while; it's gone quickly. It's to be enjoyed; it has something to say, but it doesn't mean much if it's not enjoyed. That's you. You're music. If you think you're anything else, think again. If you think you're anything else, you're getting very serious. There's nothing that isn't music. Any real musician will corroborate that. You have to find it out in life. If you aren't a musician, if you aren't born to music, you have to grasp this somehow— that everything is music. Music doesn't ask any questions. I'm not saying, "Don't ask any questions." We welcome and invite all your questions, but every answer that you will get from me will, in one form or another, be somehow suggesting to you that you are music.

You aren't as substantial as you think you are. You aren't as full of all kinds of things that seem to be there, as you think you are. You are more like music: wafts up, lingers a while [snaps fingers], and it is gone. Leaves a fragrance. Leaves a taste in the air. Gives a certain feeling, has an effect. I'm not saying it's meaningless; it *has* an effect, but it's not about questions and answers and great dilemmas and great things to be done, which doesn't mean there aren't great things to be done, but if you can see that it's more like music, you would be closer to the truth. You will be closer to reality. You will be closer to what you really are.

Most of the people who come to a meeting like this already have some sense of how they are more like music than they are like a table. How they are more like music than they are like a refrigerator, although I have met a few people who are more like the refrigerator, but they tend not to come to these kind of meetings, or, if they do, they thaw out fast.

You're more fluid than you think. You're more adaptable than you think. You're more porous than you may realize. You have more possibilities than you may ordinarily think or remember. Like music, any minute a new note, a different direction, a different melody. You are no different. You can live your whole life one way [snaps fingers], and in the twinkling of an eye, can change all of it. You can play a whole different tune anytime. You aren't in any kind of "prison" that you're required to remove. You're writing the music as you go along. Nobody is preventing you from writing a different tune, although, certainly, it can feel like everything is preventing.

Faith: What's the difference between the self and identity?

Premodaya: Where does the question come from?

Faith: I don't know who I am these days.

Premodaya: How did that happen?

Faith: By choice. The identities, the "she is this," "she is that," "I am that." I didn't want to be this or that anymore.

Premodaya: You gave up the identities, but the miserableness stayed on?

Faith: It's overwhelming right now because I feel very lost now. It's very scary.

Premodaya: So you changed your tune. But the new tune hasn't been written yet. That is why it's scary. You are more like music. What you did was, you let yourself become more like music. That's what you're saying. Very brave.

Faith: Yes, I know I'm brave but it's also very lonely.

Premodaya: What do you expect as the payoff?

Faith: I don't really expect anything. I have some hope that the pain will finally set me free.

Premodaya: You're saying, "You hope the misery will go away," right? What do you want out of life?

Faith: I would like to feel loved. I would like very much to conquer that feeling of aloneness. I've always been looking for connection and for what love is, and some "wise man" once told me, "A sense of belonging." He was a Benedict monk.

Premodaya: Well, don't listen to those wise men. He gave you very bad advice, because if love was about a sense of belonging, it's easily taken away. Easily comes and goes. Nothing substantial in that.

Faith: I know.

Premodaya: All we have to do is put you on a bus. All over. Put a blindfold on you—it is all over. Such bad advice. Don't listen to those wise men.

Faith: I thought you were—I mean, I'm *looking* for wise men.

Premodaya: Well, if you listen to me, you will get very confused. You aren't really looking for a wise man. You're looking for clarity. No wise man can give you clarity, but help is possible. Help is possible for getting more clear. The answer to your question about, "What's the difference between identity and self?" is totally irrelevant, doesn't matter. Because neither one addresses that you are music.

Faith: Well, I have a problem with the music. The music isn't in me right now. Maybe the melodies are missing.

Premodaya: Well, you are music, so nothing is missing. Luckily, you're hearing it from me, not from a wise man. So now you have to tolerate what you have done. You have to tolerate that you have thrown out all of these identities. It is a smart thing. I'm all for it, but now you have to tolerate living without an identity. But now you have to do one more thing, which is even bigger, and harder than throwing out the identities. You have to throw out all these ideas, like: "I want love," "I want this," "I want that."

Faith: That's what I heard yesterday, and I thought, "Oh, that's what I want." It was not even my idea, because I don't even know what I want.

Premodaya: That is better. Can you live with not knowing what you want?

Faith: That is a freeing feeling. There's also, "If you know what you want—" My control, you know. I don't know what I want.

Premodaya: Well, I think you want yourself.

Faith: I would like to feel comfortable with myself.

Premodaya: Oh, I didn't say comfortable. Your question was, "What's the difference between identity and self?" You wouldn't have asked that question if you didn't want yourself. It's always the strangest question, because how can you not have yourself? As far as everything you're telling me, if it can be tolerated, it will take you further. But the danger is, not to tolerate it, to have done this and then not go further, not see where it takes you. That's the danger.

Faith: I'm hanging in there to see it through, but I haven't seen the light yet. It is very dark.

Premodaya: Stop looking for the light. Maybe it will come as music. Maybe nothing will come. Nobody in the room is worried about you. I am not convinced you're worried, even.

Faith: You may be right. I'm a little impatient. I just don't like the way I have felt for three months, heavy, no escape.

Premodaya: There is always suicide.

Faith: It has never been an option for me.

Premodaya: I'm not surprised. In fact, it is not even possible to commit suicide. If you commit suicide, one second later it is all the same. Nothing has changed, except now you are dead. Other than that, it is the same.

Faith: I had somebody who committed suicide about six weeks ago and it had a big effect on me. You know, people left behind.

Premodaya: Well, it may have had a bigger effect on you, than on them, is what I am saying. I'm always vehemently against suicide for only that reason, because it won't change anything. Imagine the shock and the disappointment to a person who commits suicide thinking, "At least I'm releasing myself from all the anguish." And then they are dead, "Goddamn it—the anguish is still here." Imagine the shock and dismay of that.

Faith: It was never an option for me.

Premodaya: No, you are too brave. Everything will go forward and sort itself out and be fine.

THE CHAIR IS EMPTY

Rashad: People come to me and pour their hearts out, ask for advice, help—whatever it is. It's to the point now where I know this is what I'm supposed to be doing for my livelihood. I'm confident in what I do, but on the other hand, I worry about, "Who am I to be offering that kind of advice, providing those kinds of services?" I sometimes feel other people have gone to school or gone through intense training, and have better credentials, so part of me feels, "Well, maybe I'm not as good as them."

Right now, I'm feeling the urge that I need to apply a lot of the stuff I use to help everybody else with their problems and tailor unique to them, to work for them. I'm having the hardest time trying to do that for myself.

Premodaya: So, are you completely hollow and empty?

Rashad: No.

Premodaya: That's what's required to really help people. Step one is to become completely empty, completely as hollow as a flute. That's why you're not sure. If you were hollow, there would be no question. See, it only looks like somebody is sitting in this chair [where Premodaya is sitting]. There's nobody sitting here.

Rashad: And I know that, because when I do what I do, it's like I'm channeling something. It has absolutely nothing to do with me.

Premodaya: You have a piece of it, and you know a piece of it, but now you have to get all of it, and all of it means: that there's no urge to help anyone. There's no urge to use it. There's no urge to do anything. It's just an unplanned sharing. An unchosen sharing. See, if I really had a choice you wouldn't catch me in this chair. And I'm a very good disciple. I have two Masters and many teachers, and I'm very happy being in the audience chair. Very happy. I mean, *really* happy being in that chair.

The whole idea of being in this chair is really not my idea. Something is there for you that wants to be in the chair, that feels it should be in the chair. So first, become empty enough that that urge isn't there anymore. Then this question and these doubts and everything won't be there. Then there will be something to share, because nothing in you is in the way.

What you have (everybody sees it) is a certain kind of a lovability. A lovableness. And that, of course, attracts people. Everybody likes loveable people, and people that are felt as loving. That's your strength. That's why people come to you, because you're loveable, loving, safe, warm and friendly—all that good stuff.

But that's not enough. There has to be a real clearing there. And that's your job. You have to get to the point where anything you share is completely clean. It's not coming from some urge inside to help somebody. It's not coming from some unconscious need in you.

Hearing this, don't let me confuse you. I'm not suggesting that anybody who sits in this chair is in any way perfect. It doesn't mean you become perfect, you have no more needs—none of that, none of that. There's no such thing. As long as you're on this earth, you're a human being, and you remain a human being. It doesn't matter what level of consciousness you've reached. You're still a human being. A human being always has needs, always has wants, and always has an ego. Always. It doesn't change.

I'm not giving you some big impossible goal of become perfect, become empty, meaning: you're not being a human being anymore. It just means you're not in the way. The way the flute is empty. So that when you're with someone and helping someone, *they* are what's there. Your needs aren't in the way. Your ego is not in the way. Your wants aren't in the way. And that lovableness and lovingness in and of itself is very healing. People want that. I'm not all that lovable. I have my crusty side, my more provocative side. Everybody isn't going to love me. You have more of that quality that appeals to a bigger audience. It appeals to a wider array of personalities. I appeal to some, not to others. That's definitely your strength. I'm wanting you to really realize that: You can't buy that loving-ness and lovability, and you can't train yourself to be that way. That's a gift.

Now, it wouldn't hurt to have some training or credentials. If you read my bio, you know that I was a therapist for many years, that I've worked with a lot of people. And I was director of psychiatry at Cedars-Sinai Medical Center. You don't get that job by being a lousy therapist. But all of that, I realized, was simply training to be in this chair. I didn't know it until the chair appeared—but once the chair said, "Get your butt in here," it gradually became clear that that twenty-eight years was, literally, existence saying, "Hey, let's give you some good training so you don't mess nobody up."

I thought I had a career, but it turned out I was just an apprentice to be in an empty chair. I'm not saying that you have to go out and have a career in counseling or psychology or psychiatry or any of that. I'm simply saying that it certainly doesn't hurt to learn something professional about how to work with people. If that calls you, if there's a feeling to do that, why not?

Having said that, and I encourage you to do that—at the same time, I can tell you that my professional background has, in another way ab-solutely nothing to do with what I do now. Both are true: That there's absolutely a training to do with what I do now, and absolutely nothing to do with what I do now.

If you recognize that simply by being with people and sharing what's there, and really being with them, that there's something being given, something being shared, it becomes even more important that you figure out how you're going to live, so you can do that. Like I said, I'm very prac-tical both in how I work with people (what I talk about) and my advice to people.

I'm not a great believer in, "I will just be open, and a living will come to me, doing the things I love to do." Most of us in this life don't get to make a living at what we love to do. Some do. I'm not saying you can't be, but a lot of times people go years and years, if not decades, kind of looking for a magical solution to that issue. And in the meantime, they don't live too good. Understand that sometimes you gotta to do what you gotta to do to pay the rent. Don't forget the practical side, is all I'm saying.

EVERYBODY HAS A GIFT TO SHARE

Felix: My question is: How do you master patience when you have a lot of passion?

Premodaya: Talk about why that's your question.

Felix: I'm an actor. I have done a lot of work back in New York. I moved here and got a manager, and she's been helping me find an agency. Sometimes I get frustrated because of my passion. I feel I have something to give to the world, and I feel like it is delayed when things aren't happening at a certain time, you know?

Premodaya: What if I said, "Forget about giving anything to the world"?

Felix: It's hard. Tonight, when you mentioned the unknown, it helped me a lot, I realized that you really don't have control. I think when you do things, or you're proactive it convinces you that you do have control, because you expect results.

Premodaya: Exactly, but it's all an illusion. You're convinced you have control, but it's just a convincing. It's not true. You get sold an idea, and it looks real, but it's not. Actually, you are giving right now. You're always giving. Now, you need to know that anything that any of us have to give, we are always giving. Maybe not in the exact way you would prefer to be giving it. Maybe not in the exact form that you would prefer to be experiencing it—as a giving, as an actor getting paid, with a job, acting. But really, part of understanding for real, that whole insight that the unknown is right here, right now—that that's the only place you can be, because that's where you actually are—includes this idea of "everybody has something to give; everybody has a gift to share." It includes that.

You don't have a choice about that either. That also happens whether you want it to or not. You might have your own ideas—and you do; that's what you're explaining. Most of us do. You might have your own idea about what that should look like, what it is, what the gift is, what you have to share. What I'm saying to you is, it's a bigger mystery than that. The unknown is more happening than that, and you don't know what you're actually sharing. You don't really, actually, truly know what the gift is that you're giving. You don't even know who's getting it and what they're doing with it. At the most, all you can know is something is transpiring. There is some kind of interplay happening. That's the most you can know. And even that is not real solid.

I'm giving you the deepest possible answer to, "What do I do with the impatience?" The deepest answer is, "Impatient for what? You're not even doing anything to begin with." The real way to be more patient and to share the gift wider, is to live more in that unknown. To more and more know that you aren't controlling anything. To more and more know that you aren't doing what you think you are doing. I'm not saying stop doing, but I am saying, you don't know. You really, truly don't know the actual results of anything you do.

You could say something on Tuesday to somebody, and not know that somebody in the back of the room heard it and it changed their life. And they went out and did something, and that had an effect on their great-grandchild one hundred and ten years from now. You wouldn't know that. But that happens all the time. That's the practical way the unknown works. It simply means, you don't know. We don't know. It's bigger than us.

Know that more. Plug into that more for real. And then you can be as passionate as you want and it will not drive you so nuts.

Felix: Yeah.

Premodaya: Did I answer you?

Felix: Yes.

Premodaya: Good.

CHAPTER 10

ON SILENCE

Premodaya: "Silence" is the great synonym for all the big words: "Truth," "God," "Realization," "Self," "Soul." All the words with capital first letters are the same as silence. Silence is impartial, impersonal, infinite, eternal, unchanging, unmoving. Truth, God, silence—all the same thing. *You*—all the same thing. No true teacher has any interest in talking; I certainly have no interest in talking. All the talking is simply to get to a point sooner or later where silence can be communicated. That silence is the depth, the depth without end.

Perhaps you felt, sitting here in a more silent way in these few minutes just now, how it throws you to yourself. That can be sweet and wonderful and that can be grating and unpleasant. But whatever the experience—however it feels—it throws you inward, it throws you more to yourself. But it's not just that silence is the condition, or the optimum circumstance, for going deeper; it's that silence *is* the depth.

In so many ways you get a taste of it here and there, accidentally, suddenly, spontaneously, purposely; however, it happens, everybody experiences the profundity of it now and again, when suddenly the distractions seem not to be there and somehow you fall more into yourself. Somehow you find yourself deeper without effort; somehow things open up more. Somehow more is visible, knowable, palpable.

Everything that happens in Truth happens in silence, even if it's not noticed; even if sound is there, even if words are there, even if communications and activities are there, the real transmission, the real event, the real happening, is in the silence behind all those other things. Silence is the void, and silence is the fullness. Indefinable—but it can be felt; it can be sensed; it can be entered; it can be known. You were born in silence; you will die in silence. In between, it's also all just silence, but it seems otherwise.

In the death process, in the physical death process, one of the first things that happens is the hearing sense shuts down. You're thrown to yourself in the last moment, just by the simple fact that your physical hearing apparatus simply turns off, shuts off. In that second, you know, absolutely, that you will never hear anything again through these ears. There's a sequence—the eyes shut off; the other senses shut off; the organs shut off—but one of the first things that shuts off is the hearing. Suddenly you realize—when all sound, when all external sound, has shut off—that you're alone. And now, no one can talk to you, and it's very difficult for you to talk (even though people who can't hear can often talk). In the death process you become physically weak. You sense, you feel immediately, "Now I can hear nothing and now I can't really say anything, ever again." Now you're by yourself. The relationship in that few seconds becomes a relationship between you and silence. You know suddenly and spontaneously that there are only seconds or moments left, so there's no point in trying to relate to the outside world, to anybody who is there.

I'm trying to give you silence, always, because ultimately the only thing that can be given is silence. All the talking is required, all your questions are required, all the activities and interactions are required just so—and for no other reason—you can ultimately, in the end, move through those and come to silence. Silence is the Mystery. Not silence meaning "no noise" or "no sound." Silence meaning that which is the Source of Everything. When you finally come to silence, you have reached everything that's worth reaching. Anything that's happening—it flips, and you begin to sense that now you have to relate to silence. Now it's an inward journey, knowing not to where, knowing not how. But one thing you know in those seconds is that now your companion is silence.

This mirrors the whole life, because ultimately, if you see rightly, you see that silence is always your companion. Silence is always where you're sitting. God is silence, and you are silence. Most of us associate silence with peace. That isn't an accident. The only place you're ever really going is closer and closer to silence. Remember, silence doesn't mean an absence of anything; it means the absolute presence of everything.

Why in all spiritual groups, all spiritual meetings like this, all formats with so-called spiritual teachers, why is it always a question-and-answer format? Because the questions have to be answered, so that you can't be held back from silence. Until the questions are answered, you can't really move into silence. The question operates as a barrier. You have to bring your questions; you have to ask them; that's the process. Not because the questions themselves are necessarily important—they may be, they may not be—but so that you can empty yourself of what's troubling you, what's confusing you, what's stopping you. So that one by one the questions can be resolved, not because in the end you get the "right answer," but so that the vessel of questions that you are, can be emptied out, cleaned, purified, become ready to be filled with silence, instead of questions and chatter and wonderings and dilemmas and sufferings.

No true teacher is ever annoyed at your questions. Sometimes people will say, "I don't want to sound stupid, so I'm not sure I should ask this." You should ask it so that you can be unburdened of it. And it should matter. I don't mean ask any dumb question that occurs to you. That doesn't unburden you. But to ask what really matters, what is life and death, what you absolutely have to know: this will unburden you; this will open you to another level of experiencing and comprehending. Not because the teacher gave you such a marvelous answer—although they may, or they may give you a terrible answer, who knows? But because you were able to move the question out like a cork from a bottle, so it's not stopping you, or stopping you up.

All of that is a clearing process, and in a meeting like this there's an energy, there's an inner movement, the inner urge; Truth motivates an inner urge to put the question on the table in a way you don't feel in other circumstances. Sometimes people become quite on fire, quite urgent with their questions. That's because Truth is heating it up, heating it up so that you can more quickly move towards silence, so that nothing is rankling in you that doesn't have to be.

It seems like my answers are important, but what's important are your questions, much more important than any answers I will give you, because your questions are your unresolved mind, the mind that separates, that holds you apart. Like a wound-up thing, you have to unwind it. The process in satsang, the process in darshan, the process in the spiritual context, is to unwind that, and you do that by bringing questions, questions that you very much want the answer to. Questions that change your life.

So never worry about asking a stupid question when you're with me, or anywhere else that this kind of process happens. Never bother to censor yourself for fear that you'll say something wrong, or look foolish, or annoy who is there, or bother the teacher, or whatever. When you come just to listen, that's good. There's nothing wrong with that; that's a certain mode. But what's even better is when you come with a burning question. What's even better yet is when the question is more important than anything, when your whole life depends on it, on getting the answer, because then it means you have gotten to some level that's more essential, more serious. At that level much more is possible.

At that level, something can be accessed that's much harder to access ordinarily. At that level you will be more available to what's trying to come to you. And at that level what's trying to come to you will have an easier time revealing itself. At that level the soil is more fertile; the possibilities are more real. At that level you aren't going so much in circles, or wasting your time, or finding yourself not where you want to be. So many processes are going on; in a meeting like this, many levels are operating. We are just talking about one of them, but it has to be understood. It's good to understand this one aspect, this one particular process, the process of bringing your questions. It more quickly moves you closer to silence when sincere questions are brought sincerely. Just the asking clears a space, moves you closer to yourself. Your idea is, the answer is what matters, but it's that clearing the space that really matters.

If there's any question that anyone has about silence, I would love to hear that question.

Riley: It's hard to still your mind, it's hard for me to find silence. Unless silence is trying to still your mind. Is it hard to do that?

Premodaya: One of the things some people see, or experience, when they are searching for silence is the loudness of the mind. Is seeing how hard it is to still the mind a new experience for you or an old experience?

Riley: It was hard tonight to still the mind—I don't think I have ever stilled my mind.

Premodaya: Well, most people haven't, but the silence is there whether your mind is still or not. Silence is irrespective of conditions. Why do you want to still your mind?

Riley: I guess I don't understand what silence is. I relate to it as a void. Because meditating is peaceful and I like the peacefulness of meditating— but silence, I'm not sure what silence is.

Premodaya: Good. I have thrown a new challenge at you.

Riley: Is this silence something that you try to accomplish all the time? Is it a state you want to be in all the time?

Premodaya: It's not a state and it can't be accomplished, but it can be known. When it's truly known, then you see that it's the fabric of everything. These two questions go together, because of what happens for people when they first come across the whole notion of moving towards silence, understanding better what silence really means, what it really is. And the whole related experience of how deafening the mind is and how active the mind is and how, in the most practical way, the mind prevents any real silence—at least it seems that way. Everybody comes up against this seeming challenge and the danger, the ditch here, the trap here, is to start battling with the mind so you can still it, so you can quiet it, so you can get more silent. Then that battle rages; you can't win that battle, because as soon as you battle with the mind, the mind has won, because mind is a battle, mind is nothing other than an engagement, and a battling and a back-and-forth activity.

Riley: So, silence doesn't exist.

Premodaya: Silence is the only thing that exists.

Riley: Then I don't understand what silence is.

Premodaya: Then that's your new Zen koan. I have to tell you I'm very excited for you because if this whole notion of silence is a fairly new idea for you and if you're seeing more clearly that the mind never wants to be still, then you're absolutely coming to a whole different level. You're absolutely getting closer to something important, because you are sincere and you are serious. That sincerity and that seriousness pays off, in this form. In the form that you get to come up against something that moves you to a higher plateau. I get excited for you and I want you to struggle with it:

226

this whole question of silence and the mind. By "struggle," I mean engage with it.

Riley: Yes, I want to find the answers; I want to find the enlightenment. I don't like the word "struggle," but I will allow it to come to me.

Premodaya: Give some thought to it. What do they mean, "Silence is everything and synonymous with Truth or with God?" Chew on that.

Grant: I've experienced silence, but I still have the same question as she had.

Premodaya: This is everybody's question.

Grant: I sought basically my whole life to get to the part of silence and in the last year, I could get myself there. As soon as I get there, I realize it was just the push of the ego to get there, so the ego would think there is some pleasurable feeling there—and I realize that in silence you don't get ego pleasures. So the next thing I'm looking for is: What is there, and what is there to experience?

Premodaya: If you don't get ego pleasures, what did you get?

Grant: I guess it's a realization of the illusion of the world. I relate to what you're saying, that silence is the essence of everything, but it's also the essence of nothing, because we don't want everything. No one wants *everything* that there is to experience—and no one wants *nothing*.

Premodaya: What do you want?

Grant: I'm not sure if I want anything. I have split it into two—there's a spiritual side of me and there's this other side of me that relates in the world: it's my identity, where I came from, who I am, and what relationships I have. All of that is illusion. This other part seeks out the silence and recognition of what is illusion. It's still a question to me. So, then what?

Premodaya: Then that has to be reconciled once and for all, and that's why you're here. That's why you are at this meeting; that's why you go to things like this—because you know that that has to be reconciled finally, once and for all, so there isn't that split, so that you know without any doubt, without any confusion, and without any further questioning, exactly what matters.

Grant: Right. And along the way there's a lot of frightening stuff. It's wonderful to know that it doesn't matter what car you drive, but it's frightening to know that your children aren't really there. It's hard to even say that, but in some ways they are no different than the car. I know that ultimately now, my children are nothing more than my car. That's why I say I have this identity. I nurture them; I have a job to do with them; I love them; I take care of them. But ultimately, they are not real.

Premodaya: They aren't yours.

Grant: They aren't mine, right. They aren't the illusion I see them as. They are their own people, their own spirit. Anyway, the question is, what is that reconciliation?

Premodaya: Well, there isn't *a* reconciliation; what there is, is the demand of the reconciliation. The demand that that reconciliation be found. What I'm saying to you is that nothing else matters more than that and that that has to be reached. That reconciliation has to be found, whatever it takes, no matter what the price. Through some kind of grace, you've come to know certain essential things that most people never come to know. Having come that far, you have to go the rest of the way. Having come that far, you can't ever be comfortable staying there, because it's part of the understanding; it's not the whole understanding. So, you have to get the rest.

Grant: I'm already at the point where I realize that it's all going to come through grace, so then I'm in a place of complete surrender. But when you surrender, there's no expectation.

Premodaya: Until the next time I see you, that's what I want you to question in yourself, whether you're in a place of real surrender. I don't want you to answer it in your own mind quickly, "Oh, I know I can go deeper." I want you to really sit with the question of, "Where am I with surrender?" Can you do that?

Grant: Yes.

Premodaya: Good.

This whole subject of silence we should talk about whenever we have the opportunity, whenever it arises, because to understand this more clearly is a great challenge that can't help but move you forward, can't help but move you into a greater depth. If it's new to you, then it's a rich exploration. If it's very familiar to you, then the challenge becomes, what does it mean for your life and how you live it? And ultimately what does it mean for your perception of the Profound? Of the Eternal? So there's no position that you can be in relation to the concept of silence, that notion of silence, that isn't valuable.

CHAPTER 11

THE BEYOND

YOU ARE A HOLY BEING

Premodaya: Anyone who tells you that you aren't a holy being doesn't know what they're talking about. The emptier you get, the quieter you get, the more you taste what you really are, the more you become aware of that—regardless of what thoughts are there, regardless of what behaviors are there, regardless of what problems are there. It is not that you *become* this holy being and problems disappear and you float off somewhere and you know yourself as sanctified—*you came here sanctified.* "Sanctified" means: have problems, have to pay the rent, get angry, screw up, have bad thoughts, have anxiety attacks, do bad things, go nuts. Do you think that makes you any less a sanctified holy being than existence made you? Than God made you? Let me leave you with that thought.

TRANSCENDING YOUR OWN EXPERIENCE

Premodaya: It's always a strange experience for me—these events: partly, because I never know what I'm going to say; partly, because I have no idea how I got in this chair; and, partly, because it's always a miracle, literally, that you show up. It's very strange. How can this be? The answer is—despite everything. Despite me, despite you, despite circumstances, somehow. Somehow, I'm sitting here; somehow, you're sitting there. What I would like you to see is that just because I'm sitting here and you're sitting there, that we aren't sitting in different places. You aren't in a different position from me. I'm not in a different position from you. You can get the impression that the guy that sits in this chair, "Oh, he's the answer man." But it's not true.

You could just as well be sitting in this chair. Anybody could be sitting in this chair. Anybody out there could be sitting in these chairs, but somehow—and it's the part I call a miracle—somehow, here we are. It's a miracle, as far as I'm concerned, because I can't explain it, because I can't account for my part in it, and because I know absolutely for certain that there's no such thing in this universe as an "accident." Since it's not random that you're here, since it's not accidental that somehow you heard of ICODA, or somehow wandered in, or somehow you found yourself in whatever chair you're in, since there's no way it's an occurrence that has no purpose or no meaning, or something that just happens—since that is not possible in this universe—it's actually quite amazing. When you consider that you're here because you have to be here, when you consider that you're here because there's nowhere else you could be, and when you expand that out to any and every moment of your life, that's a whole different understanding than the one our parents usually give us, or the one society gives us, or the one that we commonly agree on, which are: some things are purposeful; some things just happen; they don't really have a purpose; they aren't so important. My contention is that that's incorrect.

The smallest, slightest thing is absolutely meaningful and purposeful, things that our mind looks at as inconsequential—every little thing. It's only our mind that makes a distinction between "the big things" and "the little things." If you pull out that judgment, if you extract that measurement, what's a "big thing" and what's a "little thing," how strange does that become if you think about it for a moment? Imagine your life with no big things and no little things, just whatever there is, whatever happens, without one being more significant than another. That's actually closer to the truth. The significance is added later by us. I would encourage you to look at that very closely, because you're likely to see, the closer you look, that it's really *you* that's saying, "This is insignificant; this is important." It's not coming from some arbitrary standard.

Yes, part of it comes from an outside standard, but the culture gives you that. This is big stuff: you graduate from college, you get a well-paying job, you buy your first house; whatever the culture says it is, "These are the big things, these are the little things." But what does the culture know? You can be wiser than the culture and look for yourself, think for yourself, and see that in almost everything, in almost every moment, in almost everything you do, almost everywhere you go, almost every activity you engage in, including every thought, that you're doing a dual process. You're engaging in it, but you're also categorizing it at the same time—"This is big, this is little; this is important; this is insignificant; this was meant to be; this was an accident; this was bad, this was good; this was pleasant, this was unpleasant." It's automatic. You don't think about it; you don't actually sit there and do it; your mind does it for you with no nanosecond of gap. What I'm suggesting is, all of that, that whole process, is to your detriment—that whole process is a string of interpretations you give yourself—that the primary effect is limiting you: limiting your awareness, limiting your seeing, limiting your knowing, limiting your understanding and limiting your experiencing. And you don't have to impose those limits.

Now, you can't just blame the culture, because there *is* a natural, built-in "tendency," let's call it, to want to categorize and, believe it or not, it doesn't come from the mind. The mind carries it out, but it comes from a sense that you somehow have to protect yourself. There's an actual urge, an actual need, an actual tendency to limit your experience, to put blinders on yourself, to put shutters around yourself, because there's some kind of sense—in a very primitive way, very early on—that if you don't do that, it will all be too much: You will be crushed by life; you'll be crushed by awareness. This can't be blamed on, "The mind is your enemy," or "The culture doesn't teach you the truth," or "My parents were ignorant." This is in all of us.

It's a very interesting subject, because the real subject is experience— experience itself. *Experience is a limitation of you.* This is not an idea that you're going to hear very often or in many places. Especially in spiritual circles, there's often the idea that experience has to expand, experience leads to greater awareness, experience leads to higher consciousness, experience leads to Truth. You need to get higher experiences—better experiences—purer, holier experiences. What I want you to consider is, it's not the nature of the experience—holy, unholy, religious, irreligious, significant, revelation or tiny bit of knowledge, experience of expansiveness or experience of smallness—it's experience itself. Not the definition of the experience, not the text or context or the content of the experience, but experience *itself*—your ability to experience—*is* the limitation.

Can you imagine life not bound by experiences, not defined as a set of experiences, one after the other? It's very hard to imagine for most of us, because we are told (and it makes sense) that it's all about experiences. What's life? A bunch of experiences. What are we? An "experience gatherer." So we're looking for bigger and better experiences. If you're on a spiritual path, you're looking for holier experiences, higher experiences, purer, more truthful experiences. And you will rarely find anybody who will disagree that experiences are good. I'm not saying experiences aren't good; I'm saying, see if you can see that experience and experiences, itself, has a natural catch-22 in it: You limit yourself to that experience in that moment because the feeling is if we didn't, it would be like we were on LSD. It would be too much sensory input; there would be too much mental input, too much emotional input, too much everything input, too much physical, too much nonphysical, too much energy, too much everything. Somehow—deep down, without ever thinking about it, without ever looking at it, without ever discussing it with anyone—we all kind of go along, evaluating, "What kind of experiences are we having in life? And how can we improve those experiences?" Whether you're trying to make a million dollars or whether you're trying to find God.

What I'm suggesting to you is relatively radical. What I'm suggesting to you is that your experiences don't matter. If you really are greedy and want the Truth, greedy for the Absolute Truth, greedy for the Truth that is the core of all Truth, greedy for God, greedy for Reality—however you want to put it—the real prize is to get beyond experience. Better experiences? Holier experiences? Great! Nothing wrong with that. I'm all for it; probably so are you; probably so would anybody you talk to; and you can get to a point where your experiences are tremendously loving and tremendously positive and tremendously fulfilling and prosperity bringing, and all the other good stuff you want to list—the list can be long, and you can have a great life. Some people do and some people don't. Most people have a mix of the two; most of us if really asked to answer, would say, "Well, I've had some great experiences, but I've had some difficulties, too."

What I'm saying is, all of that is a diversion. That whole game, that whole dialogue, that whole concern for, "What's the nature of my experience? What's the nature of my experiences?" is all a smoke screen that causes all the difficulty in trying to get to Reality, to get to what's truly True. Some people call it "getting to Self" or "Self-Realization." If you could wipe out, magically, the boundaries that come naturally with how we experience experiences, there would be no question of Truth; there would be no question of God; there would be no question of Reality; there would be no question of being separate from anything or having a question that arises in any way.

Now, I can't tell when I say these things if it all sounds very esoteric or if it makes sense to folks. What I'm trying to do is provoke you into considering something that it's likely you have never, ever considered, or anybody has asked you to consider. I'm trying to see if it sparks anything in you. So tell me how you relate to what I've said so far?

Darshana: I was involved in a program of creating experiences that were supposedly everything you ever wanted. The thing about getting in the mode of constantly creating experiences was that you were never actually present to any of the experiences you were creating; you put your mind in this mode of constantly looking for the next experience, or trying so hard to create the perfect experience, that there wasn't a whole lot of room for just being present to that which was. It was quite a roller coaster of emotions, it felt like a lot of manipulating, a lot of pressure. It made a lot of sense to me what you were saying, because I walked away from that path a while back—and now since I have been working with you, learning more and more about allowing the big, grand experience called "life" to be the experience that I'm having—I feel a lot less pressure. I feel a little saner and more peaceful.

Premodaya: Maybe you said it better than I did, because listening to your description sounded to me like we could say that that's what people are always doing. You were telling us that you were in a special course where that was the focus—to have more prosperous or more powerful or better experiences. But listening to you, I kept thinking, "That's the perfect description of how we all live." We are doing exactly that, that's my whole point. You made my point a little more succinctly than I did: that this is what we're doing all the time, and that the doing of that is the smoke screen to the Truth. At the end of your comment you said, "Now I'm just trying to allow, instead of get better experiences," and I realized there's a simple way to make the suggestion that I'm trying to make, so I thank you for clarifying that for me. The radical notion that I'm trying to impart is, that *life is not an experience.*

We think life is an experience, and then we run around saying, "Why aren't things working out better?" or "Why am I not in absolute communion with God?" or "Why is the Truth not evident to me?" or "Why am I not Self-Realized?" or "Why am I not a millionaire?"—whatever it is.

Morgan: If experience hinders us, then why were our bodies put on earth, which are essentially experiencing mechanisms?

Premodaya: Perfect question. This helps me clarify more. I'm not saying that experience hinders us. I'm saying the way we look at what we call experience, the way we define it and live it, is what limits us needlessly, is what is detrimental to most of what we want. Most people basically want peace or Truth or understanding or happiness. I'm saying, experiences can't give you those things. The tagline at ICODA is "Beyond Self," but it could just as well be "Beyond Experience." Experience, as we tend to live it, is like looking at one little piece of pie and saying, "Why isn't the pie bigger?" or "Why isn't the pie more delicious?" or "Why isn't the pie sweeter?" Well, if you look at one little, tiny sliver, it's not going to taste like much. A bigger slice can be had by loosening the definition, by loosening the experience of experiencing. This is why most formal meditations are about closing the doors of the senses, limiting the perception. That's a movement toward limiting what we call experience or experiences, so that we come closer to the core that isn't about an experience. What I'm saying is very, very wild. I'm saying that your experience is not synonymous with life, but most of us wouldn't say that. Most of us would say that life and experience are the same thing—they are synonymous. I'm saying the limitation on life is our experience.

Priya: It makes perfect sense, because our experience is only *our* experience, and there are billions of people and creatures and animals and plants and stars and air; everything could be said to be experiencing. And experience changes all the time.

Premodaya: And *you* change all the time. Not only experiences change, the experiencer changes.

Priya: Our perception of our experience isn't just an idea that we have of us and of experience; everything is just changing so we don't really see it.

Premodaya: The problem is the idea that we are having experiences. I'm not saying that we aren't having experiences, but the problem is we limit things through the lens, through the boundary line of experiences. Another way to come at it: whatever you think you get that you like from your experiencing, "Oh, this feels good," or "That makes me happy," or "This is blissful," or "I'm proud of this, this really satisfies me," any feeling like that, any experience like that, is a little tiny taste of what lies beyond experience, that that's a permeating of what isn't experienceable penetrating through experience. We believe that we won the lottery and that's what made us happy; we're ecstatic the night we won the lottery, "Now I'm a millionaire!" (The Buddhists talk a little bit about this, this aspect of it.) I'm saying, it's not winning the lottery that made you happy. It's winning the lottery that allowed you to relax enough that, for a split second, something came into your experience from beyond experience, and *that's* where the happiness originates. It doesn't originate in our experience; it originates in what the experience is *originating in*. I really don't want to sound Buddhist, but the Buddhists have talked about this from that aspect.

Grant: Taking the converse of the experience of winning the lottery, or what is named a 'positive experience.' Burning your hand can be considered a 'negative experience,' or painful at the very least.

Premodaya: The suggestion that I'm making is that whether it's pain or whether it's pleasure, whether it's wanted or unwanted, whether it's physically perceived or mentally perceived, or emotionally perceived, that entire basket called "experience, experiencing and experiences" is all an indicator of something else. And that "something else" is the origin; that something else is the source; that something else is what experiencing (including us) is sitting in, is coming from, is originating from. The provocation I'm trying to make is that we can actually move closer to that; we can actually, in sort of a leap, give up our attachment to the idea and the definition of experiencing. Everybody has had a taste of this at some point, through some kind of experience or another that took you beyond experience. I'm just trying to put out the radical notion that life isn't about what we think it's about. It's not about what we experience—it's about what life arises *in*. And the sooner and the more we look in that direction, the more we are likely not to be so trapped by our own definitions and our own preferences. This may not be interesting to anybody but me; I don't know.

Grant: If you walk down to the watering hole, and the tigers were down there and they came after you and bit you, it's not a good thing to do that again. You learn from experience so that you can experience life more fully. You have to experience in order to give up experience.

Premodaya: Maybe. I don't know. I do know that the kind of learning you're talking about is certainly necessary and is certainly valuable. The problem is, then we start saying, "This is what life is about." Then we wonder why we can't find the Truth that we're looking for. This whole notion is a stab at putting it in a bigger context so that the understanding can develop that experience itself is the limitation.

Mary Anne: Two experiences come to mind. I had my own experience of being in very high, chronic pain. There was a moment I was so desperate that I realized there must be something beyond that pain—like you're hitting a wall; there must be something beyond it—I knew there was something beyond it. I'm not only my experience. The other one was an extremely positive experience, all of a sudden time stood still; everybody, everything, stopped. It was like getting out of that experience, if I look backward now.

Premodaya: They are certainly examples of what I'm talking about.

Darshana: If you know all things, if it's all inside, then why do you have to have experiences? So, experiences limit.

Premodaya: That's a very good other way of saying what I'm trying to get to. I'm going to borrow from you and expand on it as best as I can: If all is already there and what is, *is*, and what can be known is already known, then the only limit to the living of that is experience. Experiences put a cap on what you can know, what you can feel, what you can sense, what you can be. It's not only if all is *already* known, it all *already is*. The best is already here; the possibility of whatever is possible has already happened. It's not just you already know; it's you *already are*. Whatever it is, it's already the case. This is very strange, because it's radically good news. Because it says everything you had hoped for, already is. But it's very strange because it's saying if you go to try and experience it, *that* will be the limitation, the barrier from really being that.

The question of, "Why do we have experiences?" is a significant question. It's a very religious question; it's a core religious question. If we were dropped off in the forest after birth and raised by wolves, or raised by trees, or whatever, and we didn't find ourselves in a society and we didn't find ourselves with a language, or with other people of our species to relate to, what would be our experiencing? The funny thing is, this has happened. They have tried to find this out, because there are people that were raised by wolves, or by animals. The famous one was Victor of Aveyron, discovered in the late 1700s. One physician took him in and tried to have a conversation with him, again and again, about his experience when he was wild (this is where the term "wild child" comes from). Two things are interesting to me; one is, he could never have that conversation; he could never impart or have any meaningful dialogue with the scientists about what it was like before us (what it is like *now*, knowing there are other human beings, and having interactions). They could never get an answer. The second thing that's interesting was he died suddenly, and they were never sure why. He was, by their estimate, in his twenties—so he shouldn't have died, he wasn't at the time of his time to die. To me this was very fascinating, that they couldn't get any meaningful answer—and that the end result of living both ways, was that it killed him.

Why do we have to have experiences? Maybe the answer was what Grant said: We could get to the point of not having to have experiences. I don't know the answer, but it's fascinating to me to delve into the question, because I think it's the delving into the question that opens up windows.

LIFE IS A DREAM

Prof. Alex: I'm aware that I'm running a lot, running towards or running away from things. But once in a while I will say, "Stop," and I think, "My goodness, I'm sitting here!" Sitting in the car or just all alone, and it's a wonderful feeling. Things that happened five minutes ago are gone with the Roman Empire—they're gone. And I don't know what's going to happen next; it's almost like I wake up. Is that part of a dream? I'm not sure now.

Premodaya: It's recognizing the dream that you're in. It's an awakening. And what happens when you awaken? You recognize that have been dreaming.

Prof. Alex: Osho was very helpful to me, because I'd go a whole day without this kind of episode, and I would think, well damn, why have I been unconscious all day? And Osho said: "Don't do that. Be thankful that you have moments. Celebrate that you have moments." I think that took a tremendous burden off me. I think sometimes the whole human race has one thing in common: this moment. If everyone could just stop, we'd share that moment.

Premodaya: Well, we know that cats dream. And we know that dogs dream—and we assume that most mammals at least dream, so it's not a uniquely human phenomenon. But the uniquely human phenomenon is to recognize that what we think is serious is also a dream. If you really wake up, then you stop taking it so seriously. Then you can really laugh and mean it.

Wyn: What about physical pain, though? How do you attribute physical pain to a dream?

Premodaya: Haven't you dreamt of being in pain?

Wyn: Yes. But that was a nightmare, I thought.

Premodaya: Well, aren't our physical pains nightmares?

Wyn: So how do I transfer the pain into a dream?

Premodaya: If you're trying to transfer it, you're trying to get rid of it, and that just sets up a fight and makes you more aware of the pain. If you can relax into it and view it objectively, this can make a difference and does make a difference for many people. If you start to both feel it for as real as it is, and watch it from a distance at the same time, many people report that things change when they achieve that. Experiment with it and see what happens.

It's not that this part is a dream and that part is a dream. It's not, this part is hard and this part is painful, and this part is a dream and that part isn't. It's just like a dream at night, in that we don't get to choose that we like this part and not that part. When you get to *choose* is when you recognize it's a dream. Everybody has had this experience too, when you suddenly realize you're dreaming. Everybody loves this experience, because then you start to make it how you want it. It's no different in *this* dream.

That's what freedom really means. That's that whole talk, the million things that are said about freedom in spiritual life, which is all about getting to some kind of freedom. It really means you get more choice about the dream. Why is it always referred to as waking up? Because you don't wake up *from* the dream, you wake up *in* the dream and then you get some choice. Until then, it's just whatever happens. Really waking up all the way, is stepping out of the dream. It doesn't mean the dream ends. It means you know who's dreaming.

Tonight's message was not really the idea that life is a dream, although I believe you would be wise to buy that idea. It's really to make the link for you that relaxation is what gives you the answer to these questions. It's not sharpening your intellect and figuring out the answer. It's not reading every book ever written and gleaning the answer. It's relaxing, and the answers start to clarify by themselves. The real message I was trying to give you tonight is: Relax, and then see what this life is.

BEING NOBODY IS THE BEST PERSON YOU CAN BE

Premodaya: Without taking a lot of time, pick a person that you know the least well. Pair up, and stand and face each other, but without relating, without making a big connection. Be blank with each other. Face each other without talking. Without doing anything with each other. Without any kind of agenda, or any kind of purpose, or any kind of response one way or the other. Starting to look in each other's eyes without any judgment, without any particular idea in mind. Not staring each other down—just looking into the other person's eyes, just seeing what's there, without making it into anything other than looking into another human being's eyes.

As you do that, I want you to try an experiment. I want you to have the experience—and let it deepen the more you look in the other pair of eyes—that the other pair of eyes, and who stands behind that pair of eyes, is you. Forget who you are. Forget your history. Forget your name. Forget your life story. Forget your gender. Forget your nationality. Forget your age. For these minutes, see the other life standing in front of you as if it were *your* life.

You aren't you—you're this other person. There is no you. There is only an awareness looking at this other person, and this other person is you. You're used to thinking of you, and experiencing you, and locating you in yourself, in your body, in what you call you. For this minute, be the other person, for real. Locate yourself in the other person. Forget the body you're standing in, as if it doesn't exist. Be pure awareness, pure being. If you have to think of a "somebody," then that somebody is standing across from you, and it's you. If you have to be a somebody in this moment, experiment with being that "other" somebody. No, *you*. Them. But "them" is "you."

See what that feels like. See what that experience is like, to be someone else. What comes up in you? What do you notice? How does it feel? What's the experience? But really experience that other person as "you." They aren't, in this moment, another person. The person you call "you" is standing in front of you, and you're looking in their eyes. You exist, but you exist as them. If they are a different sex, now you're that sex. If they are a different age, now you're that age. If they are a different kind of person, now you're that kind of person. Experience the other person truly as you. Not a meeting, not a relating, seeing across from you—you.

You, as who *they are*—not you as who you think you are. Is it easy? Is it hard? Does it feel good? Does it feel bad? Is it strange? Is it not strange? What happens inside you when you're someone else? What do you notice about that which you thought was static about you, static and unchangeable? Does it change if you're someone else?

And now let your eyes, without any effort, fall closed. Without looking into another pair of eyes, remember what you just experienced. Experience yourself, with closed eyes, as that other person. Going to the interiority of being that other person. See what that feels like. What's that experience like, without the reference point of another body, another pair of eyes? Is it possible? Can you feel yourself to be that other person? Do you find yourself capable of letting go of you and being someone else? Or does it seem like a strange and difficult struggle? Maybe it feels like a relief. Maybe it feels impossible. Whatever it is, notice it.

Let your eyes fall open and thank the other person who participated with you, and go ahead and take your seats.

What did you experience?

Priya: I felt I could really feel a different perspective, a different history. Not knowing things. Not thinking things. A sense of connection to everything. I mean, of my person's connection to everything.

Darshana: It felt embracing. Very embracing and love just healing. It just felt natural.

Premodaya: Did you become the other person?

Darshana: Moments.

Gracie: You said seeing without judgment. I struggled with it for a minute, but I did pick up her qualities. She became a good mirror. I'm not saying it was comfortable. It was enlightening.

Malik: I think there was a certain shyness maybe at first. Then there seemed to be a little bit of a playfulness, almost like a childhood feeling. I kind of felt, you as a girl, just looking at birds and stuff like that. There was a little embarrassment, but then it became much easier to be you, after a while. I could see your curiosity of things and, almost as you were a child.

Jocelyn: I felt the similarities. There were so many similarities. There was almost a sensation of *falling in*, falling into her eyes. And then looking out of her eyes. There were no boundaries in anything, almost like we fell into each other almost.

John: I had difficulty trying to see myself going through, to turn around to see myself. But yet, I could still feel kindness and stillness, but it bothered me that I couldn't get the job done.

Premodaya: Are you sure you didn't get the job done? If you didn't get the job done, then how did you feel stillness and kindness? To any degree, did you feel like you were the other person? Or like you were someone else other than how you experience "you"?

John: Well, you got a point. I could see myself taller.

Premodaya: Good. Close enough.

This exercise, in my mind, was not for the purpose of you experiencing yourself as someone else. Although it may seem like it, given the structure of the exercise. The purpose was for you to experience yourself as *not you*. Because the whole idea of "you" is the illusion. The whole idea of "you" is what you have gathered through a lifetime and stuck a label on it called "you." It's a bunch of disparate ideas, notions, impressions, perceptions, feelings, judgments, assumptions, definitions, categorizations, stories. Put that all together it spells: you.

But how can you be those things? Really, think about it. How can you be those things? It makes no sense. And yet we all walk around thinking we're that. What am I saying? *You're not that.* You may think you're that. You may have some felt sense you're that—which is simply a deep habit you've been taught. It's been reinforced to you that you're that: You are your history; you are your story; you are your name; you are your nationality; you are your gender. The list is endless, but somehow, deep down, you know you're not that. The one who knows you're not that, is the one that you are.

Prof. Alex: It's no different if I'm me or if I'm her. They're the same.

Premodaya: Yes, and I'm going further. I'm saying there's never a difference. I'm saying you are always her. She is always you. Everybody is always *it*. You are it. Everyone else is it. Everything else is it. "You" are a false focal point. All those other things, "I am this," "I am that," "I am tall," "I am short," "I am young," "I am old." That's what I'm referring to as "the focal point." These are the gathered strings. I'm saying the one who is holding the strings is who you are.

Prof. Alex: All that intellectual stuff needs to be let go of.

Premodaya: Or seen through. Let go is better, but seeing through is enough. You have to see that there's no such thing as a man or a woman. There's no such thing as young or old. There's no such thing as tall or short. These are attributions. They are made meaningful by the society. There are other societies than the one you may have grown up in, that see something else as meaningful. This society, American society, twenty-first century—sees male/female as very meaningful. Makes a big deal about, "Are you a man or are you a woman?" "What does it mean?" "What should you do?"

There are other societies where male/female isn't a big deal. There's not a big differentiation. There are other things that are considered primary and important, other than that. Have more cultural importance than, what gender are you? You can find examples all over the world of different cultural emphases. The lesson I see in that is that none of the emphases are correct. They're just the cultural emphasis. They're evidence that none of these things really matter. They're evidence that to get attached to an idea of a definition, "I'm a man, I'm woman, I'm young, I'm old," is limited and essentially incorrect. I'm not saying there are no men and no women. I'm saying you are at the core something far deeper and bigger than that, and, it really is the same.

I'm not saying there are no differences between men and women, certainly there are. But at the core, there aren't. At the core, you're not a body. You're not a gender. And to whatever degree you can disidentify with these ideas, to whatever degree you can become unattached to these holdings, these definitions, these categories, I say you're better off. I guarantee you, you're closer to reality. Closer to Truth.

Because this is very, very, very, "on the surface," all these definitions. This is the superficial aspect of life on this planet. Or any planet. "Are you this?" "Are you that?" Yes, I'm this; I'm that—but not really. If you believe it's real, you can't know what's more real. You have to be able to separate what matters from what doesn't. People get very upset to hear, "You're not a man." "You're not a woman." There are people who would fight you on that one.

Kyomi: The spirit itself is somehow what you are in essence, not male/female. It's just—*it*.

Premodaya: That's another perfect way to say exactly what I'm trying to say.

Kyomi: So you aren't even any "body." It doesn't matter.

Premodaya: That's the other way to say what I'm saying. You are purely spirit. You aren't definable in worldly terms. You aren't limitable in reality. You may think you're limitable, and you may limit yourself to, "I'm this," "I'm that." But even if you cling tightly, it doesn't change reality. And reality is: You aren't "this" or "that." To see that, is to start liberating yourself from all the ideas that tie you down to a certain view, and a certain experience, a certain way of being, a certain way of relating. Everybody in this room is capable of a far wider scope, a far deeper relating. To get there, you have to see that relating as "this," relating as "that" isn't necessary, doesn't add anything, doesn't enhance any experience you have.

The whole ancient Eastern method of tantra, even the sexual part of tantra—male/female union as experience of Truth, has behind it one and only one purpose, exactly what we're talking about right now—to see that none of that is real. The male and the female in union deeply enough to see that there's no male and no female. Even that there's no *union*, because there was never any separation.

These ideas have a certain utility. I'm not speaking against the utility. You know, in electricity they talk about a male and female plug. It's purely practical. That's fine. But the trouble is we don't stick with the practical. We go beyond it and give great meaning, fight wars over these definitions.

If we just used them practically: I'm tall, I'm short, I'm old, I'm young—there would be no problem at all. If we didn't identify, and just used them for their practical usefulness when needed, there would be no problem, but we don't do that. We live these ideas. We chain ourselves within these ideas so that the more attached we get to each and every one of them, the more we limit ourselves, the more we narrow our scope, the more we narrow our understanding, and the more we cut ourselves off from all other experience other than our personal experience.

In these few minutes of this exercise, many people were able to see how easy it is. It took minutes, not hours, not days, not years to have some sense of another person's experience, a person you may not even hardly know at all! That's how fluid you are. What I'm really saying to you is: You're fluid beyond your wildest dreams. Yet most of us walk through life thinking we're this static, fixed thing. You aren't a thing. You aren't limited in the ways you have been told, and you aren't limited in the ways you feel you're limited. You just feel that way. Well, see through that. Understand better than that feeling. Understand wiser than that feeling. I'm not saying that feeling isn't real, we all get feelings. I'm saying: Be smarter than that feeling, with your understanding, with your intellect, with your ability for insight—know better. Know better that you aren't these things you feel yourself to be.

The argument people make is, "But I feel it—I can't get beyond it." I'm not saying: Try to get beyond it. I'm saying: Just know better. Understand it. Nobody in this room isn't capable of understanding it absolutely. In the spiritual life people get into this whole struggle with trying to get detached. Trying to unattach, disidentify. They get into this fight with all these concepts and all these assumptions and all these experiences. You can spend decades battling with these things, trying to get pure, trying to find your essence. I'm saying: Why take that chance? Why be in a struggle for years, decades, who knows how long? You may never get beyond it. You may never feel different from how you feel yourself to be right now. But you can absolutely understand much more deeply. You can understand your way beyond it.

People struggle to have a certain experience. Sincere spiritual seekers struggle to have a particular experience, or to be more open somehow. It's possible, and for some it's very possible; for some it's never possible, and there's everything in between. I don't know which one you are. You may or may not know where you are on that continuum—what's possible for you in terms of your inner experiencing. I'm saying, no matter where you are on that continuum, you can understand your way through it and that doesn't take a lifetime of struggling with spiritual concepts and secular concepts and "worldly versus spiritual." You don't have to be on that battlefield. You can simply be smart enough, wise enough, and willing enough to see through all this nonsense of: I'm *this* and I'm *that*. Because deep down you absolutely know that you are not this or that. You can tap into it with your understanding. You can understand what you know deep down. You can understand it better.

I would put it very simply: Anything you can think that you are— know that you are not. It's good news. It means you're far more than that. It means you're something deeper and truer than that.

Nothing sounds crazier to me than nationalism, when people get all, "I'm an American." "I'm a Frenchman," or wherever. It's like jeezus, I don't want to get too controversial or political here, but when I hear the word "patriot," it's a dirty word. It's ugly. It's horrible. It means you see yourself as somehow better than someone who was born to a different geography. It means you haven't thought it through even for one second. I remember when George Bush#1 started Desert Storm. I was in a bar and grill with my wife. And these girls, these young girls (about eighteen), maybe college girls, in little skirts, nice little outfits, and they came in waving these little flags. They were collecting money. Collecting money, for the war effort, or something related to that war.

They came up to our table and they gave us the same spiel they were giving every table, and they said, "Won't you give?" We looked at them and said, "No, we don't support this." They were shocked. They had never run across anybody who would say, "We don't support the war." It just had not happened yet. Maybe it was their first night of doing it. They were pretty sheltered, I think. And they said, "Well, do it to be patriotic." We looked at them, and one of us said, "Well, we're against patriotism."

These girls went nuts. I think one of them actually screamed. They were so shocked. They had never heard somebody have, what I guess to them was such an unconventional view. They actually stopped dead in their tracks. They couldn't move; they couldn't talk; they couldn't whatever. It's like they didn't know what to do with that. One of them finally said, "Well, aren't you proud to be Americans?" I looked at her and I said, "No." They couldn't fathom this. This had never entered their world or their consciousness.

They wanted to argue; I don't think we wanted to. We didn't get into any big argument with them; we just kept explaining to them, really simply, "We're not nationalists. We're not for one country over another country. Just because we happen to live in this one doesn't mean that we see ourselves as somehow having to be against another one."

Don't get me wrong; I'm not necessarily against war, and I'm not necessarily against protecting your country. But as a philosophy I think patriotism is horrid. It really means, "My country, no matter what." And that's dangerous ground. It's that idea that gave us Nazism.

These identifications are not innocuous. On the spiritual level, they keep you bound to false ideas and keep you further from what's true. On the practical worldly level, people kill for this, for these identifications. So every which direction, it's dangerous. And to any degree that you can pierce through it with your understanding, you become wiser. You become not as fooled by appearances. You become more open to the ocean of existence that has no definitions.

Prof. Alex: What we are talking about tonight, is that in any way related to your experience with Gangaji, sudden awakening?

Premodaya: Everything is related to my experience with Gangaji. I am not capable of saying a word that isn't related to my experience of Gangaji.

Prof. Alex: I'm wondering if I let go. I had all these worries, and a nervous breakdown, "I'm sick of being Alex—I don't want to be Alex anymore." And then suddenly I was in the most heavenly beautiful place, not related to Alex, or Alex's worries, or Alex's life.

Premodaya: Well, being "nobody" is the best person you can be. Being nobody is much better than being Alex. Or being Premodaya. Or being Gangaji. Or being anybody.

Prof. Alex: That's what it felt like—very free.

Premodaya: Yes, so be nobody all the time.

Prof. Alex: Is that what happened with Gangaji—you became nobody all the time?

Premodaya: Yes, there's nobody sitting in this chair.

Prof. Alex: Osho says that. He says that he is around the body, he is just around his body.

Premodaya: However it's experienced, you're always better off being nobody. That's the best thing you can be. What does it mean to not be attached to your nationality? To your gender? To your definitions? To all this long list? It means being nobody.

Prof. Alex: It means you're free.

Premodaya: It means you're nobody. If you're nobody, there's no question of free, not free. How can nobody be free? The interesting thing is it's much easier to be nobody than we tend to think it is, but it seems really hard when you're on the other side of it and these definitions seem real, and feel real. This is why I talk about this so much; this is why I keep saying the different things I say. Because what helps, what helped me, and what it seems to me helps people, is more and more to get the practical understanding of how possible it is. It seems somehow unattainable, but it's attainable. But it's only attainable by being nobody. It's only attainable when nothing is attained because how can nobody attain anything? It's all about understanding—past ego, past self-importance, past self-pride. It's all about not having the arrogance to think, "I'm somebody."

When you're nobody, you're everybody. When you're nobody, you see yourself in every pair of eyes. That exercise we did in the beginning; that's real. If you become nobody, every person you see will feel to you like *you*. On the outside, you will still sound like a somebody.

Priya: I saw somebody today, earlier, and I thought, "He is old." Then I thought what that implied and what a limitation it was. The concept was totally false.

Premodaya: The interesting thing is the judgments still will "bling-bling" around in your mind, like a pinball machine, but you don't have to buy those judgments. You don't have to believe them. Don't think the judgments will go away. The mind is a judgment machine. The judgments don't go away. But you don't have to be in league with those judgments. You can laugh at your own judgments as mind-created nonsense. That's my whole entertainment, laughing at my own judgments.

Whatever you think you are—as soon as you notice the thought that you think you're that, know that it's not the truth. It sounds hard until it starts to be easy, until you have done it enough, until you have pierced it enough, until you have understood it to enough of a depth that it quickly starts to get easier and easier and easier. I want it to get easier for you to not be fooled by all these ideas and identifications that fool us most of our lives and fool most of the world. You don't have to live in those illusions. And it's progressive. You have to start somewhere, and it gets easier and easier past a certain point. There's a critical mass. There's a threshold. You have to pass that threshold and then it starts to get easier. The threshold is really the acceptance of the notion that it's all false.

Most of the people in the world can't do that. Most of the population of the planet can't get to that threshold. "What do you mean, it's *all* wrong? Something has to be right. Something I have to cling to. I can accept I maybe go too far with patriotism, and it's an idea I can see through. But what do you mean I'm not a man or a woman?" People want to hold on to something.

In my understanding, the threshold is the generalized notion that it might all be wrong—whatever you can come up with as a thought—that it might actually, by the very fact that you can think it, imagine it, has to be not accurate to what's true. Because the Truth isn't a thought, or capturable by a thought. A thought can help, help you move towards Truth, but only if you let go of the thought after its usefulness. I would like you to know yourself as nobody, because you will be much happier and much closer to what's true.

If you're nobody, it doesn't mean your personality disappears. It doesn't mean your ego stops. It doesn't mean you somehow have resolved every issue or every problem of being a human being. It means you're nobody, which is who you really are. Ego is still there—it just isn't your prison. Personality is still there—it just doesn't limit you. To other people, you will look exactly the same. You will look the same and sound the same for those reasons, because your ego and your personality will still be there. All your human qualities, positive and negative—however you view them— will still be there, but you won't be imprisoned in them. You won't believe yourself to be them. You will see with your own eyes that that's the most superficial part of you and doesn't really matter in any real sense. You won't become some magical being. You will just recognize who you are. You will recognize yourself to be nobody.

Be nobody all the time. Everybody can be nobody for a minute here or there. Everybody can be "not themselves" for a minute here or there. I'm saying, keep doing it until that day when you can never again be fooled into thinking you're somebody. You won't lose a thing by being nobody. The truth is: You're nobody. So why not start recognizing it?

YOU ONLY *THINK* YOU HAVE AN OPEN MIND

Gloria: I'm curious if you believe in the philosophy of a higher power or a God. Or if you feel that we can be entirely self-sufficient on our own.

Premodaya: I believe in: no beliefs. My philosophy is: don't have a philosophy. My argument is: step out of the tent. This is what my Master taught. I never expected to teach it, but that's now my role.

Gloria: With that set of beliefs then, how do you translate or process the idea that we're here, and we're solid? Maybe we aren't solid? Where we come from, or the genesis of why we are here?

Premodaya: So, beliefs are endless. You can find any philosophy that suits you. You can find an actual, developed literature and developed set of ideas or a developed philosophy that would support any direction you want to go with any question like that. You have a basic choice, and most of us don't even realize it: you can decide what you believe or you can decide what philosophy suits you—or you can be much riskier than that, and refuse all beliefs and philosophies, drop all the ones that you've been given so far. There's nobody who doesn't escape. Everybody is taught beliefs by whoever raised them, whoever influenced them when they were young. The riskier approach, the scarier approach, is to reject all beliefs and philosophies, and only accept that which you *know*, that which you know experientially, that which you know without even a shadow of doubt. That which you know through your own absolute knowing.

That isn't the same as a set of knowledge. A set of knowledge can be argued with. Knowing can't be argued with. Not because it's subjective, but because no argument can convince you from what you know. We could bring the best arguer on the planet in here—we could bring ten of them—and they could spend the next six weeks arguing with you twenty-four hours a day to convince you that you aren't breathing. But at the end of that six weeks, they wouldn't have convinced you, because you know you're breathing. No argument, no set of ideas is going to move you from what you know. As far as I'm concerned, that's a better position than "I believe this," which tends to be, "I hope it's true," or "This is my philosophy," which tends to be, "It sounds right."

Gloria: I understand what you're saying, and for me, I probably would have adopted a more wider spectrum. But I have experienced a miracle under the umbrella of a particular faith that I still don't necessarily know that that is the only way to heaven, peace, God, however you want to call it. But I can't, because I know that in my heart …

Premodaya: That's your absolute knowing. That can be trusted. That you can put one hundred percent into. Now, does it make sense based on that knowing to fan it out? If it fits into a certain way, a certain tradition, a certain historic philosophy, whatever, if it makes sense from that knowing to fan it out into the beliefs or philosophies that go with that—I'm not saying don't do that. I'm saying make sure that you know the essence of those too, for yourself. Don't settle for just believing it—go all the way with it. Give yourself to it one hundred percent.

Belief is very superficial, "I believe it." But a few torture tools, half an hour—I can get you to believe something else. I'm talking about a level that is *so far* from the superficial that you will stand on it for eternity. What you're really saying to me is you're capable of that. What's already happened to you is so real, and you know it so absolutely, that what I would like to say to you is that you're capable of knowing the essence of the rest of it as well, without just taking it as a belief, without just taking the superficial part and saying, "OK. I accept this." You can go deeper than that because the miracle has already happened for you. That prepares you, individually, to go much deeper. And I'm encouraging you to do that. What I would say to you—and I don't need to know what the miracle was or what you're referring to—give your *whole life* to this. Don't hold back; don't hesitate; don't even question—dive in completely. Then if something isn't right you will know it. Or if you took a wrong turn, it will be evident quickly. You won't lose a thing.

I'm not selling a way. I'm not promoting a particular path. I'm not advocating this way or that way. I don't care if it's Christ, or Buddha, or Joe Schmo. I'm saying, if you *know it*, then why aren't you giving your whole life to it? Because if you give your whole life to it, it will take you all the way. I gave my whole life to my Master. Not voluntarily, but anything that has happened for me, any gift this universe has given, is because of that. Because I know that from my experience, I know it's the same for everybody else. One person's path is not the same as another person's path. People are different, that's why there are many paths. But just as once an individual gets to the end of suffering—take one hundred people of whom that's true, and there will be something the same about them. They can be from different countries; one can be old; one can be young, there will be a flavor that's the same. It's the same with what we're talking about now. Take a *really* Christ-committed person, take a *real* Buddhist, take a person who has *lived* Zen all the way, take an Islamic person that has given their *whole life* to Allah—they'll have the same flavor. The heart of Truth will be felt.

If I'm selling anything, it's that. It's: If you know it, live it. Stop hesitating; stop making excuses; stop denying. I say quite often, maybe once every two/three weeks—you have to know what you know. A lot of people know, and they're lukewarm about it. They dance around it. They don't give themselves to what they absolutely know. In your case I'm saying: You can give yourself. I hope you do.

CHAPTER 12

SAY YES TO THE MYSTERY

Riley: The last time that I was here I had a really profound experience. Then later that night my purse was stolen, and it was like the gentlest way that it could have happened, and so I didn't trip; everything was fine and then later that week something else happened. And then someone who I thought I could trust turned out to be like nothing I had ever imagined before and I thought, "Is this the universe challenging me or something?" I was in such a low place, and I didn't want to get out of bed. Then Mother's Day came and it was a beautiful day, and my kids didn't even get me cards, but I was cool with it. My daughter made me breakfast in bed; that was cool. I was OK with it; it was a beautiful day; I got to hang out with my family. I realized that these ups and downs don't have to be ups and downs.

Premodaya: Exactly. Don't even go any further because you're trying to give that simple truth to other people, and if they really get it, their whole life will change. There will always be ups and downs. That's the definition of the world; that's what circumstances are. Circumstances are, "If you're up on Tuesday you only know one thing for sure: You will be down on Wednesday." It might not be exactly Wednesday, but all you know for sure, all you can predict about the world, is that if you're up you can only go down; if you're down you can only go up. Other than that, you can't really say anything.

You're sharing the deeper insight. You had a deep, deep insight and it's profound even though it's simple; the real insights are always simple. Complex isn't a proof that it's a valid insight. Really, simple is the higher proof. The insight is simply that all these things just go round and round. This will happen; that will happen; absolutely—that will never stop. If you ride it like a horse, up and down, up and down, that's how you will feel—nauseous. But if you get the insight and start to see that again and again, so that you get to a point eventually where you never forget, where everywhere you look that understanding is there that *this is just stuff happening—it doesn't mean anything*. I don't have to give it a significance it doesn't have. Then how can you be freer than that? What greater freedom is there, than that which the world and the events of the world and the events of your own life (which is actually just a manifestation of the world) can't penetrate?

Riley: But did you not create these things that happen to you in some way?

Premodaya: If they can't touch you, what does it matter? If you aren't disturbed by them, what does it matter how they got created? If they don't take you on a needless rollercoaster ride, who cares how they got created? I don't know; you don't know; Jesus doesn't know—he might know but he isn't telling. That's the mystery: The mystery is, that it's *actually* a mystery. Nobody knows. We don't know how we got here. I always go back to that—the people who come regularly probably get sick of hearing me say that. I defy you to tell me you know how you got here. Show me one person who can say they know how they got here, anybody. Buddha himself, he can't tell you how he got here. This running after some kind of self-notion that, "I'm creating it, I'm responsible for my reality"—this is a very, very popular idea that has been around for a couple of decades now, but it doesn't go anywhere; it doesn't take you anywhere. In the end you just feel bad: "Look what I created, gee whiz—"

Riley: Yes, but there are also good things that I created that I can look at and say, "Wow, look what I created."

Premodaya: That's a trap, because eventually you will say it's not good enough, or you will go to the bad things. Yes, for a few minutes you can focus on what feels positive. But the truth is you have no idea—nobody does, nobody knows *how all this is*. I don't just mean this building, and us sitting in this room; I mean this universe, this cosmos and this entire existence. Somebody said, "The totality, the oneness"—How is this oneness? How is it? Nobody knows: that's the mystery.

When you say "yes" to the mystery, when you say "I give up, I get it"—and that means not just as a thought—but when you get it, that it's absolutely mysterious, that you're made out of mystery, you arise from the mystery; you opened your eyes, here you are—you're sitting in mystery right now, all this is mysterious. How my vocal cords make a sound and your ears understand them, this is mystery—who can explain this? It can't be explained scientifically. You can't say, "Well, the ear works like this, and sound waves, and—" Yes, you could say all that and all of it's probably true, but it doesn't explain anything. The real explanation is the profound realization—thwap!—the mystery is here—and I am it; he is it; she is it; everything is it. Every atom of air in the room, every sound out there. There's nothing you can say, do, point at, feel, touch, think; there is nothing that isn't the mystery.

Usually we are fighting the mystery; we are trying to tame it somehow, trying to get some kind of sense of control. But once you say, and really mean it because you really get it, all the way, "It's all a mystery," it can never be the same after that. Then you really relax; then you really say, "Whew! There's not that much for me to do."—Then you can stay in bed.

What you're saying is you got a little taste of the mystery, or how to relax into the mystery. And it's huge—I'm telling you, it's huge—to recognize that these ups and downs aren't real; they are just "this happens; that happens; I feel this way about it; I feel that way." All that, is just stuff, very superficial, very not significant. Usually we are running around in life thinking that is what matters: "I have to feel this way; I have to feel that; uh-oh I felt this; this isn't good; uh-oh that happened; uh-oh you should not have done that." This is what the Hindus mean when they say "maya"—"It's all illusion." That's the illusion, that that stuff means anything. Stuff will always happen—that's never going to stop. What can stop is you being fooled that it means something, and the less you're fooled, the more peace will arise in you. You had a taste of it. Now let that understanding deepen and you will get a bigger taste of it. And the day will come when that peace will swallow you.

GRACE

Anna: Is grace also interpretation of the mystery? I experience grace; is it an experience of the mystery?

Premodaya: Have you experienced grace?

Anna: Yes. But something bad might happen, then I might say, "Oh, this is *not* grace" or, "Existence is going to punish me." Maybe one day I'll be in a situation and say, "This is not grace, it's the opposite."

Premodaya: Just keep an open mind. For now, wait and see; keep an open mind and see if it's really grace, because, you know, there is doubt there. Wait and see how the doubt resolves itself. It is going to take some patience.

There is not time for me to tell the whole story, so I will tell the tip of the iceberg of the story, but you need to hear this. One of the worst things that ever happened to me in my entire life was one of the greatest gifts of grace I have ever received. Whether a thing appears terrible or wonderful isn't the measure of what it is, because we don't know the outcome and we don't know the meaning: that's the mystery.

I knew it in the moment; the amazing grace of it was that I knew it in the moment. And I've had more powerful experiences of grace than that moment, but there was something very pivotal in that moment because it showed me something about the unshakability of where I was at, the unshakability of my trust in the Divine, in Reality.

CHAPTER 13

THE PROFOUND

OUR PROFOUND RESPONSIBILITY

King: Can we talk about responsibility?

Premodaya: We can talk about anything under the sun. What about it?

King: I'd like to understand it more clearly, about how you control nothing and are responsible for everything.

Premodaya: Where did you hear that?

King: I think it was described by you. But it's something I've also experienced. I think I understand how to be responsible—but I confuse the line of understanding what you are responsible for.

Premodaya: Maybe somebody who is clear about it would like to comment?

Lucas: Well, we create our reality, as I understand it, physiologically. And since we create our reality around us, we're responsible for it … I'm quoting physiology class from UCLA. They said, we don't know for sure if anything exists outside our bodies, physiologically.

Premodaya: We don't know if anything exists for sure inside our body!

Lucas: You know, he didn't go into that.

Premodaya: Well, then he left out the important part; ask for your tuition back. [laughter] You got jipped!

Well, I would say the exact opposite. I would say we don't create a darn thing. This is the view that most people sign onto in Western culture: You live in your body—there's an "inside" there's an "outside"—and you have certain perceptions and certain sensations, and certain things mean certain things, and out of those perceptions and sensations and ideas and thoughts, you kind of put together a reality for yourself.

Everybody kind of has a different point of view, a little different reality, but pretty much there is an objective reality "out there," there is a subjective reality "in here," and that's how things work. That's what our parents teach us, what our teachers teach us, what we're told in school, what our friends believe, and what everybody believes. It's what most people wouldn't argue much with.

So I am arguing with that. Meetings like this are exactly for the purpose of questioning that conventional idea, conventional construct. The reason it needs to be questioned is for the simple reason that it is never questioned—we get spoon-fed that from before we can talk. And most of us are pretty much the same, so most of us don't ever stop and think, "Well, wait a minute—how true is that? How much does that fit with my actual experience? How much does that fit with other things other people say?" It's really, in our culture, in our society, in the Western world; it's really not much questioned; we all just kind of sign off as "That's what's real.

That is how life works. That's how humans work." All I'm saying is that it would be wise, prudent, to not leave that unexamined and unquestioned, because the real question, the real statement there, is about life itself. And what could be more useful, more significant, than understanding as best as we can life itself? Our own life?

To go by a set of assumptions and ideas that have been conditioned into us and to never question it, simply isn't sensible. And I'm always for what's sensible. I think it's useful to question it. It's useful to ask, "Well, how true is that?" And then the fun begins.

Now, in a meeting like this, probably no one's going to go berserk, wanting to argue that there's something there to question or examine. But if we went out into the wider culture, where people aren't necessarily coming to a meeting that has a spiritual title—if you bring up the notion that the conventional or generally agreed-upon view of reality might not be reality, people get very upset. People feel very threatened, intimidated, and actually lay down their lives—kill and are killed—for these ideas, for "what is what"—for protecting the status quo.

Riley: Religion.

Premodaya: Religion, politics, all of it. Everything that is out there. When you think of it—and I have said this many times—what is a country? It is arbitrary lines on a map—yet people live and die in the name of country. That has always astounded me! So unquestioned, unexamined concepts can mean life and death—can be a life-threatening situation. So before we are in a life-threatening situation, let's talk a little bit about how to examine reality. Because that is really why you are here. People come to a meeting like this because they have some kind of question, some kind of interest, something has been sparked for them that says, "Well, I don't know if the conventional view does the job—it might not be working for me as well as it used to work." Some kind of question has arisen for you if you are here.

I want to say to you: Don't be fooled. These conventional ideas have not evolved for you. They have not evolved because they make life easier for you; they have evolved because they make life easier for the society. If everybody can agree or generally sign on, "Well, reality is kind of like this," there won't be much trouble. You will go about your business; if the society needs you to be a consumer you will consume, if the society needs you to be a producer you will produce, and you will have a somewhat orderly society. But if the very definition of what's life, what's real, what's a human being, is in question, that's a whole different kind of society. Don't be lulled into the notion that the conventional view, the generally accepted view of what is, is for your benefit. It's for the herd; it's for the group. It makes things easier for the group. But the group mind isn't the smartest mind. The herd mind is the lowest common denominator. So probably everyone in this room has already realized that you can do better. You can come up with a better answer for yourself than the one the herd mind supplies.

Now the quote, the statement that King was referring to, is I frequently say that we control absolutely nothing. That all ideas of "we do something" is an illusion. And I also frequently say that we are completely responsible for everything. And on the surface, it's not hard to understand how that could be confusing, how that sounds contradictory. But you have to not be fooled by language.

The problem is we're using language, and language is very, very meager. Language only touches the surface. It's all we have; it's the way we communicate understanding, but it can't really give the depth. It can't really touch the Truth. It can only indicate it; it can only give a rough idea; it's going to be approximate at best. So first you have to start with that understanding. But language is not adequate for what we are talking about: when you're talking about life, what is life, what is a human being, what is real, what isn't real, what is true, what isn't true. Language isn't going to give us an exact answer, but language can point us in the right direction if we don't get confused by it.

The first thing not to get confused by is that linguistically it sounds like there's a contradiction—control nothing, responsible for everything. But that's a linguistic contradiction. In Reality there's no such contradiction. In REALITY, everything is possible. Because Reality doesn't have the limitations that language does and that we do. Our minds are limited; Reality isn't. The first thing to understand is that Reality is much bigger than our ability, much deeper than our capacity to fathom it, to make sense of it. We are looking for that, for it to make sense. Reality doesn't care if it makes sense. Reality is not interested in our logic. Our logic is a mind thing—a very small way to look at things. Seems right, makes sense to us, but very poor.

Reality is what is. If you define Reality as that which is—what can be simpler than that? "That which is" doesn't care what you think about it. "That which is" has always been, is right now, and will always be. It was here before you, it will be here after you, and it has absolutely no concern for your comprehension. It's impersonal. What is, is. Everybody has experienced this in some form in your life, in your consciousness; where you're really up against something and you just feel that there's nothing you can do; difficult moments in life, where the bigness of life overwhelms you. You get a flavor, you get a little taste, of how small we are and how big the universe is. Once you can accept, even just from the point of view of examining it, the idea that what is, that Reality is completely unconcerned and completely not related to our view of it, then it's a little more palatable; it becomes a little clearer that our understanding is not significant. Existence is not waiting for us to understand it and say, "Ah ha, now I get it," and existence says [claps hands] "Good job, you got it."

The profoundness of "what is" is beyond our comprehension. The idea that our mind can grasp eternity and infinity is nonsense. We can't grasp that. We can get an approximate idea and, if we think about it long enough and hard enough, we get *very* freaky. It freaks us out. I don't know about you, but it freaks me out! [laughter]

If you really go into it with your whole heart and soul, I guarantee you'll freak out. Everybody in here has probably had that experience. Now a lot of people never go near that because they kind of sense it will freak them out; they don't want to go there. But probably everybody in this room is willing to go there. What I'm advocating, what I'm sharing with you is the idea that something is here that's much bigger than our logic, that's much deeper than our ability to understand it, that's much more permanent and profound than our notion of it.

A statement like, "You control absolutely nothing and you're responsible for absolutely everything," doesn't have to make sense to be true in Reality. I say lots of things that don't make sense, but they represent something that most people have felt about what's Real, what is, what's True.

What I'm doing when I sit here is encouraging you to be open to the possibility that there's something so much vaster, so much deeper, so much more unknown and unknowable than we generally acknowledge. If you can open yourself to just that concept, that idea, that there's something so deep and so big that if you truly felt it, even for a second, it would take your breath away forever. The more you open yourself to that, the more it makes sense, in a paradoxical way, that we're responsible for everything and that we control nothing. The reason is, the macrocosm—(the all, the big)—and the microcosm—(us, the minute, the specific)—are not different and are not separate. They mirror each other; they represent each other. So in you, in every single person in this room, the whole infinity, the whole eternity is right in you. It's what you're made of. It's where you come from. It's where you are right now. We're not sitting in a room in Los Angeles; we're sitting in the middle of infinity and in the middle of eternity. Time is an outcropping of eternity. Space is a little outcropping of infinity, and if you trace it back, that's where you are. That's the only place you could be. It's the only place you have ever been; it's the only place you will ever be.

Within that context (which, if you really take it in, takes your breath away), the "everything" and the "minute" aren't separate. In that sense, we are responsible for everything, because we *are* everything. We are connected to everything. Nothing in this cosmos is independent. Everything is interdependent. If somebody could wave a magic wand and the trees suddenly disappeared, we would all drop dead in one second because there wouldn't be enough oxygen on the planet. But we don't walk around remembering that we owe our breathing and our life to the trees. Well, there are countless examples like that one that prove and demonstrate beyond any questioning the interdependence of all things. If all things are interdependent and all things are in that sense connected, in that sense we are all responsible for everything. Every tree out there, is responsible for every one of us. Every one of us is responsible for everything, *out there*.

Now, if someone here could tell me how you got here, I'm happy to listen. But my contention is you have no idea how you got here. You don't—and people have heard me say this again and again, but I love to say it—you don't control one hair on your head. You can't make one hair grow one micrometer. You can't guarantee or make sure you will draw the next breath one second from now. You don't control how tall you are, how short you are, nothing. You just found yourself here. You were little and then got bigger and bigger. And you have the illusion—because it's good for the society for you to believe—that you have some control over that. But if you really question it, if you examine it in depth sincerely, I cannot imagine that you will find any example where you actually control, truly control—anything. You have to trace it back far enough, deep enough. If you don't go deep enough, it can look like control—we fool ourselves all the time. We have this belief in cause and effect. But that's, again, a very puny concept compared to what is. Compared to the vastness, the deepness, the profoundness of all that is. Our little tiny concepts do not match the depth of reality. They don't even come close. And yet, because we are mind-oriented in this culture, we insist on explaining to ourselves. It makes us feel better; it makes us less scared. It's understandable, but spiritual maturity means—and it doesn't matter what religion you are and it doesn't matter what your beliefs are—you have gotten to the point where you're willing to question basic assumptions that you have not questioned before.

If you really question them sincerely and your faith is honest, it will take you deeper into your faith, not further away, whatever that faith is— that faith can be agnosticism, any "ism." But people are often frightened to question, because the fear is, "I don't want to give up my beliefs." But again, beliefs are paltry things in comparison to what is. Beliefs are just what somebody has told us, what our mind has come up with, what we feel, but we are very, very tiny. To cling so tightly, to believe so strongly in what we come up with—if you really look at it, how much sense does that make when you consider the bigness of everything?

We are responsible, I say, for everything because we are. I'm the outcropping of reality in this chair. You're the outcropping of reality in that chair. Interdependent with everything, not separate in any way. You're responsible simply by the fact that whether you admit it or not, whether you realize it or not, whether you fathom it or not, you are in intimate relation in every second with all that exists. Whether you call it God, whether you call it Existence, whether you call it the cosmos, whether you call it the world, whatever you look at, whatever you can identify, whatever you can name, you are already in deep and intimate relation with. Whether you know it or not, whether you fathom it or not. Whether you're willing to admit it or not, whether you recognize it or not. And, in that sense, everything and everyone is responsible for everything and everyone. At all times, in all things, in all ways. One hair on your head changes, the entire cosmos is affected. I guarantee you that's the truth.

Anna: What does it mean, "You're responsible?" Does it include several actions and nonactions, several things we can do, prepare, whatever it is?

Premodaya: It means that you're willing to consider that possible truth, that all things are deeply and completely interdependent. That's really what it means.

Anna: What consequences does that have?

Premodaya: Well, that's jumping ahead. First, if you're willing to consider that possibility and go into it deeply and sincerely, obviously that changes everything. The question of consequences takes care of itself. First go, and then you tell me the consequences. See, this is what the mind does; the mind says, "Find out the consequences; find out the temperature of the water before I jump in the lake." And then what we do is we spend the rest of the day measuring the temperature of the water and we never jump in the lake. When it comes to Reality, when it comes to what is, when it comes to Life with a capital *L*, when it comes Existence, nothing can be known without jumping in. It can't be known through the mind; it can't be known through measuring it; it can't be known through conceptualizing it; it can't be known through understanding it. It can be only known by being it, by jumping in completely.

Lucas: That responsibility ... I'm completely puzzled by the statements, like, "How could God allow the Holocaust?" And then I hear very wise people say, "Well, how could *we* allow it?" And, I'm thinking you're saying, we're responsible for it, and I'm miles away from the Holocaust. In some way I'm responsible. Is that what you're saying?

Premodaya: You're completely responsible. That responsibility, by the way, goes all the way back, all the way forward. So who wants to comment on the notion that everybody in this room is responsible for any Holocaust you want to choose in history?

Tishya: I understand the idea of everything before, for as far back as man has been, or anything has been in existence—like your idea of a hair on your head changing everything in the cosmos—I have an understanding about that trickle effect. But I don't understand the half that speaks of now, then *forward*, unless what you're really saying is that who we were in another time and place, or anything like that ... I don't get it.

Premodaya: No. I'm saying that the interconnection, the interdependence is so real, so profound, so true, so core, that it goes all the way back and all the way forward. There is no way that it is limited by space and time.

Everything is continuous. Everything is part of everything else. The macrocosm and the microcosm are in each other; they're not separate. It's not there's the great existence up there, and we are down here. We're just as much up there; it's as much down here. It's all a reflection of the same thing. There are many ways to understand it; there are many ways to talk about it. You can say it reverberates, you can say it reflects, but what I would say is there's no piece that isn't completely related to every other piece. The mind can understand it that way, but it's so much bigger than that, because the mind is part of time and space. Our thinking is part of time and space. Reality isn't limited by time and space. We are, but Reality isn't. We have a limited ability to grasp; we have a limited ability to comprehend. We have a limited ability to plug into what's larger. But, we have an ability to continuously see more and go deeper, to continuously see what's larger, to continually understand more and more, with no end to it.

Tishya: How do we apply that responsibility then in our daily lives?

Premodaya: Well, I'm going to use the Holocaust example. One of my teachers, a very beloved man, Eli Jaxon-Bear, has what's almost his slogan, and truer words were never spoken. He says, "Stop the war where you are." And that's all you can do. If you stop the war where you are, you become one more spot where no holocaust can happen. To get any more complicated than that, to go any further than that, is to divert yourself from real responsibility, is to deny or confuse yourself about what is real responsibility. Real responsibility is: Stop the war where you are. What's real responsibility? If your eyes look around and you see that there isn't enough love in the world, make love where you are. If you look around and you see there's too much hunger and it offends you, disturbs you, stop the hunger where you are. You can't change the world, but you can change where you are, and every time you do, you've changed the world. This is what happens—people go off into changing you and me. People look everywhere but where they are, because that's easier. It's easier to focus on somebody else. It's easier to say Hitler did it than to say there is so much anger in me, there is so much confusion in me, there is so much hatred in me, that the Holocaust is possible where I sit. To admit that we participate, that we are that potential, is the first step. To not deny that I'm full of enough anger, I'm full of enough hatred, I'm full of enough whatever it is, that first I have to admit that it's possible where I am. Most people in a wider culture aren't willing to do that. Probably a higher percentage of the people in this room are willing to do that than if we took a hundred people at random off the street. Most people will say, "I'm not the bad guy—he is."

That's a denial of responsibility. It's saying Hitler is responsible for the Holocaust, not me. I'm saying *we're* responsible. As soon as you say somebody else is responsible, you've cut off all possibility for yourself to bring about any truth, bring about any positive change. Whatever it is that offends you, look for it in you first. Whatever it is you hate, find it in you first. Don't be small-minded enough to say it exists out there but not in here. If it didn't exist in here, we couldn't see it. All of us have everything inside us. All of us. With no exception. Every human being has every potential, so to fool yourself that you don't have the potential for anything and everything, is the first wrong move, is the first denial of responsibility. "Well, somebody else murdered somebody, but I could never murder someone." I think under the right conditions you might have to reexamine that idea.

So first you have to be courageous enough, willing enough. If you really want to be responsible, if you really want to change the world, you have to be responsible enough to admit that under the right conditions, *you* could kill someone. *You* could participate in a holocaust. *You* could vote for Hitler. I'm not saying that means you would, but I'm saying we need to admit that under the right conditions—if you were tortured enough, if you were hungry enough, if you were in pain enough—we all have the potential for everything inside us. The murderer is the one in whom the potential for murder came out. Because it didn't come out in me, doesn't mean I don't have the potential. The first requirement of real responsibility, if you really want to look at what it means to be responsible for your fellow man, is to admit the possibility for yourself that there is nothing in you different from anyone else.

The people who become the greatest heroes, the ones who save lives, the ones who change the world, they were not sitting around saying, "Wow, I'm really good, I'm really something!" They were the same as you and the same as me, and in a certain moment they responded to whatever call came. They are the same as you; they had that potential, the same as you. I have inexpressible admiration for the absolute courage of Martin Luther King, Jr. And you know what? That same potential for courage is in you, and in her, and in her, and in him, and in her. Having made the statement, that under the right circumstances we can all be murderers, under the right circumstances we can all be Martin Luther King. We can all be saints; we can all be heroes. It's all already possible; there's nothing lacking in your potential.

We are going through a time when many people are saying, "This is a worse than usual time; it seems more doomed; things are more dire." I don't subscribe to that. I subscribe to a different view. By definition, my view is the world is always in dire circumstances; the world has always been and, will always be, in dire circumstances. There will always be a pandemic on its way. There will always be a crusade to sign on for. There will always be a disaster headed our way. I don't read the news. In my way of looking at it, it wouldn't make any difference if I picked up a newspaper from March 25, 2006, versus March 25, 1886; it's the same news. So-and-so killed so-and-so; this disaster happened here and there. This war is going on in this place. The only thing that changes is the names and the dates. The details change, but the news is the same. That's really, to me, quite obvious. It astounds me when I see people poring over the newspaper, "Oh, look!" But it's the same stuff again and again. If they had a newspaper in 5000 BC it would say the same thing—so-and-so smoked so-and-so.

"Stop the war where you are," is really the only answer. The only answer that is possible for us, because that's the only thing that's news. The news is: Where you sit there can't be a holocaust; there can't be a suffering if a pandemic arrives, because where that person sits, there's a recognition of something bigger, something that has more to do with the infinite and the eternal than with what's going on in worldly terms. To me the definition of the world is a place where there's trouble. As long as there's a world, there will be a problem. Now, we have a choice: We can cloak ourselves in that problem and hunker down over the newspaper and fret about every new detail, or we can try to see and live deeper. Try to live and see what is, instead of what happens. What happens is just a recycling, the same stuff. What is, is a whole different matter. If you're standing on top of what is, instead of what's happening, you're on a whole different ground.

Jocelyn: It's fresh and new in every moment, full of surprises, and it's alive. Empty yet full.

Premodaya: Can you expand people's understanding for whom maybe that's a new concept? Comment to what that means? Why everything is fresh and new?

Jocelyn: Because to keep that constant story, to keep that worry, to keep the concern of so many things that you feel that's your life—to keep all that in constant update is exhausting. It serves absolutely no purpose, and once that's really been seen and that's been let go of, then you don't want to go back to having those concerns again. They're pointless. It doesn't mean that problems don't arise; life still has its momentum and takes whatever course it will take, but you've taken your hands off—your hands aren't on the wheel, and you're really not in that panic anymore—so you let go. It's really not a problem anymore. Nothing's a problem, but problems are still there.

Tishya: You're saying you're not buying into that reality, so to speak, not that you're ignoring it as a world concern, bird flu for example, but it doesn't apply to me? I choose not to live in the anxiety of that, so therefore it's not my immediate reality?

Premodaya: No, because that doesn't work, because that's denial. The anxiety comes out some other way. You can't close your eyes, but what you can do is understand more deeply. In the late 1800s early 1900s there was a massive epidemic on the East Coast. Literally hundreds of thousands of people died on the Eastern seaboard, particularly in New York City. There was nothing the public health officials could do. They did their best, it was partly a hygiene issue, but it was an epidemic of disastrous proportions. If bird flu comes along and hundreds of thousands die, it will be the same thing. And other times in history, in other places, same thing. So first look deeply at how the world works, and then see if from that deep looking there is a different understanding.

What Jocelyn is talking about is the understanding that we have all been taught. We have all been inculcated and conditioned to tell ourselves stories about what is going on. That's how we make sense of things. We tell ourselves a story—this happened and that happened, and I was born in this and that place, and then this happened, and I met so and so, and then that happened, and then I went to this school, and then I got that job—as if that's reality. As if that's the definition of what you are. The only real message that I'm trying to impart is that you aren't that. You aren't your story; you aren't your thoughts; you aren't your feelings of the moment; you aren't your ideas; you aren't your beliefs; you aren't your concepts. You are much more than that; you are far more of a potential than a particular story. The story is your mind's idea of what happened.

To believe that story you have to not look at the limitless potential that's in everyone, that's in you, that we were talking about a few moments ago. What we do is we forget all that, we forget the limitless potential, and we believe in what happened to us on Thursday. That's a poverty-stricken point of view. It's the point of view that we are taught to have, because it's orderly. But now and again a person wakes up to the notion that maybe what's orderly isn't what's most important. Maybe a person gets a taste— everybody in this room I guarantee has had that taste—that there's something in me that's deeper than that. There's something in me that's more real, that's closer to Truth than what happened to me when I was twelve, than who my parents are, than what country I was born in, than what I'm going to have for lunch on Thursday, and how I'm going to live, and when I'm going to die. There's nothing that you can say about yourself and your life story that is anywhere near as significant as what you are. The story is almost arbitrary, because somebody with a slightly different frame of mind would interpret the story radically differently. It's not hard to understand. The slightest little twist of mind and the same set of events, and the same story becomes a whole different story.

A different way to say it: You are more than a point of view. We live our lives as if we are a point of view. What I'm encouraging you to do when we have these meetings is to not limit yourself to point of view. You can't plug into eternity from any point of view. You can't feel the depth of infinity by standing in a particular point of view. That works for getting a job, buying a car; it doesn't work for answering the basic questions of life. Who am I? What is life? What is this world? What is God? What is real? What's the Truth? To get real answers to those questions, which are everybody's questions, you have got to change how you ask the question. You have got to first develop the willingness to not be a prisoner of point of view. Point of view is just where you're looking right now. If you happen to be sitting up there [pointing to a section of ceiling] you would have a whole different point of view. If you happened to be up there [pointing to another section of ceiling] you would have a whole different point of view.

See how arbitrary point of view is. Don't limit yourself; don't tell yourself you're your point of view. Your potential is so much huger than that. Point of view is this second what you think you can see. So much more is possible for every person. You have to start to get the idea, the understanding, the seeing of how much is really in you, how much every human being represents. We sell ourselves short all the time, we really do. Really becoming more spiritually aware, more spiritually attuned, means starting to see that you're not this limited, flawed, poor thing that needs to be fixed or brought around or disciplined or whatever. Really being responsible includes recognizing how much is in you.

Everybody has had moments in their life: moments of crisis, moments of trouble, moments of problems. Something comes up, some set of circumstances arrives, where you have to act; you have to respond. A potential has to come out that ordinarily doesn't come out. Usually it's a moment of crisis. Some local catastrophe happens—and by catastrophe, I mean, in your life. You walk by a bad traffic accident where people are groaning and screaming, and you respond. Some friend of yours has some event happen and calls on you for help. Whatever it is—it can be dramatic, it can be undramatic—but by the time you're at least in your later twenties, very few people have not had this experience. And if you think about what that's been in your life, probably in remembering it, you will make some kind of observation that you went beyond yourself, that you didn't know you had it in you. That you helped or responded or did something in some way that you might not do ordinarily.

That's the part I'm quarreling with: I'm saying it's perfectly possible; your potential is so huge you can be heroic ordinarily, all the time, not just in these dramatic moments. You don't see that about yourself. You limit yourself to the societal notion that you don't have much potential, that in moments of crisis you may or may not rise to it. But I have worked with people too long to believe that. I have seen what's in people too clearly to believe that. All that's needed is a little reorientation, a little change in point of view in how you regard yourself and your own potential, and to not see yourself as this little tiny thing that can't do much. That's being responsible. Recognizing that the moments you were your best self, nothing special was going on. You didn't dial up "Heroes-R-Us" and get some special courage or some special ability or some special responding power in that moment—it was right there—it didn't go anywhere since then. You didn't call on anything that wasn't already in you. You just have to see it. You have to see that if that was there, and the circumstances allowed it to come out, nothing new was created. It was there before; it's there now. You actually have to be willing to live more courageously, to admit that. To admit it first to yourself and to say, "I *can* be more than I might allow myself to be. I *can* be more than I have been told I can be. Because I have already seen it in myself." That's being responsible.

I'm talking about simple potential. The potential in every human being, without exception. You have every potential in you. No human being has ever done anything on this planet, ever, that you don't have the potential for. Because if it is possible in somebody else, it is possible in you. It has to be. Now, when you first really get this, it's really scary. Because you feel, "Whoa, what does that mean? What do I have to do now?" But really you don't have to do anything other than admit to yourself that there is no 'best self,' there's just you. And whatever you've thought of in moments in your life as your best self, when the best in you came out; you can bring that out any moment you choose to. There's nothing stopping you. There are no 'best self' police standing on every side saying "Hey!"

But in a way, there is—it's the society. The society says, "Don't make waves." "Keep the peace." "Do what you're supposed to do." It's rebellious to let out that potential; it's dangerous. It takes a certain courage, it takes a certain willingness to live more dangerously, because who knows what you'll do, who knows what you'll say? Who knows how you'll respond to what you maybe before chose not to respond to? Who knows? But if you experiment with it, if you take seriously what I'm saying and experiment in your own life, my contention is you will see very quickly that it's not really dangerous, that it doesn't make an upheaval in everything. It just takes you closer to who and what you really are. We live in a society that's full of messages about your limitations. I'm trying to give you the opposite message, because you've been oversold on the idea that you're not much.

I'm telling you that's a lie. The powers that be, the society, control you better if you believe you're not much. Then you will do your job; you won't make trouble; you won't question authority; you'll obey the law, and I'm not advocating you don't obey the law. I'm not advocating anything other than you see that you may be more than you've been told you are; that there may be vested interests, political interests—by "political" I just mean the herd, the group, the society; that it's in the interest of society that people be homogenous, that people all agree to all the same kind of ideas and don't go off in different directions, since that's just less orderly. That's harder to control. That's harder to run things, and the society has a need to run things, but do you want to live a life where society runs you? Or do you want to look deeper and see if there might be more in you, more possibilities, more reality—that it might be possible to get closer to what is, to what's True, to where God sits than you've been told.

See wider, see what's available to be seen if you're willing to look, which is: This can happen and that can happen but that doesn't make you who and what you are. You aren't what happens to you. You come before that; you have an essence that has nothing to do with what has happened to you or will happen to you. That's what you have to find. The only reason people come to a meeting like this is to get some help on finding it. I say this again and again: That sets you apart from most of the world. Most of the world doesn't want to find that. It's too much trouble; it's too difficult; it's too frightening; it's too anything. Substitute anything, any word, any adjective you want. It's not easy to move out of step with convention. For me it was easy because I had a very unconventional life. My whole goal when I was younger was to be conventional, but I couldn't pull it off. I couldn't figure out how to blend in more. I walk in the room; I don't have to do anything; I stick out like a sore thumb, but that's because I carry this energy of an unconventional history. There's nothing I can do about that. It always astounded me to hear that other people are trying to be rebels, trying to break out. I was always trying to break in.

It wasn't hard for me to see some of the traps of conventionality, and that turned out to be a gift in my life even though it didn't feel like it for years. But whether you have a conventional history, an unconventional history, no matter what the story of your life, be willing to see you're not the story of your life. That's only a story. If you were born in a different place, a different time, it would be a whole different story, so what? Don't confuse yourself with the story. You are not your story. When you're your story, when you believe you're your story, suffering is inevitable. Because stories have good parts, bad parts, ups and downs. If you start to realize the truth of how you're not your story, to the degree that you can see that for yourself, your suffering begins to lessen, because you become identified with what is, more and more identified with what is, rather than your interpretation of what is. Our interpretation always includes that's good and that's bad. When it's good, great; when it's bad, you suffer. Now, the truth is when it's good, you suffer, because if you've sold yourself the notion that it's good, the only thing that can happen next is something bad. It can only go down.

Riley: And then you're going to look for another good.

Premodaya: That's right. It becomes a hamster in a wheel; it goes on and on and on. That's the whole Buddhist concept of the wheel of samsara. But it's really true that our interpretation determines our level of suffering. If you really want to not suffer, it isn't, get a better interpretation; it's, stop interpreting altogether. Find the way to be with what is instead of your interpretation of what is. The suffering isn't in what is; the suffering is in your interpretation of it. If you don't call it good, and you don't call it bad, how are you going to suffer? Now, easier said than done, but first you have to understand that it's really that simple. First those ideas have to come into your consideration.

I'm selling you a very radical notion. I'm trying to sell you the idea that it's possible for all suffering to end for any person on this planet. But it carries a price. The price is you have to be willing to give up all interpretation. You have to be willing to give up any idea of good or bad. You have to give up choosing, which sounds very different from what it pans out to be when you really go there. It always scares people when I say give up choosing. I don't want to scare anybody, especially you.

THERE'S SOMETHING MORE TO BE FOUND

Premodaya: Politics is one thing and all the other concerns of life are another thing. And what happens is, people get caught up in those things, and we all have our favorites: politics, sports, entertainment, fashion, science, literature, whatever. Whatever floats your boat. What happens for most of us is we forget that that isn't what life is about. We start to believe and we're taught to believe, that life is about life, that life is about the quality of the life that you live, and the quality is measured in a variety of ways, depending what you believe: he who enjoys himself the most in this lifetime led a good life; he who had the most moments of happiness; he who got the richest; she who had the best sex—whatever it is. We all have our measures of what's the measure of the value of this lifetime. At the end, at the last moment, when you're breathing your last breath, and you know it's your last breath, what will you be saying to yourself as an evaluation of this lifetime?

It's my view that if what you're saying to yourself is about this life, you will be dissatisfied. You will feel the life didn't make it somehow, didn't meet the mark. Maybe even you'll panic that death is coming in a moment and this life hasn't really been lived. What I'm always saying to people is: "Where are you in relation to that which is eternal? Where are you in relation to that which is infinite?"

When I'm dead I want to be quoted as saying, "You are standing right now at the intersection of eternity and infinity." It's not something that happens after you die—one second after you die, you find yourself in eternity and infinity, you go to some heaven or some hell, you go to whatever, you reincarnate, you go to some other realm, whatever idea you have about what persists or doesn't persist, what happens or doesn't happen. It is not about *then*, because whatever is then will be whatever is now. You are sitting in eternity *now*. The space you are in is infinity *now*. The span of time you are in is eternity *now*. My contention is: You are not going to go anywhere you aren't already. You are not going to become something you aren't already. Your chance to become whatever you can become, is now.

The trouble is, life as we define it conventionally, culturally, societally, becomes a distraction, becomes a movement away from what I would call "what matters." As far as I'm concerned, and some of you may quarrel totally with this idea, it doesn't matter how happy you are in this life-time—you can have a miserable life and still have gone deep spiritually. The measure isn't, "How much fun did you have?" There is nothing wrong with fun; I'm all for it. I encourage every one of you to have as much fun as you can. But if you make that the measure of your life, I say you're on the wrong track. Have fun, but don't make it the measure of your life.

The measure of your life is how much did you anchor yourself? How much did you find, how much did you plug into, that is eternal and in-finite—that doesn't wax and wane depending on what happens, that isn't dependent on forces you don't control, or any particular set of inside cir-cumstances or outside circumstances? What I'm really saying to you is, everything is circumstances, and if you focus on the circumstances, you miss what matters. The circumstances are what they are—some of us are tall; some of us are short; some of us are rich; some of us are poor; some of us are smart; some of us are stupid. When you compare it all, there isn't that much difference in all of it. The difference is: Are you dazzled by cir-cumstances and go running after this and chasing after that? Or can you plug into to what's real, what really matters? And you can do that whether you're stupid or smart; you can do that whether you're tall or short; you can do that whether you're educated or uneducated—no particular set of circumstances is required. No particular criteria have to be met to search for Truth, search for Reality, search for God—whatever is the right term for you.

Let me say it a different way: This life is meant to be the stepping stone to the Profound, and we live in an age and in a place where the highest value for most people culturally is to be entertained. It's become, in my view, an entertainment culture. Now, there's nothing wrong with entertainment, but if life is about "How much can I be entertained?" and it becomes an addictive need to be entertained every nonworking moment, in my view at least, that ain't life.

The Profound really does require a certain amount of meditativeness, a certain amount of peace, inner peace already, a certain amount of willingness and ability to not be blindly following the culture, blindly following every marketing trick, blindly following everyone who wants to sell you something or has something that they want you to blindly follow, including spiritual teachers. It's about developing the recognition of what matters. And it's so easy to be distracted in a thousand ways. Everything in the culture is about distracting you. There are other cultures that are more supportive of the Profound, but we're not in one. And we can read books about the Navajo and read Indian philosophy, but we're not in those cultures.

I want to encourage you to go deeper. If you're in this meeting, you've already seen that the culture only goes so far, and that there is something profound; there is something more to be found, to be plugged into, to be cultivated. I'm saying, go further. You're already folks who have gone further than the average person on the street. Go even further. Recognize that this life—I'm saying something very radical—this life, is not about this life. When the moment comes that you leave this life, this life was not about how good a life it was. It's about how far did it get you toward the Profound. Even a little way is a greater life than a life filled with happiness that's spiritually bankrupt.

I'm not saying anything that hasn't been said a million times by all kinds of folks, but it needs to be said a million times by all kinds of folks. Most of us don't get it until we have heard it so many times, in so many ways. There's an inner call that tells us this, if we're lucky, but still it has to be heard a thousand ways, a thousand times, to get our attention, to get us to realize that these distractions really are distractions, that this life really is not about the superficial, that there is something to sink your teeth into that is real, that isn't something you enjoy when you're thirty or forty, and then you couldn't care less when you're fifty or sixty. Those of you who are under forty, just wait—you will be very surprised. The things that you care deeply about right now, you won't care one iota for in twenty years. Your whole priorities and agenda will change. I guarantee it. I have never met anybody who at sixty wouldn't validate that. It's not rocket science. You have different concerns at twenty and thirty, than at forty and fifty, and then sixty and eighty.

That tells you that these things are shifting and don't really matter, because they matter on Tuesday but not on Thursday. All I'm saying is, find what matters *every day*. Find what matters when you were two, when you are twenty-two, when you are eighty-two, when you are a hundred and two. Find what matters that never doesn't matter. *That's what your life is meant for: to find that.* And along the way people have the idea, "I'm looking for inner peace," "I'm looking for happiness," "I'm looking for spiritual contentment," "I'm looking for the Truth," "I'm looking for God." Whatever idea you have along the way, fine. Everybody has their pull. There are as many pulls as there are individuals, so to fight about "my pull is more real than your pull"—not much point.

All religions and all real spiritual paths, spiritual traditions, are pointing to the same exact thing: That which truly is, truly matters, doesn't change from day to year to decade to century—that which is the core of everything, if you can get to the core. It's only for the most intelligent, the ones who are able to discern, discriminate that there is something beyond, there is something that matters more, there is something that is deeper. Most people can't get to that, and there's nothing wrong with them for that. Be glad you're someone who can. Don't judge the ones who can't— they're at a different stage. They just aren't there yet. It's always about *yet*. It's always about different people are at different stages of understanding.

If you're a little further than someone else, it means you have gone a little further down the road. They aren't worse than you and you aren't better than them because they are a little further back of the road. Don't worry about anybody else. The only one you can ever, ever, ever really take forward is yourself. All I'm saying is, there's really is somewhere to go—keep going!

Does that all sound very vague somehow, or not really? I can't tell, because when I'm talking, I'm listening to myself like, "What's he saying?" I have to check with you whether I went anywhere.

[long pause]

Did I confuse anybody?

Lucas: When you talk about "the Profound," could you also be talking about God?

Premodaya: Sure, but "God" is a loaded word for a lot of people. It doesn't really matter: you could say "God"; you could say "Truth"; you could say "the Profound"; you could say "Reality"; you could say whatever fits for you.

Lucas: I see God as primary and everything else is important but is secondary, like jobs, money, fame, fortune. It's good, but it's secondary. I think every seeker sooner or later comes to the point, when there's really nothing else.

Premodaya: You see; I have been talking for twenty minutes, and you said what I said in two sentences.

Premodaya: What brings you here tonight?

Jacob: To go deeper. Not identifying with my body. Trying to get beyond my mind.

Premodaya: What would happen if you went deeper? You say, "I'm here to see about going deeper, to go deeper." What changes if you go deeper? What do you get? Is it relief from pain or is it something other than that?

Jacob: It grounds me. My practice allows me to shift the brain from looking at something as a problem to just another adventure in this life.

Premodaya: How is that working so far?

Jacob: It actually is working. It's taken me quite a few years, but I'm just now getting to the point where I do see it working. That's compelling me more to want to continue with the practice, to want to make the effort every day, to not jump on to my work on the computer, and to take away the fear of being homeless.

Premodaya: What's that about?

Jacob: That's about security, money, finances, the body, the taking care of the physical needs.

Premodaya: Is there any chance you could become homeless?

Jacob: No, but that's just my need to have that angst.

Premodaya: Right. You know this didn't exist thirty years ago, this fear of homeless. I hear this all the time from people. I hear it from people who are more well-off financially than I can imagine being. It's an effect of our time. It's an effect of how the society has morphed. Is it really all about fear? Because listening to you it sounds like it's all about fear.

Jacob: That's what drives it, and I know intellectually that fear is wasted. You can live your life without fear. There's no reason to have fear; there's no reason to have worry. I realize that intellectually. It's getting beyond the intellectual that is the stumbling block. But by going deeper, by having a practice, I can "let the mind go" and let it do its thing, and observe it and say, "OK, it's wacko, I'm nuts, I'm crazy" but that's not who I am, that isn't my identity. This is classic Nisar, it's basic sense. That's my practice with Nisargadatta, which is readings every day and trying to hear what he's saying.

This is probably my seventh reading of the book, and now I'm basically realizing that intellectually, there's enough evidence to me that there is something beyond this physicality, or identity with this body or what I want to project based on my being, my background, my issues or whatever. But I am seduced by my mind, and I forget it sometimes. And that's where the fear comes back in.

Premodaya: Well, that's the reorientation that I was talking about just a few minutes ago. That's the orientation to the eternal and the infinite that says, "This can't be *it*. Just this? This life can't be it." You're just saying it in a different way, and it's the profound beginning of that which is profounder. How easy it is for you to enter that fear, to confront that fear that's there?

Jacob: Stay with the pain? It's very hard; I run from it. I'm still worried it's not going to work, but I have no choice at this point. I can't go back.

Premodaya: Perfect. That's the best thing of all in terms of what you so openly shared with us. Now you have no choice. You had choice, and you picked the right one. Most of the country isn't looking at Nisar, they're looking at NASCAR. You picked the one that takes you to what matters. Now it's only forward whether you want to or not. Is it possible to enter that fear right now? If you closed your eyes and relaxed, would you be able to enter that fear? Would that fear come up?

Jacob: Probably not, because I meditated quite a bit this morning, and I did longer practice than I normally would. Probably not, is the answer.

Premodaya: Would you be willing to do an experiment and just see what's there right now, without any preconceived notion? I'm not looking for fear; I'm not looking for any particular emotion or feeling state or condition or circumstance of anything. Let's just see what's there right now, because what Nisargadatta is talking about is direct experience, and what you're talking about when you say "fear drives me" is a visceral experience that becomes habitual. It's like the base.

Jacob: I can go there if you want me to. I have a fear right now of being in front of all these people, not wanting to make a fool of myself, or embarrass myself. I can feel that viscerally right now.

Premodaya: Sure. Are you willing to take the chance of making a fool of yourself and just seeing what's there right now? Just closing your eyes, relaxing, and seeing, just seeing what's there, just seeing what the direct experience is, aside from this superficial fear? Because you are sitting up here and you are doing great and you're talking very cogently and whatever you are feeling about it, there's not much real effect. So just see what's there and share with us what happens. When you drop in, when you go deeper in this moment, what happens? What's there? What do you find?

Jacob: But when I go deeper, when I meditate, I get beyond that, so then the fear sort of dissolves. By sitting here silent, all of a sudden, my fear is worse.

Premodaya: Don't jump out of it; let's see where it goes right now. Relax, close your eyes and let yourself fall into yourself without any going anywhere, without any doing of anything, just falling inside, literally without effort, without an intention. It's really just relaxing. And just letting yourself fall in, letting yourself get comfortable in your body, in your mind, not looking for anything in particular, not rejecting anything that comes up, not moving in any direction other than falling inward. And then, as you fall more and more inside, noticing what's there, noticing where you are, noticing what comes up. And without leaving that, without opening your eyes, without going into a monologue about it, simply letting us know what that is as you fall even deeper.

[long pause]

Premodaya: What are you experiencing, without leaving it?

Jacob: The flowing of my breath, and thoughts, didn't really go anywhere. The disconnect I have is that if an emotion or something comes that's painful for me—if I do focus, or I do close my eyes and try and go deeper, then it dissipates, I don't stay with it. But I know you have to stay with the pain. In order to disperse it or alleviate it, you have to go beyond the pain; you have to stay with the pain. But I can now shift into a place where the pain shifts away on its own without having to stay with it—it seems like. I don't know if that's a disconnect or if that's supposed to be that way.

Premodaya: The bad news is, it's all about getting away from something. What you're doing is truly fear based, clearly. You know that; I'm not telling you anything you don't know. But maybe it's not as clear to you how, because of that, it's about getting rid of something. It's about making something disperse. It's about getting the pain out. It's about not feeling imprisoned by the mind. It's a kind of a getting away from. Now that's the bad news.

The good news is, you couldn't have a better teacher than Nisargadatta to deliver the message that really is going to have to get to you, one way or another, sooner or later: that you will only go around in circles. You will find ways to feel better; you will find ways to push the pain further away. There will be less moments of pain in this lifetime. You will find ways even to truly progress spiritually in real and deep ways, but it will be like going in circles because it's about getting away from something. And nobody has said it better—there are a few who have said it as well—but certainly, in my mind, nobody has said it better than Nisargadatta—that it's about allowing everything. It's about what is.

We did a meditation the other night; the title of it became: "What Is, Is." This is his whole message. Nisargadatta's whole message—and it's really meant for very intelligent people, so I'm not surprised that you're attracted to it—and the real message is: What is, is. Adjust yourself to that. See the reality and the profound truth of it.

It sounds so absurd, "Well of course, what is, is." No: What is, *is*. You don't change a thing. Nisargadatta is really saying stop deluding yourself that all the things you want, all the things you prefer, all the "druthers" in life, amount to anything. What is, *is*. We all have our preferences.

You're saying, "I don't want this much pain. I don't want this much fear. I'm trying to find a way out of this fear." Somebody else is saying, "I want to be happier." Somebody else is saying, "I want to be richer." Somebody else is saying, "I want to find my soul mate." It doesn't matter what. Everybody's running around most of the time saying something, thinking something. You have keyed in that the mind is a source, and that's a more advanced level. You understand that it's coming from somewhere: It's not just a given. And what Nisargadatta, as far as I'm concerned, is saying is: "All of that is just what *you* prefer."

Very valid, nobody can't not understand why you prefer it. Who wouldn't rather be rich than poor? Who wouldn't rather be successful than unsuccessful? Who wouldn't rather be more spiritually advanced versus less spiritually advanced? But what he is saying is, it doesn't matter what you want. It doesn't matter what you think. It doesn't matter what you are preferring. It doesn't matter what your desire says of what your interpretation says or where you think you are or where you think you aren't. Because the Truth is: *What is, is*. Doesn't matter what you think about it. Your job is to find out what is, so that you are not fighting with it. He is really saying: "Stop running."

I just want you to hear one thing. You have a very sincere heart. You are a sincere searcher. You are willing to risk, clearly. You are an adventurer, and if you are willing to include your fear, to stop running, to stop trying to make anything go away, then you're living Nisargadatta's formula. His formula is: Allow everything. You've got the right teacher. You've got somebody who has written one of the great books of all time (I know he did not '*write*' it). There is no lack of Truth in that book but it has to be rightly understood. The trouble with the mind is, the mind reads a book and interprets it to *its* comfort level.

Jacob: Nisar isn't comfortable. That's what's great about the book, you can never read it at your own comfort level because he won't allow you, and that's the brilliance.

Premodaya: I don't disagree with you, but if the main motivation is fear based and is about trying to make something go away, then the one thing that will not jump out clearly from that book is that it's about allowing everything, including what you don't want. I'm just interpreting now. I'm saying what I hope you'll do is take out the division between what you like and what you don't like, what you hate and what you love, what you fear and what you want, and just look for what is instead of what you *hope* is there; and see that it's not just fear, because you already knew that. That it's about keeping something away, pushing something away, making something less, and that will keep you in that mode. That's Sisyphus. That's Sisyphus pushing the rock. I'm encouraging you not to spend the rest of your life pushing the rock, and instead to allow everything that is. And my belief is, that if you can do that, everything will open.

My hope for you is you don't wave it away with a true statement that hasn't been lived yet.

Jacob: Well, I think you're very perceptive, and thank you very much. For me it may not be this lifetime, but I'm going to keep going, no matter where it leads me or what it may be.

Premodaya: Make it this lifetime.

Jacob: It may not be this lifetime. It may, but—

Premodaya: Make it this lifetime.

Jacob: Well, I'm working on it. I'm here, right?

Premodaya: You gave people a beautiful example because life can become about conquering the fear. Life can become about eradicating the pain, and it can be done. The trouble is you *can* conquer fear. The trouble is you *can* lessen a painful life, and then that becomes all that life was about. You die, and it turns out you lived a less painful life, or a less fear-based life. I'm saying that's the booby prize. That's not good enough for eternity and infinity. There's something more valuable and more mysterious than just improving this life. That's a modification, an improvement of this life. Most people spend their life—most intelligent people spend their life—trying to improve this life, and at the end what they get out of it is a better life, which isn't that much in the face of eternity.

There's something profounder that can be gotten, and it's much harder to get outside of this life than in this life. That's my experience. You have real limitations after you die that aren't there now, believe it or not. The physical is actually a mode that allows you to move in certain ways you can't move when you aren't in this body. Real meaningful growth is very, very difficult outside of this sphere, this body. This really *is* the opportunity. Conventionally we hear the opposite: "Oh, I will be free after I'm dead," and "I will be not in the confines of a body." Well, there are confines with being in a body. There are aspects of limitation, but there are also aspects of ability to move and act that aren't there when you leave this body. No matter what you believe about after-death states, reincarnation, the end or the not-end, of what persists, the opportunity is now.

Every teacher has said that, for thousands of years, for good reason. But the more esoteric part isn't always understood, or isn't always said or isn't always known, that this body is not the enemy. This body allows you to act. And this mind is *in* the body; the body acts as a container for the mind that limits it. Otherwise, you're just Jell-O all over the place.

The whole reason you can focus, can get somewhere, can advance inwardly; the whole reason you can advance spiritually, is because this mind and this body exist in this lifetime. The body is really the enhancer of the mind. My experience is, when you die, mind remains, and then you're really stuck because you can't go anywhere. There's no body to move somewhere, to do something, with whatever the mind has put its attention on. Then you're not in the same degree of control as when you're in a body. Then your mind determines your reality and your experience in a much more direct, much more haphazard way, unless and until you reach that profounder point while still in the body; unless you anchor yourself, find your place in eternity and infinity, here now—before your mind determines it for you because it doesn't have the control the body gives you.

The body is actually a gift of control, it's like the steering wheel. It's not the enemy. It's not what keeps you locked in the car; it's what allows you to go somewhere. Conventionally, it's thought of as what has you locked in the car; you want to get of the car. No, it's the steering wheel. It's what allows you to get somewhere.

My experience has been that when you die it's like you're in a car with no steering wheel. You can't really go anywhere. That car is floating in space, so you don't get to choose. This is why so many spiritual traditions are based on disciplines, are based on learning how to discipline the body, discipline the mind. The idea is, discipline it before it controls you. There's nothing wrong with that, except people often get lost in the disciplines, and the discipline becomes the point instead of why the discipline is valuable.

You don't have to spend your life on a mountaintop disciplining yourself—body and mind, every second to reach it. It's really what Nisargadatta says: Recognize that what is, is. That's what all the discipline is trying to take you to, that you are no longer following *your idea* of what reality should be. "Well, I don't like the fact that I don't have a lot of money." "I don't like the fact that I'm forty-five and still single." "I don't like the fact that I have six children I have to take care of." Whatever it is. Existence doesn't care that you don't like it. *What is, is.* Existence isn't concerned with whether you're happy or not happy. *What is, is.*

There's nothing wrong with being happy, and it's much better than being unhappy, but your focus can be on making a happier life, or your focus can be on finding what is, which will have the result that you're no longer fighting with existence. Your chances for happiness go way up when you stop fighting with existence. It's one of the nice by-products. But if that's your purpose, then all you'll find is how to be happier. You won't find what is. If your purpose is to avoid pain or have less pain, then that's what you will find, but you won't get to what is. So that's why I said to Jacob, better to allow everything and see what is.

Jacob: And that's the conundrum, how do you get to that point?

Premodaya: By giving up all notions that you have, and seeing what's left. It's very hard—nobody wants to do it. One by one, giving up everything that is an idea, a belief, a concept, a learning, a knowing, giving up everything that has been poured into you that feels like yours but turns out to be borrowed. Everything has to be examined. You've chosen the intellectual looking way. That way says, "Is there a Jacob?" There's a man named Jacob; does that name hold up? No, there's no Jacob; there's just *this*. There's this person who thinks he's a male; is he really a male? There's no such thing; male and female is our interpretation. These very basic things have to be looked at sincerely, and I believe you have the sincerity to do it. Have to be looked at very sincerely and questioned to the very core: Is there such a thing? Does this exist? I have the idea that I'm an American; is there such a thing? I have the idea that I'm a female; is there such a thing? I have the idea that I'm forty years old; is there such a thing? What does it mean to be forty, versus twenty, versus eighty, versus dead? And one by one, you go through every sacred notion that you have that defines you, and if you look at it in true sincerity, if you truly, truly with your heart and soul open yourself to it and are willing to consider what really is, each one drops. You recognize that you aren't a male or a female. You even recognize that everything you think you are is just a story about what you think. That's the perfect way to start, because most of the world does not know that intellectually.

Most of the world believes every idea that they have about themselves, because they have been taught to believe it. They will die and kill for it. "I'm an American, Goddamn it," and "I'm a Frenchman, Goddamn it." You have gotten to the stage where you know enough, you're intelligent enough, you have sincerely examined enough to know that it's ridiculous to die and kill for the idea that you're an American. It's just an idea. That doesn't mean if somebody is breaking down your door and wants to kill you that you're not going to respond or even kill them first, but it does mean you understand, intellectually, that it's just an idea; it's an arbitrary line on a map. There's no such thing as an American. It's an idea.

If you can have the wherewithal and the courage and the willing-ness—the last one is the big one—the *willingness*—to look at every aspect of what you believe, everything that lives as an idea, rather than as a living reality, if you really go deep into it, it will drop; you will see that it has no substance. When you get to the ones that mean the most to you, that is a painful, painful process, because you have to actually go into that which you don't want to let go of. What's left is the ability, the greater ability—to whatever degree—to see what is, to be part of what is. To not be living in an idea about what you think is or would like to be, but what isn't. Because only what is, is. Existence is never going to bend itself to what you would like it to be. *You* have to get to *it*. It's not going to get to you. It doesn't care. It's impersonal. It's not that you don't matter, although ei-ther interpretation is closer to the truth: you matter completely; you don't matter at all. If you matter completely, then you really have to get to what is. It can't come to you; it's not the nature of it to come to you. You have to go to it. And what prevents you is any idea about reality that is just a concept, a belief, an idea that isn't your direct, living knowing. See, what is, is alive. Reality is this aliveness right now. How can aliveness die? How can aliveness go anywhere? You're part of the aliveness that is. You have to know that.

It starts with the intellect. People are always wanting to rag on the intellect as the enemy of the spiritual. You've got a great start. It starts with the intellect. First, you have to understand it. If you don't understand it, you can't go anywhere. But it's not enough to understand it—you have to give yourself to it. It has to operate in your life, in you, because it's alive; it's not another idea. You can make it an idea, you can make it a concept—that's what religion is, a concept about what is God, what is Real, what is Truth—and *even that* can lead you somewhere real, but you have to be willing to *go* somewhere, not just talk about something, not just think about something.

You have to be willing to give yourself up to it. To the point to where your head feels like it's going to explode, your heart feels like it's going to come out your throat, your feet and your hands are burning, and you think you're going to lose your mind and die any second. Because that's how searing it is to come closer to what is, so it's only for intelligent people, courageous people who know it's worth going toward, because there will be difficulties. You won't go hopping and skipping; it's not love and bliss. It's the arduousness of Truth; it's the all-consuming fire of what's real. You will be burned. You will be burned away. What will be burned away is everything you think you are now. Every idea that isn't the Truth burns away, if you allow it, if you're willing, if you keep moving toward it. It's not about what you want things to be. It's about *what is*.

You have to do the moving. You have to recognize that what is, is. You have to give yourself up to that. It's not about how you think it should be. It's about you developing the ability to see what is.

Jacob: Is that surrender?

Premodaya: It becomes surrender. The more you move toward it, the more surrender happens to you, because in the face of what is, how can you do anything but surrender? Anything you try to do that isn't surrender will either be painful or will be felt to be not the right direction. It could even be pleasurable, but it will be felt as the wrong direction. This is what they mean in the ancient texts when they say "tremble before God." They say, "Go before God and go trembling." That's what it means. "Trembling" means go in surrender; don't go as a big ego, "I'm going to get my way." When you're in the presence of God, you're not going to get your way—God is going to get God's way.

It's already that way, because what is, is. We just don't want to admit it to ourselves; we have our own agenda; we have what we want; we have what we prefer; we have what we are comfortable with; we have what we hope life is about—what we hope our experience will be about. We are all trying to get a certain experience. What this says, what Nisargadatta says, and he's one thousand percent right, it's not about your experience, you will experience whatever you experience. Irrespective of what you do or don't experience, what is, is. Adjust yourself to that. Orient yourself to that. The more you do that, the closer you are. What happens is, mysteriously enough, there's what you can think of as a magnetic force that the more you are willing to do that, the more what is pulls you in, makes it easier. It's like you're rowing a boat; what if somebody starts pulling it in with a rope at the same time tied to the front? That's how it works, at least in my experience. You become more something that the Truth wants to pull toward itself.

Anything that isn't helping you recognize more what is and that what is, *is*, doesn't matter. What matters is anything that moves you toward recognizing that what is, is. Anything that makes that real for you, not in a *convince yourself* way, but in a *seeing it*. It makes me think of a lighthouse; anything that isn't moving you toward the lighthouse is moving you away from the lighthouse, and only the lighthouse *is*.

On the one hand, people respond to this as very scary, and understandably. On the other hand, it's simply the real situation you're already in and have always been in, and cannot be in any other situation. You can only be in the situation of what is. That's what it's saying it's saying: You're already there. It's not over somewhere; it wasn't yesterday and it's not next week; it's what is. It includes what's here now; it includes last week; it includes next week; it includes when you were six and it includes when you are dead. It includes everything without exception but it doesn't include anything that isn't. And what *isn't* are your ideas and thoughts and notions and concepts and beliefs about what is. That's the prison. That's why there is this polarizing notion in many spiritual circles that the mind is the enemy. The mind isn't the enemy. That's a misguided notion, but it comes from something real. Ideas and concepts and beliefs when thought to be real, when lived, taken as reality, when the map is mistaken for the territory, that's what they are getting at. You don't have to drop the mind; the enemy isn't the mind. Going beyond the mind means seeing that these are just ideas, that they have no reality to them.

Reality is organic and alive and palpitating and the real deal. It doesn't have anything to do with our ideas about it. Ninety-nine percent of what I do with people or the work we do at ICODA, whether we realize it or not and whether the people we work with realize it or not, is about somehow getting you beyond these ideas, somehow getting you to see through—one by one, every one we can get to—everything that is an idea, a concept, a belief, something you're holding on to that actually can only be something you learned somewhere along the way, which means some-body else gave it to you. People think the spiritual journey is about going somewhere, about learning something. It's about letting go of everything that has been learned up until now, because all that is borrowed; it doesn't belong to you. Somebody gave it to you—your parents, your friends, your schoolmates when you were six. It's all borrowed knowledge; it has noth-ing to do with what's real, and it operates as the barrier to being OK with what is, because you've got an idea that it should be something else, but it's never going to adjust to your idea, because what is, *is*, and it isn't going to change because you'd like it to.

That's the first stage. The second stage is where you recognize that "what is, is," includes you. When you experience that that is not separate from you, and that if you're a raving lunatic, if you yell at your wife, if you steal cars, if you drool every time you sleep, if you can't say a sentence without a four-letter word in it, that none of that precludes you from being and recognizing what is, which isn't separate from you. That is stage two, but first do stage one, where you're willing to let go of everything.

Jacob: Which is not worrying about the outcome.

Premodaya: If you right now could stop worrying about the outcome, could let go of all results in regard to everything, you would be there like *that* [snaps fingers]. This is the problem. The problem is it's always instant, but we only get there through what looked to us like the steps to get there. So, giving up the idea of results is the same statement as "what is, is," recognizing what is, is. It doesn't matter how you get there, as long as you get there.

THERE IS NO 'WHY' IN EXISTENCE

Premodaya: There are really only two reasons to come to darshan. One is because you need an answer. You're invited to ask whatever question is important to ask. Not just an idle question or curiosity about this or that, but something that matters to you, something to which the answer is really needed. The other reason to come to darshan is the energy. To bask in the energy that this kind of meeting includes. Now, the guy in the red chair always gets wrongly the credit for the energy, so don't be confused; you brought the energy. Whatever you feel, whatever feels good to you, whatever feels like it's not your everyday condition—you brought that into the room. You carried it in with you. There's no magic spray in the air. Or, if there is, the other way to look at it is: If there is, you did the spraying. By all means, the best questions are life-and-death questions, the questions that finally getting the answer to is a life-and-death issue for you. If you have one of those questions, I would love to hear it.

These meetings are unscripted. In that sense, whatever it is, isn't even a metaphor for life; it's exactly like life. You don't know what is going to happen in the next second. I think that's part of what people like about these get-togethers, but the problem is that we fool ourselves that these meetings are this way but life isn't. Life is somehow something that we tell ourselves, "We know what's coming in the next second. We know the past; we have some sense of at least the immediate future. We have some sense of right now." What I'm suggesting to you—in fact, what I'm emphatically insisting to you—that all of that is an absolute delusion. All of that is a self-deception. All of that is a societal teaching that has nothing to do with the truth. None of us has absolutely any idea what's going on. Any thought that you do is at best a delusion, and at worst a semi-intentional self-deception. The quicker you see that, the closer you are to what's real. It's not a thought people like to take on, because it calls everything into question. One of the questions someone wrote, a very simple one, "Why am I here?" is the question. Now, I don't know if the person meant, "Why am I here in this room tonight?" or "Why am I here on this planet?" or "Why am I here in existence at all?" But the answer is the same to all of them—you'll never know.

You will absolutely—I guarantee you, no matter what, never know why you're here. No matter what. No matter if you live a thousand more lifetimes and reach the highest spiritual peak and know everything that's possible to know—you will never know why. It's not the wrong question; the question is right; this question is everybody's question. What I'm saying is, it can never be answered, because the question only exists for human beings, and it only exists for human beings from the aspect of the limited mind. It's a mind question. That isn't a criticism. Only the human mind asks, "Why?" Existence—any word you want to use: Existence, Truth, Reality, God, the Universe—whatever, insert the word that's least offensive to you, or the most all-inclusive to you—the Universe doesn't deal in "why."

It doesn't exist in existence. There is no dimension of "why." That's a human mind fabrication. Now, it's very tricky, because it's everybody's fabrication. There's no culture that doesn't have it. There's no place on the planet, no people on the planet, that don't deal in "why." But nothing else ever deals in "why." No tree has ever asked, "Why?" No aspect of existence has ever asked "Why?" Has ever concerned itself with the question of "why." No armadillo has ever turned to Ms. Armadillo and said, "Why, honey?" It just doesn't exist.

So, I want to give you unsolicited advice: as completely as possible and quickly as possible and really as possible, to see through all whys and literally abandon them. That is a circular path. "Why" only takes you to more questions of why, which have many vicissitudes. Well, "why" leads to "how," and "how" leads to "when," and "when" leads to "where"—but it's all the same, going nowhere, because the universe won't cooperate with your "why." You can come up with an answer—you can actually fabricate or think that, "From the sky, a great answer has been given!" The mind is powerful. You can come up with something that will seem absolutely true and real, maybe even change your life, and it'll be false. There is no "why" anywhere in existence. I'm not saying facetiously the answer is "because;" I'm saying seriously the answer is "because." It's the only answer—there's no "why." There's no answer to that, because the question is not relevant to anything that exists and not considered by any aspect of existence, other than the tiny little subsection called "the human mind," which loves that question because it's like fuel to a rocket. It keeps the mind going. You can ask that every minute of the day, every day of the year, every year of your life—and never run out of things to think about. So, "Why am I here?" Not possible to address, no matter what. If you become *God*, you will not have an answer to "Why am I here?"

Now, I don't know if this is good news or bad news. I would like to hear from whoever is interested in sharing their thought, whether this is good news or bad news, or whether I'm just nuts. I mean, I do need to know when we have these kinds of discussions whether this computes for folks, because I'm not here to give speeches.

Priya: I didn't write the question, but to me it's good news, because it has always seemed that it's wrong to define everything in terms of something else. To define everything in terms of some future place. That any meaning has to be intrinsic every moment. When people say, "Everything has a reason," they are mostly thinking something good is going to happen in the future, and that doesn't make sense to me. All sorts of things happen in life that are only "right now."

Brook: I tend to get into the mode of just, what is. "Why did he do this?" "Why did he do that?" The reasons don't matter; he did it—either you accept it, or you don't accept it.

Premodaya: Good.

Riley: I believe that I'm here to spread love to every little thing, and to love everything, and to make this world better. I get irritable sometimes and can be ugly sometimes, but it makes me really happy to know that *that's* why I'm here.

Premodaya: When you hear me say there's no why—is that good news or bad news? Or you just disagree?

Riley: I don't really get hung up on why.

Premodaya: OK, so it has nothing to do with why. That's what you're saying, that you have a sense of purpose and it has nothing to do with the question, "Why am I here?"

Riley: "Why" is so that I can give as much love in whatever creative way I feel like is fun.

Premodaya: I'm suggesting that that isn't an answer to why. That's just, in your words, what is. So "why" isn't a dilemma for you; "why" is only an issue when it's a dilemma—when it has to have an answer. That's how most people live—as a question, "Why? And I *gotta* have the answer, at least sometime before I die. If not by Thursday, at least before I die."

Brook: Are you telling us that we will never have the answer, and it's OK?

Premodaya: No, I'm not saying it's OK. I'm only saying you will never have the answer. I'm not making a value judgment about whether that's OK or not OK. I'm just saying that "why" doesn't exist in existence as a question; it only exists as a question in the human mind. I'm just pointing that out.

Brook: Is it an aberration in the human mind?

Premodaya: It's a process and the human mind is a question-machine. What happens for most of us, particularly in a culture like ours, is we get stuck on a certain question, and most people are stuck on "why." I'm saying that's unfortunate, because "why" will never have an answer. See it as a unicorn—as something that the mind can ask, but doesn't exist in reality. A word for something that doesn't actually exist: unicorn—but because a word is there, we think it exists. We think it's valid; we think there's an answer. This is a question that has no answer. The first thing to understand is that. Anything other than that is going in the wrong direction—is just going in a circle of "why."

Anna: I didn't write the question, but for me, it was related to, "What is the sense of my life? What is my purpose? Why I'm here? Where do I go? What makes my life worth living?"

Premodaya: Everybody wrote that question. This is everybody's question on one level or another, at one time or another; this is everybody's question, "Why am I here?"

Anna: It's not bad news for me that there's no "why" and there's no higher purpose that I am heading to, or have to head to, or something written in the book where I should be one day, or not at all.

Premodaya: I didn't say that. There's another question somebody wrote: "Does God give me my life's mission or do I just need to figure it out?" And the answer to both (that's two questions; two for the price of one)— and the answer to both of those is "Yes." Now are you confused?

Anna: No, I'm not confused at all.

Premodaya: So why are you not confused by those seemingly conflicting questions?

Anna: First of all, I know we're living in the unknown and what is going to happen to us is grace, and I'm responsible for what I can be responsible. At the same time, there's nothing I can decide or choose. It just is and it's just unfolding, and it's the mystery we are living in.

Premodaya: It's an interesting experience to sit in this chair because I get to have the experience of somebody saying back to me what I say, again and again. This is very subtle, because it doesn't mean that there's no value to asking why and it doesn't mean there's no usefulness or purpose to consider-ing the meaning of why. I'm really being very specific; it means: Recognize that there's no answer, no ultimate answer, to the question of "why?" It's not the same as, "It's a dumb question," or, "The question has no meaning." The question has meaning; it's the right question, but at some point, you can't go anywhere with it; what I'm suggesting is that you get to that point as quickly as possible, that that becomes a jumping-off point.

Jasmine: I obviously don't know your philosophies like some people here, but I'm concerned about how people live their lives. I completely agree with the things that you are saying, but applied to what? When Brook was saying, "Why did he do this? Why did he do that? He just did." Well, maybe "why" isn't necessarily the most important question, but "how" I think is very important, not "how" in "How do you do this?" As you were saying before, words, language, culture, are limiting. To a certain extent, I think it is important to embrace that we have that and to try to work with it. The only reason I bring up concerns; does this mean that we don't try to change the world? Maybe that isn't what you're saying at all, because I ask "what" questions every day; my whole life is about curiosity. When I apply it to a specific situation, when I apply it to society or culture I feel as if those things are important to pay attention to and to question and to constantly try and change. This process may help that process of change, but I'm just hoping that people don't give it up because there's no answer and it just is. I feel very sad if that was the case.

Premodaya: You don't have to worry about people giving it up. That's not going to happen. No matter how hard I try to get people to give it up and no matter how successful I might be or might not be, most people will not give it up. You're completely safe in that area; don't even spend one second worrying about it. It's really not general. I think you're hearing me rightly, but at the same time I want to point out that I mean it very specifically. What you said is, "I can see it. I don't actually disagree with it in the general, but applied specifically I don't see that, really. I think there's a usefulness to 'why?'" This is a very subtle point—I appreciate that you make the point because it helps me make even more clear the subtlety of this. The "why" that you're talking about, the specific "why" in the world, in society, in interaction, isn't really the "why" we're talking about. That's really "what." It sounds like "why," but it's really asking "what?" "What's going on? What's happening?" "Why" is a very specific level; it really only means, "What is the meaning?" That's all it means. It doesn't mean, "What's happening here?" If you apply it to a given situation in daily life, we almost never ask, "What is the meaning?" We're really asking a more practical question and that's the problem—we never look for meaning; we look for practicality. We look for practicality because we're lost.

If we start questioning the meaning too much—which is the essence of the spiritual search—it gets painful, it gets difficult. Everything gets called into question; everything gets seen as "up for grabs." Our most cherished notions, our most deeply held beliefs, our most dear and cherished ideas, suddenly are up for grabs; suddenly may not be what we thought they were. This is scary stuff. The people that come to a meeting like this, usually, aren't very uncomfortable with the question of "why?" But if you think about the general world, there's not a lot of encouragement; there's not a lot of support to really ask, "Why?" To really delve into the meaning of whatever's going on. The support is utilitarian; the support is, "Let's look at 'what.' Let's look at what the pattern is; let's look at what the events are." It's a more materialistic mindset.

I'm saying a very strange thing. I'm saying, at the same time and in the same breath, that there's no answer to the question "why?" and that in that sense, it's a purposeless question or a question that leads you nowhere specific, and I'm saying, at the very same time, it's the only important question. Not in the specific sense, not in the sense of, "Why this?" or, "Why did he do that?" "Why did she do this?" It doesn't matter—the world is much bigger than that; the universe is bigger than that. It doesn't matter why this happened on Tuesday, why that happened on Thursday, why this city decided this, why this country went over there. Ultimately, what does it matter? Ultimately, it's all a wash, right? Just get far enough in your perspective, just fast forward ten thousand years—what does it matter? Just beam out to a billion planets and what does it matter?

That's the "what." This is why we're talking about this, because everybody has some degree of confusion. It's impossible not to be confused about it. "Why" is mistaken for everything that isn't "why," and usually when that's the case we're thinking, "what?" but we are calling it "why." We are telling ourselves that we are questioning the meaning, when all we are doing is looking for safety, looking for an answer that satisfies us, that we can hold on to, so that we aren't swinging in the wind. What I'm saying is, you're always swinging in the wind, you've always swung in the wind, and you'll always swing in the wind. That's where you are, and the more and the quicker you question whether that's true or not—and if you find it to be true, accept it—the closer you are to what's real, the closer you are to what's true, the closer you are to what is beyond any understanding of "why."

"Why?" is the most important question, because it's the beginning of everything that matters. Until you seriously, with your whole heart and soul, ask, "Why?" there's no real spiritual search. It always begins with, "Why? Why am I here?" That's the only way it begins for anybody, but that's also where it ends, because "why" can't take you to where you want to go, "why" can't give you the answer, "why" can only take you around in a circle. I hope for each and every one of you that circle doesn't last a lifetime. It doesn't need to and the only way to start getting beyond it is to start to see what's really meant by "why"—what you're really asking when with all your heart you look up at the sky and say, "Why?" You have to know what you're asking; you have to know what your real question is, and it's very deceptive. You can ask "why" and be asking something very different from what you think you're asking, so you have to find out your real question. If you really dig into that, with many people it will turn out to be "What? Help me understand what's happening," and that's not the search for Truth; that's the search for safety. That's the search for, "Help me position myself the right way on this planet, in the material realm." Now, I'm not against the material realm, but I am against people living there. It's not a good place. It's fraught with dangers; it's beyond insecure, and when you swing in the material realm you bump your head a lot, so I'm suggesting you can swing somewhere else.

Brook: Thinking of people I know who have been so stuck in, "Why?" I think by them getting an answer, they are trying to validate themselves, "I'm right." To make change, I don't think you have to know why. If something's not working, you can change something without having to know why it is the way it is.

King: I struggled with "why" for a while. For me, it was a life-and-death question. I had to know why, and I was not going to move from it. I came to an answer, which I know to be true for myself, because I have experienced it. I saw that "why" is not only unknown but unknowable. What that did was allow me to get out of the way, because it was the mind asking why and the mind coming up with answers, until I saw it was unknown and unknowable. And when I got out of the way, it freed me up entirely for whatever was necessary. Everything changed for me dramatically; the world changed where I was.

Jasmine: You said that what I was questioning is what's going on, and what's going on is trying to get into safety or …

Premodaya: Or trying to change the world.

Jasmine: I feel you can ask why and get away from the material world, and still try to change the world. And I think it's almost necessary. The people in this room; we are some of the most privileged people in the world; we can do so much.

Premodaya: You're right. We're the cream of the planet. Nobody here is ever going to starve. Nobody here is going to spend three-quarters of the day standing knee-deep in a rice paddy, just to have something to eat tonight.

Jasmine: Maybe we don't need to ask, "Why is it so?" but, again, I go back to "how"—looking at history, looking even at what the country is doing. It may not be important in the scheme of the universe, but it's important in people's lives: who's dying in a different country or how we're contributing to the death of trees, or using plastic bottles and buying new clothes every day. There are things that we can do in our life. Maybe I'm really misunderstanding, but every time I hear that that is not important, I'm not sure if you mean it's not important, in the sense of, it doesn't tell us anything about why we're here, or spirituality?

Premodaya: I'm saying something more radical than that; I'm saying it can't be done.

Jasmine: Changing the world isn't possible, so don't try?

Premodaya: No, I didn't say don't try. I said it can't be done.

Jasmine: If that were to encourage someone to not try, that's their decision, but I would honestly have a problem with that.

Premodaya: Yes, well, my job is to create a problem for you.

Jasmine: Well, that's fine, and my job is to question people who are privileged and don't use it to change.

Premodaya: The dilemma is that none of what we're saying implies, or in any way suggests, that anyone should do anything differently. The dilemma is, it's hard not to take it that way. What it really means is—see the truth, see the reality, so that whatever you do is based on something real instead of on our interpretation or what we have been told is real. It means see for yourself with your own eyes. It doesn't mean don't do something that your heart tells you to do. It means: *Be sure it's your heart telling you to do it.* Now, just so it's on the record and for no other reason, my view is, the world has never changed. Hasn't happened yet. The world has always been what it is and will always be what it is, because that, to my understanding, is the definition of "world." Now, we can tell ourselves that we're changing something, but my view is: We don't have that power. The only power we have is to change *inside*, and when you change inside, the world changes. You can change the world, but only where you're sitting. The amazing thing is when you change the world where you're sitting, the whole world changes. I'm not saying, don't be an activist; I'm not saying, don't have an ideal; I'm saying—see beyond both of those; see beyond the idea that changing the world changes something.

Jasmine: I still want to do it.

Premodaya: I'm not saying don't do it. I'm saying, understand something more essential about what's really here. World is just one level; world is the material level. What I'm meaning to impart is—understand that when you talk about changing the outside world, you're talking about the material level of things. There are other ways to approach existence. Does that make more sense? These are fantastic questions. This discussion is as important as any discussion can be, because everybody needs to have this answer. Everybody needs to know what "why" means, and how to respond to their understanding of it. Without that you just are doomed to confusion.

Anna: I remember once there was a question, "How can we stop the wars in this world, the conflicts, the crime?" and you answered, "Stop the war within you. That's the only way." Is that right?

Brook: "Let there be peace on earth and let it begin with me," that's the only place it's ever going to happen. When you change, it affects everything around you, and that's how you make it work.

Marley: I have done activist work also and I would never stop doing it just because this is the material world and it won't change, because I think that gesture of giving of yourself, is of something much larger. I don't think it's a conflict. If it's important to you, do it, because it's connected to something bigger. I think it's a higher level of consciousness, a higher level of existence. It took me a long time to come around to that; it was a lot of conflict for me, and I'm in a more peaceful place about it.

Premodaya: That would have to mean that you stopped concerning yourself so exclusively with "why." If you were not in a peaceful place about it, it means on some level, in some way, you had to be preoccupied with "why." And somehow "why" diminished in its hold on you. That's really what I'm talking about. We can be so easily trapped in "why" and not even know we're trapped. This is very, very complex and subtle stuff, because "why" is woven through everything. All I'm trying to do is pull it out and give it some clarity, so that any trap that any part of you is in, in relation to "why," can find a little more the doorway. I'm suggesting that we are all trapped to some degree in this question, "Why am I here? Why, why, why, why?" You don't even have to add more words, but it's really, "Why do I exist? What is life, what is death? Why this way? Why in this form? Why does it feel this way?" You know, there are a thousand questions within "why," all of which are everyone's question, all of which have to be addressed. You can't not go into this question—you're living it; it's existential. You can ignore it; you can refuse it, but it doesn't mean you aren't living it.

Riley: I just don't feel like I am. Do you think I'm in denial?

Premodaya: How sure are you?

Riley: About as sure as I can be.

Premodaya: Then there's no problem. As long as you can say, "I'm as sure as I can be," there's no problem. The only issue is if it's a problem. And for many people, at many times, it's a problem. Good for you that it's not. It may have been at some other point; it may be at some other point, but right now you're saying it's not, so be glad there's no problem.

The other question was, "Does God give me my life's mission, or do I just need to figure it out?" And my answer, my response, was "yes and yes." Now, this has to be a very sophisticated gathering because nobody is saying, "Well you can't say that; those two are conflicting." It seems that most people here get it that those two are not conflicting.

Brook: I'm trying to figure it out. I'm sitting here totally confused.

Benjamin: If God gives me my mission, then how do I know what he's given me? I still have to figure it out, and there's the brief supposition that I and God are separate in the question.

Premodaya: My contention is that there never has been, and never can be, one breath that you draw … that nothing can ever happen, ever has happened, or ever will happen, that (if we go with the wording of the question and use the term God) isn't God's will. (If somebody is irritated by the wording, just change it in your head to the words that fit for you.) That you absolutely are part of the Divine plan. And yes, *there is* a Divine plan, but that plan is unknowable, unfathomable, unreachable, and there's no possible way to put any part of your arms around it. It's as unfathomable as the Martian language; there's just no way for us to plug in. That's my contention.

Marley: If we are part of it, why is there no way for us to plug in?

Premodaya: Let's try to understand it more specifically. There's a way for you to *be* it, but there's no way for you, as an idea, as a mind, to comprehend it. There's no way for you to plug in, in the sense of, "Aha! Now I know what the Divine plan is." It would be like an orange asking for the square root of pi. It just doesn't work this way, although it seems like it's how it works. It seems like we ought to be able to grasp, "What is God? What is God's plan? Where do I fit in it?" I'm not saying you can't live it; I'm not saying you can't grasp it in the way that is graspable for us as human beings. I'm saying that whatever *that is*, whatever we *can* grasp, is so far away from what it really is, that for us to have the arrogance, and simply the ignorance, to think that we can "get it"—I mean understand it, is just like an orange asking to take a physics class. There's no point; there's no way; there's no possibility. You know, an apple can't ride a horse.

Marley: I guess I can't let go of the concept that everything is knowable. Is that arrogance?

Premodaya: No, that's just …

Marley: Ignorance?

Premodaya: Ignorance. That's the apple saying, "Bring the horse." That's beautiful, because that's my whole contention that takes us right back to where I first opened my mouth. What I'm saying in the simplest terms is: In terms of mind-understanding, nothing is knowable. That doesn't mean you can't understand what you understand. That doesn't mean you can't know what you know. Those people who have been at ICODA for a while know that one thing I say frequently is, "Everyone knows everything." We even had a workshop titled that. What I'm saying is, recognize. I'm encouraging you to recognize that it's so far beyond all that, that "what is" is so far beyond all that. Plug into that unknowableness, plug into that unknownness, and many things that are upside down will go right. Instead of plugging into, "What can I know?" plug into, "There's so much I can't know," and your eyes will see more clearly. I'm actually giving you practical advice, although it sounds impractical.

Brook: What you're saying is just accepting.

Premodaya: Accepting is a good word for what I try to talk about.

Brook: Like gravity does, what gravity does. I don't need to know about it, know why it does, it just does.

Premodaya: What I'm saying is more basic. The point I'm trying to make is, not only is there no point to you knowing about it, you can't know about it. There's no way for you to know about it.

Shiloh: How do you know you can't know?

Premodaya: By going as far as you can into plugging into the unknowable, by—using Brook's word—"accepting" it, as totally as you can. When you have accepted it with your absolute capacity, when you have accepted it to the absolute limit of your ability to accept it, then a switch gets thrown in you and everything changes. You reach a threshold, and you get thrown beyond that threshold. Until you get to that degree of acceptance, it doesn't make much sense. I'm not saying you can't know anything; I'm saying that what you can know is unfathomably tiny compared to what's absolutely unknowable. Unknowable doesn't mean it isn't there or you aren't living in it—unknowable just means with this apparatus, there's no way. An apple can't ride a horse, the apparatus isn't right. How does he hold the reins? How does he hold on to the neck if there are no reins? There's no way.

Premodaya: Does that help?

Shiloh: Yes, it's almost like the only way to answer that is poetry.

Premodaya: Yes, art and poetry, is one human answer (a cultural human answer) to what we're talking about, or let's say, response. Poetry, painting, all the arts point that way and, when we are sensitive to whatever art we are sensitive to, they give us some flavor, some moment of standing in the unknowableness. I'm saying you can plant both feet in the unknowableness and live there every minute of the day. For some of us music takes us closer; for some of us painting takes us closer; for some of us dance takes us closer; for some of us the sunset takes us closer.

You can be even closer than that—you can build your house there. You don't have to go to the museum. If you build your house there, something happens, something changes. And that change is possible for everybody. Everybody can build their house there. You pass through the confusion; you pass through the horror; you pass through the fear; you pass through whatever it is that human experience and existence requires passing through, and then something unimaginable and unfathomable takes over, and it takes over in such a way that "why" is never a trap again. Many people in this room are very close to that possibility. My real job is to push you over the edge of that possibility, so if I stir something in you by saying these things, then I'm doing my job good.

Priya: It feels like if you surrender totally to God's will or to the unknown that then, what one would have called one's mission will just ... there's nothing else to happen—but that.

Premodaya: Has that happened to you?

Priya: I feel like it's happening, but I don't feel like it happened.

Premodaya: Because you feel like it's happening, you have some sense of it in some way, like you're doing now, to speak of it. Because you're, let's say, in process. It's a speculation based on observation so far, or experience so far, or feeling so far. My suggestion is, drop the speculation and that will in itself, amount to further surrender. As far as I'm concerned there's no more beautiful word on this planet than "surrender." If you really surrender, aren't you surrendering "why"? Aren't you surrendering the very question "why?" Are you really surrendering anything other than just that?

Priya: It seems like you're also surrendering asking for anything.

Premodaya: Although it seems very hard until it starts to get clear—part two of this question, it's not hard to figure out what your life's mission is, but if it isn't already clear to you, it doesn't really get clear through the figuring-out process which, after all, is mostly mental. It gets clear through getting clear about it, which happens a million and one ways. The distinction I'm trying to make is, if you aren't sure what your life's work is, what your life's mission is, what your purpose is in this life, it will not come to you by figuring it out; it will come to you by allowing it to come to you. Now, this too is very tricky terrain. It's a good thing we have these meetings now every Thursday, because it can't be done in an hour and a half. This is very tricky terrain linguistically.

I will say a little bit about me. As the example, I will use myself. Most people here know something of my history. I worked in the field of psychiatry for over thirty years and had no idea (in fact would have vehemently argued with you) that that was all training for sitting in this chair with you and opening my big mouth. So somehow, being with you is in some way the mission of this life, somehow that was getting worked out, prepared for, trained in for thirty years before any manifestation of what it was going to be used for.

All I can say to you is, I have absolute clarity that the work I do now has been assigned and that it's some kind of mission. Having said that, that's not the point; I also want you to hear that I have no feeling of mission, that I'm not concerned with any kind of mission, toward you or anybody else, and that anything that gets carried out involves me in only the most peripheral way, which means my cooperation with my sense of what I'm supposed to do. Now, if that confuses you, it should. I'm just trying to give you the sense, the flavor, of how subtle it can get, how inexplicable, unexplainable it can get, because I can't explain to you why I'm sitting here, I really can't. Hopefully you can.

Jasmine: You're just sharing yourself, and people get it. I think the greatest teachers, everybody—you just open your mouth and you share of yourself and somebody else can learn from it, get something from it.

Premodaya: Well I don't refute that, but what I'm trying to get at is that it's more wacky than that because if it was up to me ... But it's not. What I'm really using myself as the example for is, if you can start to see—because there's nothing going on that isn't equally true of you—that none of this is up to you, my contention is you're better off. My contention is you're better off, because I know I'm better off. By better off, I don't mean materially, because I'm not better off materially, just the opposite. But you'll be more in tune with whatever that Divine plan, however that Divine plan includes you. I can say that with absolute assurance, but without any kind of ability to tell you what it means. I really want you to get how completely it has nothing to do with me. My contention is your life has nothing to do with you. The sooner you start to see with your own eyes, with your own heart, that your life has nothing to do with you, the clearer everything else will get.

We are trying to talk about what can't be talked about, but it can be provoked; it can be cajoled; it can be hinted at; it can be felt behind the words. So we have to have these kind of strange-sounding discussions to get to some foot onto this. Many people have told me they would like to have my job. Of course, I know that they must be nuts, because my job is to sit in this chair and make sure nobody is sitting in this chair when I sit in it. Now, who would want that job? As much as it may seem different, I swear to you there's no job benefit to this job. There's absolutely no advantage to sitting in this chair. Some of you have heard me say this before— you know I'm a lifelong disciple—I would rather be in that chair. I'm very comfortable in the disciple chair. But it doesn't matter, because now it's my turn to sit in the big chair. Who knows why? As long as you want to sit in this chair, it will never happen. Now, I have a quirky personality, so I'm the kind of guy that never for one second wanted to sit in this chair. I don't like responsibility. I want the easy way, so it is unimaginable, unfathomable, and pretty close to impossible that I would be sitting in this chair. Certainly unpredictable. And that turns out to be right—because nobody is sitting in this chair; this is an empty chair. What am I saying? *You* can sit in an empty chair, too. There's nothing special about me, except that there's nobody sitting here, but that's completely one breath away for you, too. There's nothing special about it, there's no special criteria that has to be met, that you can't meet.

Do you have a mission? No question. I guarantee you that you have a mission in this life. I don't know how to say it other than, "I guarantee it." I don't know what good my guarantee does, but there's no question, from my eyes, that you have an absolute unique role in the Divine plan. Can you figure it out? Not with your brain. Can you find the method for it becoming more clear to you? Absolutely, but it won't be by figuring it out. It will be by some other method, other than brainpower. If it's not clear to you, it will be by some other method. I'll give you one clue that occurs to me, which is, that if you know any piece of it whatsoever, any piece, any aspect, if any part of it is ringing in you, absolutely know it to be true, absolutely trust that fragment and follow that fragment towards the bigger picture. Trust that fragment like mother's milk, because what we tend to do is know a fragment and then say, because we don't know the whole answer, "Well, that fragment doesn't mean much." That fragment means everything. That fragment will take you all the way. If you have a fragment, and most people do, embrace that fragment with your whole life and you will quickly and without a lot of fuss and muss, discover your one-hundred-percent mission. But if you question it even a little bit, if you don't give your whole heart to it, it can't lead you all the way. Give your whole heart to it, trust it, and it will lead you to the whole answer.

People will frequently come here, and they will talk about this, and they will say they have no idea. But when you talk to them a little bit, when you question them a little bit, they actually have some fragment of an idea. It doesn't take more than that. You have to trust it; you have to follow it further; you have to start going into it, start living it, start living from it, start implementing it, and suddenly the horizon is much closer. I suspect that's the situation for the majority of people here tonight. I suspect you may have been telling yourself for a long time that you don't really know what your part is in the Divine plan and I suspect that's a self-deception. I think that most of you who are here tonight have at least some vague sense. Embrace that sense one hundred percent; it will be right.

KNOW WELL, THAT YOU *ARE*

Premodaya: The only reason we have these meetings is to have an opportunity to be together and, in whatever form works, communicate (notice I said "communicate," not "talk about") about what matters. Really communicate what matters; because everybody is communicating something every second of every minute of every hour of every day of every year. You can't not be communicating; even if you're sitting silently by yourself with no one for miles around, you're communicating something.

We are always in this sea of communications. We very much like radios; we're always transmitting and we're always receiving, and we are more or less aware of one or the other or both sometimes, or not much. The kind of folks who are interested in coming to a meeting like this tend to be, usually, more aware of what's coming in and what's going out than, let's say, the average person, who wouldn't be caught dead at a "spiritual discussion."

The interesting thing is, there's always a communication going on. On every level (no matter what, whether you're aware of it or not) including from you to yourself, including from your body, your mind, your psyche, your soul, your consciousness—to you. Again, people who might be found at a meeting like this probably have some interest or have thought about or have some experience with tuning into that—trying to connect more with what's already being "text messaged." The interesting thing is, there's no better transmitter for you to receive from, than you. It isn't some cosmic message coming from out there; it's not some essential truth being beamed across the universe (although those things are always there, too) because it's not really about the form of it. It's not really about the actual mechanisms; it's about the essence; it's about the message and the meaning.

If you really become ultrasensitive you will become like peoples of other cultures or peoples of other times, particularly ancient times. You'll see messages everywhere. You will hear messages from all directions. We have become very ignorant; we have become very poor culturally in terms of understanding how everything, always, is telling us something. In the general culture, if we there's some discussion or someone reads something about omens, symbols, and foretelling things or reading into things, it's generally seen as superstitious or as ignorant or primitive. Well, what's primitive, what's ignorant, is not recognizing the basic fact of that. What's ignorant is not recognizing that everything carries a message and it's not about how loud is the message; it's about how sensitive are you as a receiver? How much have you honed your understanding so you can interpret the message rightly?

For some cultures a tree has much to teach; for some societies a mountain is a source of information; cloud formations have something to show; weather changes mean something more than just weather. But we have lost all that; now we just dismiss it; "it's unscientific; it's unintelligent; it's outdated." That's our loss; in my opinion, that's our loss. Everything is alive! If everything is alive, and every thing and every moment and every situation, is a communication, obviously it's our loss if we say, "No, that's not going on." Instead, in our culture, in this day and age, in this country—we are barraged with literally an incalculable level of meaningless worthless messages: "Buy this; eat that; go here; spend that; buy this car; smoke these cigarettes; eat this pie; buy this condo!" It's *all* advertising; it's all commercial; it's all business transactions. Could it be any more worthless? No human body, no human being, no human organism has ever been meant to be barraged all day long with verbal and written messages, everywhere you look. Go find a place in any city where there isn't a billboard, where there isn't a soundtrack, where there isn't some kind of message being aimed at you, beamed at you, pounded into you all the time, even in your own home.

This is a level of stimulation that has never been seen in any culture, in all of history, any time on this planet. We don't know what the result is going to be of this kind of organismic systems overload. People born today—who knows what it's going to be like fifty years from now, given this unnatural level of stimulation? Of messaging about nothing! If the message mattered, if it was something more than "buy this car instead of that car," it might make some sense; you might be able to make an argument that there's some point to it, but my contention is there's no point to any of it; it's just about selling me something. It can't be right; it can't be good, to be barraged from morning till night every day, ceaselessly.

So, this is unique in human history that we are swimming in a soup of worthless and meaningless messaging and, at the same time, worthwhile messaging, messaging that is the message of Universal Truth, is available, is also going on, is also being communicated in every breath by every living thing. By you, by everyone you have ever met, by every thought that occurs to you and every feeling that has ever arisen in you, by every experience and every circumstance, but we ignore this, in general.

Your body, your very body, is a finely tuned message center transmitting nonstop to you and to everyone and to everything. Your blood circulating is no less meaningful than the biggest widest rushing river and what it has to say about existence, if you listen. Essentially, primarily, and above all, the message at the base is, "Here we are." The message is, in its simplest form, "I am," whether the "I" is a rock, whether the "I" is a tree, or whether the "I" is you, or whether the "I" is the entire galaxy. It would be even more precise, more accurate, to take out the "I" from the "I am" and just say "am."

Lucas: This "am-ness"—it eludes me. I've always identified myself with people around me, what they're thinking, and with other people, and it's like

I'm too scared to really take a stand and say, "I am, I am!" I tend not to do that. I tend to say, "What are you thinking?" Except in crisis, a force in me comes through and takes over, and then, after the crisis is over, it disappears.

Premodaya: Yes, in a crisis "I am" doesn't care what you're doing; it takes over, it can't wait for *you*.

Lucas: Right—a very powerful force. It's like I'm too scared to really put it together and bring that out and be public with it.

Premodaya: Isn't that strange? Because, nevertheless, whatever your attitude, whatever the fear, whatever you think you're doing or not doing with it, it is what it is. You are! No matter what your stance toward it is. That's the strange phenomenon of it.

Lucas: It's a lot of thoughts of timidity and stuff, and that's what I'm going by.

Premodaya: Irrespective of all thought of timidity, you are!

Lucas: Yeah, I don't feel that.

Premodaya: Irrespective of what you don't feel, you are!

Lucas: That makes sense.

Premodaya: Whether it makes sense or not, you are! This is a very essential point—that whatever you think or feel or know or do about it, has nothing to do with the fact that you *are*. Which is more essential? The fact that you are, or what you think about it or what you think you're not doing right with it or how you feel you can't plug into it or how you feel timidity is going on? Which one matters?

Lucas: That's obvious. I just wish I wasn't plagued with all this stuff.

Premodaya: My whole point is, to see how you *are* matters so much more than wishing you weren't plagued with all this other stuff.

Lucas: I think I'm looking for God; maybe I'm looking for me.

Premodaya: Irrespective of whatever you are or aren't looking for, you are.

Charlie: What you were talking about, what you were pointing at, I experienced as a shift in perception. A movement away from conceptual understanding (using words and talking) to nonconceptual. And by the very nature of nonconceptual I really can't talk about it, so I'm going to just be, letting the words sort of swim up. What swims up is—I am the reality that I'm trying to understand and at some level, being is easier than knowing. We simply are; there's no work at all involved.

Premodaya: Really, being is all you can do. You're talking about being versus knowing, and I agree with you. Being can only be; knowing isn't involved. Knowing is like icing on the cake, but ultimately, you can't say anything definitive about what you know. You can't say anything that can be ultimately and absolutely defended, but being needs no defense; being needs no explanation. Being is inviolable. Knowing; you can twist it around.

There's nothing wrong with knowing; I'm not saying there isn't something to be known, but ultimately what's to be known is being, because every question and every answer is resolved in being itself, in the fact that you are. Nothing else is more primary than that, so why not be concerned, why not put attention on, why not try to understand better that which is most primary? My terminology most typically is—"That which matters most." That's what we have lost sight of in this culture, if you ask me.

We have billboards telling us what we should buy. Cultures, for example, that have totem poles; that's also a kind of billboard, but a totem pole represents the elemental forces of the universe and its advertising I AM; EX-ISTENCE IS; the UNIVERSE IS, remember it, take a moment and notice it. It's not saying buy this car or these clothes. We've become a very poor society that we never communicate about what matters. We send no messages purposefully, generally, broadly, in the culture about what matters; we only send messages about how to get your money. So it's up to you; you have to decide for yourself; you have to be the counteracting force in your life if you're going to start hearing messages that matter more, above and beyond the messages of commercialism. Nobody can make that happen for you, other than you. You have to decide what matters; you have to attune yourself to what's significant; you have to decide what you want to be receiving.

Casey: Wouldn't that be falling into judgment if you were to say, "I want to receive this, but I'm not going to receive that."

Premodaya: It's not really judgment; it's discrimination. You have the responsibility to discriminate, to discern, to make a discrimination about where you want your attention. It's not judgment in the same sense as when we judge, "This is good or this is bad," or "I want this but I don't want that," or "Give me pleasure but keep out the pain." It isn't judgment for that reason and on that level; it's discrimination, responsibility, about whether your attention is going to be focused on what matters or what doesn't matter. Only you can make the final decision about what matters and what doesn't matter. Now, my argument would be that the majority of people in our culture, when push comes to shove, would decide that the commercial message matters quite a bit, but I don't think most of the people in this room would agree with that. The majority, the popular opinion, isn't necessarily the best opinion. So really not judging (in the negative sense) means being more discriminating.

Casey: But how do you draw the line? At what point are you going to stop discriminating? What if you're questioning yourself every which way? I know it's mind that's asking that question, which is something that it should not do.

Premodaya: No, there's nothing wrong with mind. Mind isn't the enemy, mind isn't the culprit. There's no line that needs to be drawn. If you start focusing more on what matters and start focusing less on what doesn't matter, no line is needed. It will sort itself out through your own intelligence, through your own experience, through your own increasing wisdom that comes from that process. See, that's the mind's question, "Where do I draw the line?" It's saying, "I don't trust myself to not fall into the kind of judging, the kind of judgment that is counterproductive, that keeps me separate, that makes me not recognize what matters." I'm saying you can absolutely trust yourself. If you're sincere and you start actually discriminating, actually saying "No" to what doesn't matter and "Yes" to what does matter (to whatever degree), if the proportion changes, if you're going in the right direction, you can't help but be benefited; you can't help but get more clear; you can't help but develop clearer eyes and better ears; you can't help but become more sensitive, and then the question doesn't arise, "Where do I draw the line?" because your own increasing sensitivity will not take you the wrong way.

The fact that you're here (and I don't mean here, this meeting, me, ICODA, I just mean any gathering of this type), the fact that you're here is the proof that you're smart enough and sensitive enough already to go further. No more proof is needed and no more proof could be more valid than that. All that's needed is a little more trust that you're smart enough, that you're not going to fall into some swamp if you start putting your attention a little bit more on what matters and a little bit less on what doesn't. It's an experiment you have to run with your own consciousness and then you start to see.

Even the culture isn't the culprit, because the culture does what the culture does. That's why I'm saying it's your responsibility; you can't sluff it off on the culture and say, "Well, the culture's screwy, and too bad for me, I was born in this culture." You're smart enough; you don't have to buy the cultural line; you don't have to subscribe to the societal party line. In fact, it's your responsibility, it's your obligation, to do better than that. That's why you come to a meeting like this; that's why anybody comes to a meeting like this—that's why I come to a meeting like this. That's the only reason anybody ever shows up; it's because something in you, some part of you knows very well that you can do better and you're trying to do better. What I'm saying is more revolutionary, is more radical—I'm saying you're doing better! You just have to start seeing that. You have to start trusting that that still small voice, or that unquenchable yearning, or whatever it is for you, isn't just real, but trustworthy.

I'm in the strange position (due to my job description, but also what my eyes see, puts me in the strange position) of often being much more confident in you than you are. Much more struck by your actual already-present wisdom, already sincere heart, already Truth occurring, than sometimes, clearly, you can see. So I have to argue with you and somehow convince you, somehow cajole you into a little more considering that it isn't so far away, it isn't so ethereal, and that you're much closer than you tend to think. All of that is based on the hard fact that—you are. It isn't some idealistic, hopeful attitude on my part; I'm not that type of guy; those who know me know that. It's because I see you! And if you could see with my eyes, you would see it too, and my whole purpose is to encourage you to let your eyes become more like how mine have become, not because mine are better than yours, but because everyone has the same potential to see more clearly.

You're always shining, you're always radiant, you're always love itself, you're always wisdom embodied; and I don't give a flying yahoo what you think! Until you see that more for yourself, as much in yourself as in other people, then you will continue to argue with me that something is wrong. "Well, I don't have this enough" or "This isn't working for me yet; how do I fix it?" or whatever. I will play that game with you because that's in my job description, but don't for a moment think that I'm in any way deluded about who and what you are.

If you disagree with that point, not every word I say, but that one point, if you don't see that you are radiant consciousness and that you are a sacred being, no less and no more part of the Divine than anything and everything else, then just understand that is all I'm trying to do is to help you, get you, to see that and know that. For the simple reason, and for no other reason, than I can't help seeing that and knowing that anymore. I don't have the ability to shut it off anymore; it's been taken away. Please God that it be taken away from you too! It's completely possible, and it's not far away and it's likely for most of you, in your lifetime. So you can keep listening to your own inner dialogue that says, "I need more of this and less of that" and "Here's what's wrong and here's what needs improving" (and see where that gets you), or you can listen to me and just a little more consider the possibility that God doesn't make mistakes, Existence doesn't mess up, and you are an expression (no matter what you think), you are an expression of Perfection itself.

Lucas: I have to admit I'm a very loving person. Since you used the word "love" it suddenly became a little more clear, I am.

Premodaya: I have a very hard job; I have to pretend I'm listening to you, and I have to listen to all this nonsense knowing full well that you're out of your mind, because unless you're in some way saying, "I AM and what is IS, and I see the perfection of it," then you're just in some way, deluded. The whole point is that delusion doesn't have to last your whole life; that delusion can be sorted out. If you're willing, if you put some effort into it, if you use your mind, if you open your heart, whatever the method, whatever the path—you have to do it. I'm one of those folks whose job it is to help people do it, but I can't do it for you.

Grant: It depends on my starting point, where I bring my attention from: if I have a focus on things outside of me or from the I AM spot. If I start with the I AM spot it's like driving a car with a clean windshield, so all the outside stuff seems to shift and come into more clarity coming from a spot acknowledging I AM. I don't think there's a separation between what the world is doing or the I AM. It's just the orientation, whether I come from the I AM through the outside world or just stay in the outside world.

Premodaya: That's the point that we are talking about made in a different way, made in a very clear way, about attention. Where do you put your attention? You have a choice about that; you have an absolute ability to choose where your attention goes. You're just explaining that your experience of that is if you put your attention on I AM, on the factualness of existence, then you get a different result than if you put your attention on more peripheral things.

Grant: Well, the peripheral things seem to be more rewarding if I come from the I AM part first.

Premodaya: Same thing. It's a good point because it points out how the direction is so irrelevant. Just remember one thing; we are taught from the very beginning to always put our attention outward. From the first moment you pop out, everything is drawing your attention outward. That's why you forget yourself; that's why you forget the fact you are. That's why you end up talking about timidity or about fear or about whatever ends up being the story. It's quite radical to start to recognize that the attention, the focus, doesn't have to be one hundred percent going out, that the arrow not only can point that way [pointing outward] but it can point this way [pointing inward, toward himself]. That's what I AM is; the I AM is turning the arrow around and starting to focus in the other direction. This is all that's meant by all the traditions and ancient wisdom paths and meditative systems and yogas and everything else; it's all just about reversing the arrow, reversing the direction, about turning your eyes inside out and reversing the habit that we all have (because we're taught it from day one) that our attention goes outward. We are in essence habituated to be moving to the outside world, and I AM is the inside world.

When that's reached, the division drops between the outside and the inside. That's the possibility, for that division to be recognized for what it is, as an arbitrary boundary, as an arbitrary idea, that we all have signed off on culturally, but reverse that arrow even just a little bit, and everything changes. Suddenly you will understand what couldn't be understood before. Nobody can turn your eyes around for you, but you can be willing to put your attention a little bit more, a little bit more purposefully, with a little bit more awareness, a little more discrimination, on "Am I focused on what matters? Can I focus a little less on what doesn't matter?" Your intelligence knows exactly what that means, and you can absolutely trust yourself to get yourself there. The whole universe will help you, but you have to do it.

TRUTH CANNOT BE SPOKEN

Premodaya: If you're here at a meeting like this, you must be in some way or shape or form interested, to whatever degree, in what people refer to as the Truth. Now this is a very serious problem, because the fact is that the Truth can't be spoken about, can't be put into words, can't be communicated, can't be conceptualized. So what are we doing here? Well, this is the whole problem—if we came here and just sat in the Truth and didn't have a chat, and didn't interrelate, nobody would be sure what's going on! And the mind would grab that and say, "Well, there's no Truth here, there's nothing to be learned here." So we're all stuck with words, with trying to communicate that which cannot be communicated about. But it can be felt; it can be known; it can be experienced; it can be discussed to a degree, with the understanding that that discussion isn't the Truth, that it's only a rough groping towards something.

This is a continuous problem; it's always a problem, because it's so easy to mistake the talk for the Truth. It's so easy to not recognize that the map is not the territory. We have to make do; we have to make do with what we have, which is words, meetings like this, each other, some kind of interchange. At some point it has to be understood more clearly that the Truth does not live in words, and the ability has to be evolved, has to be developed, to feel beyond the words, to get the message that isn't being said out loud, because it can't be; nobody can. Now if I just came here and sat here, nobody would come, but some day in some way every person who's sincere about finding what they have to find gets to the point where they realize for the first time, more or less, that it isn't in the words; that it isn't an idea; that Truth, Reality, God, whatever you want to call it, isn't a concept; it isn't a *thing*, isn't something you can grab and hold in your hand and stick in your pocket and keep.

We are all in a strange situation; here we are gathering together to talk about what matters, talk about that which is the Ultimate, but it can't really be talked about. It can only be groped toward. In the face of the Truth, in the face of that which is most Profound, we're all little babies crawling toward it—that's the most we can hope to achieve. Any idea other than that, is us fooling ourselves, fooling ourselves that we can put it in a box and tie a ribbon around it and do something with it—because it isn't even an "it," so how can we put it in a box? You can't *get* Truth. If it was an "it," you could get it. If it was an "it," somebody would have packaged it already; there'd be a Truth store on the corner and you would have to save your money because I'm sure it would be expensive. Then you could go and make a purchase and you're all set! But because it's not an "it," it's very difficult for any human mind to grasp it in its non-graspable nature. Because we are all trained, we are all conditioned to turn everything into an "it." That's what the human mind does automatically, to make it into a thing. Even the word "God" has a "thing" quality to it; it's not really abstract for most people. For most people, when you say the word "God," whether they have a negative reaction to that word or super-positive reaction to that word, it still takes on a thing-like quality. God is a person; God is an energy; God is a whatever. The mind immediately puts a package around it and gives us some kind of image, some kind of sense that "thingifies" it, that makes it into an object, that makes it something that we can somehow capture.

The first thing to understand, more than anything, is you can't capture the Truth—but you can be captured by it. You can't grab it, but it can grab you. If you recognize the true proportion of things, if you recognize how tiny we are and how vast the Truth is, then you get some kind of sense, some kind of feel for how it's possible that the Truth can get you, but you can't get it. Some people define God, or the Truth or Reality, as the Whole, as all which is, and I have no quarrel with that definition. So how does a person grab all that is? You can't, but *all that is* can grab *you*. The whole trick is to become grab-able. The whole trick is to melt enough, become porous enough, become fluid enough, become soft enough, that it can flow toward you, instead of the wacky idea that we are somehow going to get it. Until that's better recognized, we stay stuck in concept—meaning our idea of it, and our idea of it means it's an idea and nothing else—it's not God; it's not Truth; it's not Reality; it's not what is; it's not the Ultimate. It's our idea and nothing else. We fight wars over that; we kill for that; we die for that—all for an idea. If you happen to have been born in China you have one idea; if you were born in New Jersey you have a different idea; if you were born in Winnipeg you have yet another idea. If you speak this language you have these kinds of ideas, and if you speak that language it's a different set of ideas. Ideas are really quite arbitrary. If we put you in a room and feed you three times a day and keep you there for a month or two and talk to you every day, we can change your ideas. You'll walk out with a whole new set of ideas if we structure it right (and some governments are very good at this) and all the ideas you thought mattered to you will change, because concepts aren't hard to change.

If you can plug into the notion that the Truth is not a concept, God is not a concept, Reality has nothing to do with what our concept of what Reality is, then you're starting to grope your way in the right direction, but most of us don't even come close. In the average lifetime we stay stuck in concepts; we never question that our concept of something may not be in any way significantly related to whatever it is.

This is why in spiritual circles all the talk about the mind, and "you have to transcend the mind and go beyond the mind" it's correct, but it's rarely talked about intelligently, in a way that gives the real understanding, which is not really that the Truth is beyond the mind—because it's even beyond that—but simply that you have to get beyond the mind in the sense that you have to get to the point where you recognize somehow, whatever form that takes, that concepts can't get you there. Concepts can't lead to that which is Ultimate and Profound, because concepts are just our ideas. They can be right ideas; they can be wrong ideas, but they are still just ideas. Even if they are the right ideas, even if they somehow suggest what may actually be, they can never go far enough to actually take us to the door that leads to the real Truth, to actual Reality, to real God, for the simple reason that our idea is just our idea. Even if the whole world agrees, if everybody on the planet says, "Yes, that's right," so what? In fact, usually if most of the planet agrees, you can bet it's way off, simply because most of the planet never gets to the point where it's realized that concepts, by definition, are severely limited.

"Beyond the mind" doesn't have this highfalutin meaning that most of us give it when we hear that phrase. It doesn't mean some grand mystical realm where something lives that's greater than what the mind offers in its ability to conceive, its ability to conceptualize. It simply means the recognition that the Truth has no concept attached to it; it's much more alive than that. It's much more profound than that; it's much deeper than that; it's much vaster than that. It's much more related to what's eternal, to what's infinite, to what's incalculable, to what the human mind can't ever wrap its arms around. "Beyond the mind" means give up the idea that you can have an idea about it. Understand that any idea you have about it isn't it. I'm not saying don't have ideas about it; it's not possible to not have ideas about it. If you have a mind, you will have ideas about it. Just don't believe them; don't bet on them; don't put those eggs in your basket.

Anna: So, you can get it by experience and a deeper understanding. If you get a glimpse of the Divine, that is also the mind, but it's not a concept.

Premodaya: The best way I know to get it, is to recognize that you can't get it, and that's really what I have been saying tonight.

Anna: Any "profound experience" would add to a new idea, to a new concept?

Premodaya: That's up to you whether it adds a new idea or not, but if you start from the simpler, more elemental position that you can't get it, then you're much closer to understanding and/or experiencing how it works. Then your groping may bear some very significant fruit, because if you recognize—not as an idea, not as a belief, not because I say so or some book says so—but if you get it for yourself, that you can't get it, automatically your position changes. Then automatically, without trying, without doing anything, somehow you rearrange yourself, or more accurately, you get rearranged—something shifts, so you aren't putting your effort into getting it. Somehow, something opens in you that makes you more receptive. The trying to get it keeps you in a position that's not really receptive. Anything that makes you more receptive, makes you more available to the Profound. Anytime you're trying to get it doesn't mean your efforts are insignificant or aren't good, but you'll be more effective the more you're able to make yourself receptive in any way possible.

"Receptive" implies a lot. It implies open-minded to a degree most of us never consider, because usually when we say "open-minded," we mean open to this set of ideas, and this set of understandings, or this set of stuff, but not necessarily *any* set of stuff. The more you become receptive, the more you're open and open-minded in the real sense, the more you're not stuck in assumptions; the more you aren't operating from a preconceived set of ideas that expects something in a certain way. Because the Truth can't meet your expectations; God can't satisfy your concept of God. That's diminishing God to the level of a thing. That's diminishing the Truth to a commodity—and the Truth don't play that!

Raj: How is this mental habit of operating by assumptions broken? It's one thing to maybe realize that we attach concepts, but perhaps it's difficult to break.

Premodaya: How close are you to breaking it?

Raj: I can't answer that. I don't know.

Premodaya: So that means you think you're far away, right?

Raj: I try not to think about it too much. I try to be open, but I find myself reactive and that's how I would describe at least one phenomenon of attaching concepts. At one point it really disturbed me how reactive I was really, and now I don't really get too happy or sad depending on what the reaction is, but I still am attached, because I would like to break the habit of attaching the concepts. I've always thought it similar to how physics tries to measure absolute zero and that by measuring absolute zero, they add that little tiny bit of energy such that it's not absolute zero. I try to not think about it, but that itself is just that tiny bit of thought that doesn't allow me to break the habit.

Premodaya: Well, it's a fantastic question from a very sincere questioner, and I enjoyed every second of listening to you because every second contained that sincerity. In your case what has to happen for that attachment to assumptions and concepts to end has already happened, the ability, the willingness to question everything and to simply see that one is operating from—I'll use your word because it's the right word—habitual assumptions. The vast majority of human beings on earth aren't, and in their lifetime aren't likely to ever be capable of making the statement you just made. The statement that, "I'm operating, and I see that I'm operating from habitual assumptions, and I see that doesn't take me where I want to go and I think I should do something about that; I think I should cultivate some way to not live in those assumptions. I think I should cultivate some way to see beyond the concepts that I can sense, that I somehow know are limiting me." To get to the point, at any time in a lifetime, to be able to say that, is ninety-five percent.

The vast majority of people never get even to that. That's the beginning, and they never get to the beginning. In your case, you're so well on your way that even if you wanted to turn back and undo it, it's too late. You understand too clearly that assumptions can't lead to what matters, that assumptions are just conditioning. It's already so clear to you. Now let it get clear that once that has happened like it has for you, you can afford to relax a little bit. Your mind, your ideas, your intelligence is not the enemy. In spiritual circles, very commonly the mind gets targeted. Thinking, like you said, "I try not to think." Well, you must have read somewhere, heard somewhere in some spiritual something, that thinking can't get you there, so better not to think—thinking causes all the trouble. What I want to say to you is: Don't make thinking the enemy, because your thinking has gotten you to the point of recognizing the limitations of thinking. That thinking hasn't hurt you; it's helped you. There's enough intelligence, enough sincerity that thinking is really not your enemy, so don't make thinking the bad guy. It hasn't sunk you; it has helped you; it has lifted you. Now you know—partly as a result of that thinking—that thinking can't take you all the way, but thinking can help, that's why I say, don't make it the enemy. Understanding always involves some kind of thinking. As long as you already know that thinking isn't the whole ball of wax, thinking isn't the boat that's going to get you to the other shore, then you don't have to worry about thinking as a problem. You can risk thinking; it won't take you in a wrong direction because you already know that thinking isn't enough; something more has to happen; something more has to be in the equation than just thinking your way toward it.

I'm really saying to you that your question was, "How do I break that habit? How do I become less attached to my own thoughts?" What I'm saying to you is, that's going to happen for you because what has to happen for that to happen is already the case for you. The best advice that I know for your situation is relax; stop worrying. Stop trying to follow well-meant spiritual advice about the mind and thinking, and just trust much more where you have already come to, because you've come to a point that can be trusted, and with a really open mind, see what comes next. Don't worry about it, don't worry so much. Worrying is trying to think your way out of it. The capacity has already been developed for what you're asking for. Now cooperate with whatever else comes along that your own intelligence shows you is moving you forward, or can move you forward.

I can't say this to anyone and everyone. I can only say it to someone who has already seen with their own eyes that all their assumptions must be wrong, not because they are wrong assumptions, but because by definition, assumptions are wrong; they are too limited; they are preconceived; they're not organic; they're not part of the Truth. You have already seen that with your own eyes, no matter what you have read or what you've been told. The way you speak shows clearly you have seen it for yourself. That's ninety-five percent. The rest flows from that. Really start trusting yourself. Let me put you on the spot. When I say really start trusting yourself, do you think you can do it?

Raj: I don't know.

Premodaya: An honest answer. Only one who would say "I don't know" should really trust themselves. Anytime you want a booster shot of encouragement to trust yourself more, come see me, and I'll remind you to trust yourself, because you can afford to. You won't steer yourself wrong. Your own sincerity will keep you in the right direction. I trust you. My job is to get you to trust you as much as I trust you. I can see who I'm talking to. When you can see the same thing, you will have no issue about trusting yourself. Just a little bit more trust, and you will see that it works. Your intellect is not your enemy. What a sweet guy, huh? [addressing attendees].

Other thoughts, questions?

Kendra: What do you think of "ignorance is bliss"?

Premodaya: I think the person who said it was some idiot.

Kendra: Well, who said it?

Premodaya: Some idiot, who really had his stake in staying ignorant. Because if you promote the idea that ignorance is bliss, then every idiot can fool themselves that they are happy just like they are. Ignorance is not bliss. Ignorance is just ignorance, and the Ultimate can't be known by remaining ignorant. Ignorant means you settle for whatever is easy. You don't think things through; you don't grope your way. Forget about beyond the mind, because if you're ignorant you aren't even using the mind, let alone going beyond the mind. A human life is not meant to be ignorant. You're meant to find your way; you're meant to come to something that matters; get to something of real understanding so that your life isn't meaningless. But since most of the world isn't interested, since most of the world doesn't want to try, since most of the world is easily dazzled by the material—by all that doesn't matter, by all that isn't going to take you anywhere substantial, anywhere meaningful—the notion has to be sold that "ignorance is bliss." Otherwise everybody has to experience themselves as a fool. And no fool wants to do that. Only intelligent people want to know their foolishness. The real fools want to see themselves as wise, as smart, as knowing something. They say ignorance is bliss; they cover it all over to make it OK to just stay where you are and never grow.

Kendra: But then someone like Raj for instance, doesn't he feel a little bit lonely being surrounded by ninety-five percent of people who are more drawn towards "ignorance is bliss"? Also, some of us at least seem to live just fine, because living with your shutters closed, what you don't know can't hurt you. Whereas he is more aware of things, so life will be a little harder for him.

Premodaya: You're not really talking about Raj; you're talking about yourself. It must be true for you that you find it difficult to be around most of the world in their ignorance because you aren't ignorant. So it must be frustrating to you to see all the ignorance around and to have to interact with people that you know are asleep at the wheel, and not trying to grow and not really plugging into what you know to be important. My encouragement to you is don't put your frustration on poor Raj, recognize that it's your frustration, and it's a very understandable frustration. Nobody in this room has any difficulty understanding why that frustration would be there. The antidote is you have to have a really open mind toward even ignorance; you have to see for yourself; you have to develop the ability to see the meaning of someone else's ignorance (and it's certainly rampant) rather than see it as "look how ignorant he is or she is," you have to start to see the meaning of it. The meaning of it is a message to you: "I can see how ignorant he is; I can see how ignorant she is; thank God I'm not that ignorant. Thank God, at least in my life, I have gotten to a point—I have been open-minded enough, I have been intelligent enough, that I'm not stuck where they're stuck." You have to take the encouragement from the ignorant person that you're not that.

Kendra: I have a hard time with that.

Premodaya: That's a shame, because it means you aren't giving yourself enough credit. It means you aren't kind enough yet to yourself to see yourself where you have really come to, that your own intelligence does set you apart. Most of the world is willing to stay ignorant. You aren't in that category. There *is* a loneliness in it; you do feel not part of the majority. That's inevitable, but the good news is, you're not one of the ignorant ones. You have to give yourself that encouragement; you have to give yourself that credit. Otherwise you get stuck (that's what you're describing); otherwise you get stuck in the battle in your mind of, "Why can't they see it? Why can't they give up their ignorance? Why can't they try harder? Why can't they become just a little more intelligent? If I could do it, why can't they do it?" Well, who knows, maybe someday they will. For right now, when that's in front of you, what you know for sure is you have gotten beyond that. It would be nice, it would be less frustrating for you, if in the face of that ignorance you could see your own intelligence and be encouraged by it. That at least you aren't in that position anymore, and will never be again. The whole world can be ignorant, but at least you aren't one of them.

Kendra: But then people conceive you as intimidating and you end up being alone.

Premodaya: Maybe. But if the world sees you as intimidating, then you have to try a little bit harder to show the world your softness. For people like you and me, that isn't easy, but you have to try. When people get to know you a little more, they see that what they thought was intimidating (the intimidation they felt) was not justified. They have to have the chance to know you a little better.

Kendra: I disagree, because if they are mostly ignorant, how can they even realize that?

Premodaya: Because even ignorant people have eyes to see. If they know you a little better, they won't think you're intimidating. It's those that don't know you that think you're intimidating. Once they know you (now maybe you aren't letting them get to know you)—but if you let them get to know you a little bit, they will drop that idea. So don't be so hard on them. They can't help their ignorance. And be much kinder to yourself, that at least you aren't willing to settle for an ignorant position, that you're striving for more intelligence, more of what's real.

Yes, it means you won't be able to have a meaningful or significant relationship with some people; they can't meet you where you are, but you can meet anybody, anywhere. There's more to people than their ignorance and their lack of ignorance; you can find other things to love about a person and other ways to connect. First you have to be a little kinder to yourself, a little more willing to see that even if they think you're intimidating, you know that your heart is more sincere than that. The intelligent people will see you for who you are.

Morgan: We're talking about being receptive and allowing ourselves to be in the space where—

Premodaya: Don't go further. Once you've said the word "allowing," don't go any further. Not even "allowing ourselves," not even "allowing to be," just allowing, nothing else—allowing. Really receptive means allowing without any qualifications, without allowing this or that, just allowing. Whatever it is, whatever comes, whatever shows up, whatever happens, whatever enters in. The real receptivity is having no condition for what comes in. Then if you don't like it, you can throw it out. You can reject it after, but first see what it is; that is the real allowing.

Morgan: What is that based on? How does one deal with intellectualizing or questioning or "overthinking" new information?

Premodaya: It's based on the exact opposite of liking. It's based on recognizing that our liking—which is simply another way of saying preferences—that our preferences are just as much conditioned as any other set of assumptions we have. Those preferences, what we like and what we don't like, is a whole other set of assumptions—also arbitrary, also culturally determined, because if you're born in China, you don't like the same things as if you're born in Rhodesia. If you start to see that your preferences are exactly the method for not allowing; if you see that what you like and don't like is the actual barrier to allowing anything. If you see how that actually works, and really you can see that by thinking it through; if you start to see that one's own preferences are in a sense arbitrary, in a sense taught, in a sense not yours, not natural, you weren't born with them; if you start to see all that, you start to not cling so much to having your way: "I like this, I don't like that; therefore, I don't want that, but I do want that." If you start to be a little easier about your own preferences, then what you're asking about starts to happen. You start to automatically have a sense of allowing that's broader, wider, because you aren't so married to your own preferences. Most of us stay very married to our preferences until that time when what I'm talking about happens, when you start to see for yourself that preferences keep you limited. They don't lead you to what's most important. They serve to keep you in the same position, not moving to a wider position. That's why in the 'Beyond Self' Training program we spend a lot of time, there's a number of weeks devoted to getting beyond preferences, learning how to detach a little more (and only a little is needed).

Once that process starts it tends to grow by itself because as soon as a person has the experience of what benefits come from being a little less focused on one's own preferences, it naturally increases because you see that it benefits you; you see that it takes you much further much faster. So, don't trust your own preferences so much. They are the limitations.

This happened for me when I was quite young. When I was eighteen I went backpacking in Europe. That's what everybody did in those days, all us hippie kids, and it really changed me forever. I don't think anything that has happened could have happened without that trip. I spent the whole summer, and I really went with a tiny little knapsack. I was just a dumb kid, hitchhiking around Europe. Now, if you really have no big plan and you just start hitchhiking around, in the days when it was safe to hitch-hike, anything can and does happen. So you get stranded somewhere; it's ten o'clock at night, and you're out in the middle of a field and the nearest town is not walking distance. I learned a number of things that summer. I learned that I could sleep fine in a field, or on a rock, or in a doorway. I didn't have to have a bed. I slept just fine. One time I remember I slept in a cornfield, and it was pouring rain all night long. All night I was soaked. I didn't get sick. I slept fine. I was wet. Without intending it, accidentally, so many attachments were seen through because of that experience, because everywhere I went it kept happening. I kept getting stranded, and I saw that I didn't have to eat every single day. I saw that I didn't have to have a chair to sit in. Now, up until then, I really thought something terrible would happen if I didn't have a comfortable place to sleep, that if I went a day without eating, I'd be starving, it would be terrible—but it wasn't! I would get stranded, no place to get anything to eat; I wouldn't eat all day; I just kept walking, and nothing bad happened. I slept in the rain in a cornfield; nothing bad happened. And one by one it started to dawn on me that all these things—I didn't have these words then, but it started to dawn on me somehow that these were attachments, and that they were really bogus. And really, what is all that? Preferences.

We have been taught, most of us, to have a preference to have a bed to sleep in. Well, it turns out that's not really required, you can sleep fine without it. We have been taught to have a preference that we should have at least two or three meals a day. It turns out I could have no meals a day and feel just fine. I didn't know that before because I never experienced going a day with no meals. I never experienced not sleeping in a bed, or at least a sleeping bag, something—but just to lie out in a cornfield, I had never experienced that. It opened my eyes to something I had never considered, that all these things weren't really necessary. They weren't absolutely required to be OK. This was a huge revelation. I wouldn't have believed it had you told me; I had to experience it. Something changed permanently from that summer because of that. Some kind of level of fear that I apparently always lived with dropped away.

I'm only giving that example because it shows the process; the process is the same no matter what. The process of seeing through one's own preferences is the same. It doesn't matter how it comes or how it happens to you. It can happen—again, I'll say the intellect isn't the enemy, because it can happen purely intellectually. You can just think your way through that and get to the point where you see "my preferences aren't the be-all and end-all I thought they were."

I learned it the next year again because I lived for a while on an Israeli kibbutz. I lived in a commune, and I was shocked when I found out what the system was, because the system was that you eat communally. That means they divide up the work based on what people are good at or what people like. They have people who are the cooks and they have a communal dining room so you don't choose what to have for breakfast, what to have for lunch and what to have for dinner; the cook chooses it. When they first told me that the first day, I said, "This is terrible. What do you mean I don't get to choose what I have for dinner?" I thought this is the end of the world, because they're going to serve something for dinner that I'm not going to want to eat and then what am I going to do? But it didn't work that way. It turned out that they served really good food and that anything they served, if I tried it, it seemed to be pretty good. And it only took two or three days for me to finally recognize very quickly that the system works fine. I don't have to choose what to eat; it doesn't make that big a difference.

I wouldn't have known that. I really was shocked that first day they told me that. I really thought that if I have to eat what somebody else decides the meal is, "this is horrendous," because I was very spoiled. It didn't take much to see that preference about what to have for dinner doesn't matter much. If it's something I might not prefer, so what? It's still good. That's what I learned very quickly. So, what, it's still good. Because of that I got to see that my food preferences don't count for much; they don't matter much, and that attachment dropped away. So the process is the same, having the experience of not getting your preference and seeing again and again how often it's either just as good or even better than what you would have preferred. When you start to see that with your own eyes, the attachment drops by itself.

Just look in your own life to be a little more experimental, and when you would have chosen something, when you would have exercised a preference (really, I'm giving you this as a suggestion) pick the opposite; do the opposite instead and see if it isn't just as good. Seeing that just a few times for yourself, the attachment shrivels up by itself.

Casey: I'm actually in a place right now where I'm trying to believe more in my preferences because my background was quite the opposite. That's part of my journey and I think my question is really about questioning. It's about what to do about the intellect, and about coming to a road or having choices, and having the intellect almost get in the way, overthinking, moving forward.

Premodaya: Once you start to see that all the overthinking in the world doesn't afford you any more control or give you anything different from what was already going to happen anyway, it's not so much of a problem. This has to be gone into in a little bit more depth than we have time for in the rest of the night, because it's a very significant question for not just you. It's the natural tendency of naturally bright people, and as I was saying to Raj, it's not the enemy. The enemy isn't the overthinking; the enemy is not an enemy at all. The tendency to overthink is simply a symptom. It's simply a sign that some kind of fear is there, some kind of feeling of being cut off from what's natural or what's intuitive or what the heart knows is operating, because the feeling is "I have to figure it out and then I won't go the wrong way. If I figure it out, I'll be better off." This means the fear is driving the show—either doubt or fear or both. The majority of us have this issue of wanting to control it. It's really about control. Figuring it out, overthinking, is about trying to control it. The majority of us live with, consciously or unconsciously, a sense of fear and doubt about how to go forward, so we try to think our way through, and we know, if we're bright enough, that somehow this isn't the best way. We are all in the same boat in that we don't trust ourselves enough, because we have the idea, somehow, that it's up to us, that we have to figure it out; we have to make it happen; we have to control it to such a degree that it's somehow so in our hands that we can take such a terrible wrong turn if we don't do it right. This is everybody.

What I want to say to you as the last thing of this evening is—and I don't know if it's good news or bad news—but that just isn't true. We don't have that kind of control. We don't have that kind of responsibility, for the simple reason that you aren't the author of this life. You didn't get yourself here; you didn't get yourself born; you don't make your heart pump; you don't make your lungs breathe; you don't make your mind operate; you don't know when you're going to leave this planet; you don't know how *one thing* operates, how one hair on your head grows. You can't explain it. You don't do it and yet it happens. You find yourself there, but you are not doing it.

If you're like most of us you have some wrong idea that somehow, you are doing it, that somehow, you're responsible for it, that you have to figure it out, you have to make sure you don't take a wrong turn. You have to be on guard, be watchful that some mishap doesn't happen because you didn't calculate well enough, because you didn't figure out good enough, because you didn't think it through sufficiently, because you didn't bring everything to bear that you should have or could have, and this is just tragic and unrealistic. If you had gotten yourself born, if you made your heart pump, if you could make one hair on your head grow, it would be valid, but all that other stuff is happening without you, without your involvement, without your thinking, without your controlling any tiniest part of it.

My hope for you is, you get more to the point where that's clear to you that you're not responsible for it, and that somehow it has, at least until now, always taken care of itself good enough. That you can let go of the reins and stop worrying and start trusting existence that here you are and it's going OK enough; you're breathing, and the sky hasn't fallen down yet—that somehow you can start to trust even just a little more what's really going on, which you don't control at all.

CHAPTER 14

YOU LIVE IN THE UNKNOWN

Premodaya: Imagine that you don't know what the next moment is going to be. When I'm sitting here talking, I have no clue what I'm going to say. I don't know what the next word is going to be. Imagine not knowing what the next moment is going to be for you. If that's easy to imagine, that's good. If it's hard to imagine, then that's a problem, because that's your actual situation.

You don't have the slightest clue about one second from now. You have not the tiniest bit of control over one second from now. You don't know if you're going to be breathing. You don't know if you're going to be sitting up or face down. You don't know if a meteor is going to come through the ceiling. You don't know if your heart's going to explode. You don't know anything beyond this very second, right now, and even that, you're probably not too sure of.

But that's your real condition. That's what people are running away from—facing that that's the actual fact. I wanted to say "the Truth," but you don't have to get highfalutin; it's a simple fact. You can't say anything about what's going to be one second from now; if your heart will be beating, if your lungs will be breathing. You may have nine fingers three seconds from now—you don't know. You literally have no way. You literally have no say. You literally are the music coming out of the flute. This note may happen next—that note may happen next. You don't know.

I'm not suggesting that you walk around constantly focused on that and all freaked out because if you look up, a safe might be coming towards your head. What I am suggesting is that you at some point—and why not now?—fully get it, that that's the truth. Fully get it that that's your actual situation. You are truly in a situation of the unknown. You are right now sitting in the unknown. We tell ourselves, "We're in the known—the known world." Wherever we are telling ourselves we are, it's a lie. It's a delusion, a commonly agreed-upon social compact, agreed-upon delusion. Illusion. There's no United States. It's lines on a map. There's no California. It's lines on a map. No such thing. If Hitler had won, this wouldn't be California. This would be "Hitler-ana." It's arbitrary. Agreed-upon names and lines on a map, on a piece of paper. Don't believe so steadfastly in these things. They aren't true.

See the truth. You aren't sitting in Los Angeles. You aren't sitting in a room. You are smack-dab, sitting right now and always, in the very epicenter of the unknown. That's where you are; that's what you were born to; that's where you've always been. That's the only place you've ever been. That's the only place you can be.

Isn't it better to know where you are, than to be walking around with illusory ideas about where you are? I'm not saying forget this is Los Angeles. I'm saying first know, primarily know, that you are in the unknown. Because nothing can be known about the next second and nothing is for sure about this second.

If you really face that, and really get it, fully get it, viscerally get it, psycho/physio/biochemically get it, that you are in the unknown and of the unknown—if you really get it in your cells, if you really open yourself to that truth—it'll change you. Something will happen. Something might happen for you, that will be very different for him, and very different for her.

Whatever it is, it will be closer to the Truth. You will be closer to the Truth, because you're closer to what's real. You will have more understanding and more of a right attitude towards what's real. What's real is: You're in the unknown. That's more real than that you're in Los Angeles. When that is more real for you, even for a second, it changes everything. How can the perspective be the same after that? It changes.

Serena: Does awareness take you out of the unknown? Is it a knowing? Is awareness knowledge?

Premodaya: There's a difference between knowledge and knowing. Knowledge you can read in a book. Knowledge is identifiable. It's agreed upon. It's a thing, like a table is a thing. In that sense it's not really happening. It's not really alive. You can be a scholar; you can have knowledge. You can know a lot of things about something.

That isn't the same as knowing. Knowing is alive. Knowing means: You know it more than you know you're breathing, or as well as you know that you're breathing, or that you're sitting here. It's beyond questioning. It's beyond doubt. It's something you absolutely know.

The first thing is, don't confuse knowledge and knowing. When knowing turns into knowledge—usually by us taking something that somebody else knows for ourselves, and then it becomes knowledge—it's not very helpful. It can help with some things, in some ways, but it's kind of a stale thing. First, understand the difference between knowledge and knowing. Knowing is always alive. It's always here and now. It's always fresh. It's always nourishing.

Your question was, "If we become aware of it, can awareness become knowing? Is that knowledge?" That's why I have to first explain knowledge and knowing. "And does it then become not being the 'unknown' anymore?" Interestingly enough, the answer is "no." Because when we say the unknown, it has nothing to do with our logic. Our logic—meaning the ordinary everyday, what we think of as logic—says, "There's the 'known' and the 'unknown.'"

We tend to think of it, at least in Western culture, as: "The 'unknown' is kind of here and the 'known' is kind of there. It's kind of these two things that are about the same size." Really, it's nothing like that.

Think of the unknown as this space [drawing a large circle on a blackboard]. And think of this space as a billion-zillion universes. This space on this blackboard is the "unknown." And this dot of chalk on the board is the "known." Think of that dot as one gazillion-billionth the size that it is on the blackboard. What I'm saying to you I know to be true. It's not knowledge. This is what I know: The known is an infinitesimal tiny, tiny, tiny little subset of the unknown. Here is the important part: *It always will be.* In our culture, we have come to the idea—mostly because of technological advances, knowledge advances—that we will know more and more, and as we know more, the unknown will get smaller.

The unknown doesn't change. The unknown is the totality of eternity and infinity. That's my definition.

How is us knowing something going to change that? How is that going to shrink? That doesn't shrink. It doesn't come; it doesn't go. It doesn't shrink; it doesn't expand. It just *is.* That's why the answer is "no." It doesn't change the proportions. The proportions are what they are, and the unknown and the known do not have a causal relationship with each other. It's not like, "More known, less unknown." The known comes out of the unknown.

This is the mystery. The unknown is a mystery, but not a mystery we are going to solve. This is why in all serious spiritual paths and philosophies, they talk about surrender—whether they use this word or not. There's no real spiritual way that doesn't involve the idea of surrender. This is why: Because you have to surrender. All you can do in the face of recognizing that the unknown means "the unknowable" is surrender to it.

There's nothing else you can do. There's nothing else that makes any sense. When you really get it, there's no impulse that arises other than surrendering to it. It's bigger than your concept of "big." It's deeper than your mind can grasp the notion of "deep." It's more than your mind can conceive in the word "more."

The emptiness isn't empty. It's complete emptiness that's absolutely full. The silence has every sound—and every sound has complete silence in it; every silence has every sound in it. It is so *happening* that there is really nothing to do except—get it. Get it that it's happening. It's happening right now as "you." As this room, as Los Angeles, as the earth, as this cosmos.

YOU ARE THE UNKNOWN

Premodaya: This is the challenge: to be vulnerable. This is the fear: "Well, if I'm vulnerable, what will happen? Something could happen. Something could enter, something I don't want." But that's all nonsense. You're already completely vulnerable. Any thought to the contrary, any sense that you're not is your illusion. It's your desire, your hope against hope, your self-made story that you control something about your life. But you don't know how you got here. You don't know how you're leaving here. You don't even know how you're staying here, in this moment, right now. You control nothing. But here you are! So something is going on.

My whole point about control and this whole idea that the unknown is happening right now is that you're in it—right now. I'm very practical. My whole point is: It's the case already, so why not recognize it? Why not see that it's true? If it's really already the case, it's better to know that. And if it isn't the case, it's better to disprove it and be sure. But my contention is: Nothing can happen that isn't already the case, so what's there to lose?

People who have been around ICODA know that I love to talk about the unknown. It's almost my favorite topic because it really alludes to everything—and the whole society is structured to deny that. Almost by definition, society can't support that. What kind of society is it that goes around saying, "Everything's unknown and we control nothing"?

There's a natural politics to this planet that society represents. I'm saying: Don't mistake that for the truth. That's just the practical side of how the world works. That's what's happened, we've mistaken it for what's real. We have forgotten, and forget easily, that there's no protection from what is. There's no protection from life. There's nowhere to run. There's nowhere to hide. We can turn away and deny and say, "We control something." But I don't buy that.

My teacher Gangaji says, "Face everything." Whatever comes, face it. That's practically her whole message, her whole teaching. Face whatever comes. Meet it directly. It's a beautiful teaching because something is coming all the time. And whatever it is, whatever it looks like, it's the unknown. Every second is the unknown. You are the unknown.

You don't know the next second! You don't know if you'll be breathing. You don't know how many hairs will be on your head in the next second. You don't know who is going to walk through the door. You don't know what's going to fall through the ceiling. Anything can happen any and every second. Yet there's a need to feel secure. There's a human push for protection, so we forget that something can fall through the ceiling at any second. We tell ourselves, "Nah—it's generally safe." Well, as far as things falling through the ceiling, it is generally safe. But as far as what that represents about the unknown, and what we do and don't really control, it's a delusion. It's a lie. It's a self-soothing lie. Life is much more powerful than that. Life is much bigger than that. Anything can happen any second.

Anna: I have two questions. One is how to overcome the fear of the unknown.

Premodaya: It can't be overcome. It can only be met, experienced.

Anna: The second question is about the protection pattern of always trying to control something. It's a conditioned pattern. How can I get rid of it? Allowing it, knowing it's there, I think is maybe even greater than the fear, because it's more happening constantly and automatically. More distressing than the fear that sometimes comes and goes.

Premodaya: That's big progress, that's a huge step forward to be able to say that. Anyone who can say, "I'm *more* distressed—seeing the level of conditioning I'm operating from—is more distressing to me than my own fear and terror," you have arrived at a very good place. Don't leave that place. Stay with that. That's good news.

THE MYSTERY OF LIFE

Premodaya: I would like to share with you that from time to time, during this strange progression that somehow put me in this chair, it suddenly changes. Something else starts happening. The energy changes, and something else is demanded.

It has happened again. I do not know what it means, but I can see that it is a greater requirement on me, a greater requirement to work harder, to touch deeper, to cut away what has to be cut away. Those of you who have been with us for a while know that I never know what is going to happen. I never know what I'm going to say or do. And when it is like this, it gets very strange, because when the energy changes—when a new demand comes along—then it's like a rollercoaster ride. I go, "Oh, my God, what is next? Now what? Now what kind of strange thing is going to happen?" I am just warning you.

Is there anything anyone particularly wants to hear discussed tonight?

Dylan: How the change can happen subtly, as well as dramatically. Because that is what I have been experiencing in the last couple of weeks. It's not like things change dramatically, they are just changing, and it is easy. I wanted to generate some income in a different way and it happened quite easily. It didn't seem like there was a lot of time or effort or energy spent on the change.

Premodaya: What has changed in how you perceive things and what you are aware of? What has changed in your awareness?

Dylan: Part of it was I listened to one of those CDs that I bought here, "You Are A Rocket Ready To Launch." The example on that was: If you want a different car, just go get it. Don't spend a lot of time doing it—just do it. And so, I applied that principle to see if it would work with generating more income in a different way, and it did. It wasn't a big deal.

Premodaya: That's the point. That's a change in awareness. You became aware that not a lot of time and energy has to go into what needs to be done in life, in the world, on the material level—everyday problems—everyday things that need to be done. Because the point as I recall on that CD that I was trying to make is that we spend most of our life energy on things that don't require that. And then there's not much left over for what's important, like Truth, Eternity, God, Salvation—little things like that. We spend most of our life focused on what doesn't need our focus anywhere near as much.

This is the earth. You have to have a roof over your head and some food to eat and some clothes to wear. And this is L.A. You've got to have a car. You've got to have some stylin' clothes to wear. [laughter]

All that has to be taken care of. Spiritual endeavors don't mean you don't have to take care of business. In fact, it more means you have to take care of business, so you can take care of your spiritual endeavors. But you don't have to spend your life on it. You don't have to spend your life on getting a better car, getting a bigger house, getting a prettier wife, getting a richer husband. And most of us do. Most of us spend our life on that.

Your awareness must have changed, that, "I don't have to spend this much time and energy." Nothing changed; only your awareness changed. Nothing changed about how the world works. Nothing changed, believe it or not, about how you do things, because everything is the way it is—but your awareness about it changed. It feels like—it appears like things got easier, but they were always this easy.

All that extra energy that most of us put on all these other things, that's *us*. All that doesn't change how things are. All that effort, all that concern, all that focus, doesn't bring it any closer than the minimum effort of focus needed to bring it. That's why it's such a waste, because only the minimum is needed. On the material plane, only the minimum is needed, whatever that may be.

For some things it's more than for others. If you want a million-dollar mansion, yeah, it will take a little more. But there's a threshold. Once you hit the minimum [snaps fingers], that's it. It's not like you magically made it appear, but you met the material requirements to get there. What people do, what almost all of us do, is we go way beyond the minimum. We don't recognize that only the minimum is needed. You don't have to spend eighty-eight hours thinking about the new car you want. It takes about a few hours at most to decide, but most people spend eighty-eight hours. That serves as a distraction from everything else—everything that can actually change your life.

There really aren't any subtle changes or any dramatic changes. There's just changes. The changes happen whether you attend to them or not. If you sit in a room and never move for the next year, a lot of changes will continue to happen without you doing a thing—I guarantee you. But we occupy ourselves and tell ourselves that these occupations, these activities, these movements, these strivings, make the difference—cause and effect. Well, you have to do your part, but they don't necessarily make the difference.

We get caught in this idea that it's all up to us, and we miss how things actually work, how things are going on all the time without us—how change happens, whether we want it to or not. If we like it we ascribe the change as due to our efforts. If we don't like it, we tend to ascribe it elsewhere. All I'm really saying is: Consider that you can cooperate with change, but you can't cause change. Change is bigger than you are. Change comes with being here, with simply existing. Every single day of your life you wake up completely different, but you didn't cause it. We live in a very strange, strange world and, to not have to confront the strangeness of it, we spin a whole set of stories to explain what's going on.

That's the whole problem—the stories are just stories. It's not what's going on. What's going on can't be explained. It's completely mysterious. It's not mysterious in the sense of it's an "unknown." It's mysterious in the sense that it's an unknowable. It's a real mystery. A real mystery can never be solved, can never be answered. It can just be experienced.

We tell ourselves the explanation of how and why and who and what, so that we can feel more secure that things aren't so strange. But things are *so* not about *us*. It's us making ourselves the center of the story. But we aren't the center of the story. We're not any more the center of the story than a blade of grass is the center of the story. We're not any more the center of the story than the wind is the center of the story. Or if you like it more positive, we're just as much the center of the story as a blade of grass or as the tallest mountain or as this galaxy.

Now, this isn't a fault. We're taught this from the time we arrive. We're given an explanation of what's life, what you are—here's your name; here's the family you were born into; here's who we are; here's what you need to understand; here's what is correct. And it's all stories! None of it has anything to do with the mysterious, inexplicable and unknowable nature of all of it, including you. There's nothing wrong with the stories, unless you believe them. I mean they're entertaining; they're enjoyable (unless they're horrifying).

The subtle or dramatic nature of change is the name of the game. It doesn't matter if it's subtle or dramatic—that's a point of view, and you're along for the ride, whether you signed up or not. It's like you wake up and find yourself strapped into the rollercoaster. That's basically a simple definition of life. From that point on, if you ask me—and that's everybody's experience—it's all about trying to get comfortable, trying to make sense of it, trying to not have the ride be so wild.

But it's a wild ride! The proof is, in the end you'll die. You'll be torn apart. The rollercoaster will take off into outer space. You thought it was wild going up and down; wait 'til it's off the track! But you'll be calmer then, because you'll be acutely aware that there's nothing more you can do. You'll realize completely that you can't change a thing and the ride is going to go—whether you want to go or not.

That's already your situation. Every teaching for thousands of years is simply to point out that this is already your situation, that this isn't something that happens when you die or are in some high state of consciousness or in some altered state or whatever. It's all already the case. Any change that can happen, in that sense—and this gets very hard to wrap your mind around, but it's true—has already happened. Can you wrap your mind around that?

Time is our idea. If it's possible for it to be, it already is. We parcel it out into sections of time, but it's continuous. There is no "sections of time." There's just time. I'm not saying forget about time. Time is what we are stuck with. But see beyond it. I mean, what's change? Change is time. What possible idea of change or concept of change or understanding of change could you have without time, right? But then, factor in: There's no such thing as time. There's just *what is*. And we parcel it out for ourselves as "This is this time; this is this space; this is what's happening; that's what happened before; that happens later; this isn't happening." None of that is true. It's all at once. That's the only way it could be. Either existence is or existence isn't. And here we are. Existence *is*.

If you don't complicate it with ideas, trying to analyze it and understand it and put a rope around it, then it makes sense that existence just *is*. It's all together; it's all happening without any divisions. One of the main divisions, we call "time." One of the main divisions besides that, we call "space." Within that, we have divisions: past, present, future; here, there; further away, closer. These are all ideas. They don't exist in the mystery of reality. Reality doesn't care about your ideas; it doesn't care about ideas that have been around for tens of thousands of years—still dead wrong. They can be around for tens of millions of years; it doesn't make them more right, more correct. The Truth is just the Truth—all at once. There isn't this basket of Truth and that basket of Truth, or this existence versus that existence, or this part of existence and that part of existence—existence doesn't have any parts.

All these ideas and concepts and so-called "understandings" have a utilitarian aspect, and if we stayed with the utilitarian aspect—the useful part, the part that helps us in whatever way it helps us—then we are fine; then there's no confusion and there's no problem with it. The problem with it is, we start to believe it in place of reality; we start to take it as reality; we start to define what is, through those concepts—then we fight about it. That's the only problem. The problem isn't concepts. Concepts aren't a problem. Concepts are what the mind does best; the problem is we take them seriously. They're not symbols of the Truth; we take them as *the Truth,* and a symbol can't be the Truth—a symbol can't be the reality; the indication can't be the thing itself. The sign to the men's room *isn't* the men's room—you pee on the sign, you'll get arrested.

What I'm really saying to you, is that everything we see, and everything we experience, and everything we feel and everything we perceive, is a sign of the Truth, a symbol of it, a representation of it. The proof of God is that you feel it, not that it can be demonstrated objectively. We live in a universe of symbols that we mistake as objects, that we call objects, that we give solidity to when no solidity is actually there. Physics has proven decades ago that a table is just empty space, even though it seems solid to us. This isn't even news.

All these changes are going on all the time, but we aren't really keyed into them because we aren't sensitive enough; we are too focused on what we perceive as solid. This is why I know, personally for me, that some change is happening in how I have to work, what's required of me, because I don't take it as solid. I don't take an internal sea change as specific. I just know something's happening and it's going to require something different from what's been required so far. But the signs are clear: I feel completely different; I perceive completely different; I respond completely different. In that sense, it's very dramatic, but it's actually very subtle. You can't see it, but I'm aware of it—it's not like I look at all different.

I'm using myself as the example—that's going on with everybody all the time. But you may or may not be more keyed into it, so that you're to some degree aware of how everything is shifting all the time. You aren't standing still; you can't be—you're on a rollercoaster; how is it not shifting constantly? If you're on a rollercoaster, everything is changing every second. One second later you're in a different view entirely; your stomach is in a different place. The trick is to get to the point where you aren't resisting the nausea, because if you accept the nausea, if you allow that, if you allow yourself to go, "Wooaaoah," it quickly turns into something much nicer than nausea, it quickly becomes joy and ecstasy and fun and bliss and excitement and every kind of adventure. And I'm not a guy who likes rollercoasters, but I am a guy who recognizes that I'm on one, and I would like you to recognize that. You don't have to like it; you don't even have to cooperate with it (most people don't), but you at least have to recognize it. And the smart money cooperates with it and enjoys it.

You're on a mysterious ride and you don't have the slightest clue— nobody does—about what it is, what it means and how it happens; nobody knows a thing, nobody. It's completely a mystery. That's what I'm encouraging you to accept. That's what I'm encouraging you to see with your own eyes, to figure out, any way you get there. I don't care how you get there, but to get it: That it's first and foremost, and last and finally, a mystery—and nothing else.

Any explanation we have for ourselves is a temporary breather from the ride, trying to forget that the rollercoaster is moving. So if you're willing to live without explanations, you're closer to the Truth. If you're willing to live with the sense that, "This is a mystery and I'm strapped in"—as far as how I look at things, you're closer to the Truth.

Different factions come along and they say, "The guy who is running the rollercoaster is wonderful and beneficent and is fatherly and will take care of everybody in the end." That's kind of like the Judeo-Christian religious view. Then there are other folks who come along and they say, "It's a demonic, terrible guy running the machine and he'll give you a terrible ride." That's a different point of view. You can have a positive view of life, you can have a negative view of life, but none of that matters. What matters is to see that it's a mystery—because you can't accept it until you see it, until you plug into the mysteriousness of it, until you let it permeate. And then, immediately, if it actually permeates, what can you do? You see there's nothing you can do; you see that to have an idea that it can be controlled by ourselves is ridiculous—wishful thinking.

There's an automatic profound humility that occurs once it's seen. If it's seen, it's accepted. If it's accepted, it changes you. If it's accepted at the core, it changes you. It makes you humble. It puts you in the proper proportion. It takes away the grandiosity and the crazy ideas that we are these big things that control and change everything and make things happen. We don't make anything happen. In a positive way, it cuts you down to size. All the arrogance gets blown away in a puff of smoke, and you become humble, in the most positive sense.

Humble in the positive sense means you recognize that something grand is going on. You feel gratitude that you can even recognize it. You start to see a sweetness you never saw before, in everything. Those are the *real* subtle changes, when everything becomes different, when everything you see, you see differently, when every sound you hear, you hear differently, when every feeling that's in you starts to feel different—all very subtle. It sounds dramatic when you describe it that way, but there's nothing dramatic about it. And, probably, most of the people in this room have had some taste of this (if not more than a taste).

Most of humanity is living with the idea, expressed or not, that somehow, some day, some way, everything can get explained. All I'm saying is: Drop that crazy idea. Nothing that really matters, that really means anything, will ever be explained. What really means anything? This, existence, life. Who is going to ever explain this? It's beyond explanation. Explanation is an idea of the mind, a way the mind categorizes. "Let's explain it." Life can't be explained. Life is way beyond your mind, any mind, all minds. Life is not a mind phenomenon.

We bring our little categories up against the Grand Mystery and say, "Well, let's take a stab at it." It's crazy—there's no point in it; it goes nowhere. Then you get philosophies and religions and schools of thought, and all kinds of stuff, which are all just attempts to explain what can't be explained, what will never be explained, what can only be felt, intuited, and lived and experienced. It can be related to, but with your whole self, not with just your mind trying to turn it into an idea, and that's what we do, most of the time. Then people complain about being confused. I guarantee you, if you never use your mind again you'll never be confused. There's nothing wrong with the mind; just don't use it to explain the mystery that has no explanation—that has to be lived—not explained.

You're already living it. You're already on the rollercoaster. You have never not been on the rollercoaster. You will never not be on the rollercoaster. Accept that, and you have accepted everything. But you have to feel it. You have to know it's true. I don't mean, 'just accept it as an idea,' or 'because I say so,' or 'because somebody said so.' You have to know it. You have to know the truth of it.

Casey: I feel like I've gone through layers of it. Sometimes it feels exhilarating and other times going into almost feeling nauseous.

Premodaya: Yeah, it can make you feel that you're going crazy, because that's what we're defending against. The whole attempt is to not feel like you're losing your mind. The more you let it in, a moment comes—it really doesn't last long, necessarily, it can if you protract it—where you have to feel like you're losing your mind. There's no other possible experience—in fact, that's the sign that you're really letting it in. If you don't get to a point where you feel like you could go crazy thinking about this or hearing this or pondering this or considering this or feeling this, or whatever it is, then you aren't letting it in. That's a good sign. If you vomit, it's an even better sign.

This is the promise of serious spiritual inquiry—you will get sick; you will feel like you're losing your mind; you'll get dizzy; your stomach will do flip-flops; you will have a panic attack. Something along those lines is the sign that you're actually, seriously opening yourself to something. Without those signs you're probably spinning a mind game or telling a story.

Monique: What if you feel like you've already done all that; nothing pretty much surprises, or nothing makes me feel like, "Oh, I can't." It wouldn't bring that feeling to me at this point in my life, whereas before, it would. But now it's like, "OK, yeah, I can see that."

Premodaya: Good.

Riley: Does that mean we are enjoying the rollercoaster ride?

Premodaya: It means something has gotten through; you have allowed something that most of the world is working very hard not to allow. Imagine giving this little speech that I just gave to the Rotary Club or to the Elks Club or the Daughters of the American Revolution. They'd throw eggs at me. They would say, "You're nuts!" They would say, "This isn't anything; it has got nothing to do with anything real. This is nonsense." This isn't for popular consumption; this isn't for most of the world; this isn't for everybody. This is for the people who are ready and willing to consider that this is an alternate reality, already. Those other folks can talk about an alternate reality, but they make it alternate. *This* is the alternate reality.

If it's true for you, what you're saying, then you have already seen for yourself that you're in the alternate reality and that there are possibilities beyond conventional ideas. So good for you; it means you're in the rare few on the planet, and it means you have a higher responsibility. It means because you're in that smaller minority you have the potential to delve much deeper. Most people can't delve very deep; they stop right about at the surface. You have an onus, a responsibility on you, to keep going, to go deeper, to know more, to experience more fully what can be experienced, because you become the residual, the vessel for that Truth. You become the place where that deeper understanding can reside in this world.

You may have no idea—in fact most people don't—how much effect that has, just the presence of people who can accept what, to most of the population of the world, is unacceptable, who can have a broad enough mind, a clear enough understanding, an open enough heart, to hear this and not reject it out of hand. That ability puts you in a different category energetically, let's say, for want of a better way to say it. That's what I mean by, "You become the vessel." You don't know what effect that has, but I guarantee you it has a huge effect. Somebody is affected just being in the same room with you. You don't know it; you don't feel it; you don't necessarily have an awareness of it—but that doesn't mean it isn't happening.

Sometimes because I sit in this chair, people say, "I feel your transmission." Everybody is transmitting all the time. *Everybody is a transmitter.* It really means you have a higher responsibility, because you're transmitting something more important, more real, truer, if you can accept these more unconventional notions. So I said, "Good for you." But it's more than good for you: it's good for everybody. But you have to recognize where you are. You're the only hope. Somebody who believes life is about getting as much money as you can—they aren't the hope of this life. They can't be. There's nothing wrong with them, I'm not criticizing them—but they're transmitting something that doesn't go anywhere.

Riley: What can one deliberately do to increase awareness, to become more plugged in?

Premodaya: Fully accept your powerlessness; become completely powerless. Become completely nobody. Become no one and nothing. Become as humble as a blade of grass. That's the real answer. Disappear—so that only what is inside a blade of grass, is left in *you*. You will be bigger and richer for it. Usually, I give a more long-winded answer, but that is the answer. Then everything—whether you decide it or not or want it or not—gets given over and used by existence, for whatever purpose existence has.

Before that happens, it looks like one thing. After that happens, it doesn't look like that at all. In other words, before that happens, we have some kind of notion about what that would look like, feel like, be like, what it would mean, what it means for us, what it means for anything. All that's nonsense. All that's speculation at best. We read about what other people's experiences are, but it doesn't matter. Somebody else's experience isn't what's going to be your experience. But then, on the other side (post- not pre-) all these questions and concerns disappear because it isn't relevant anymore. It isn't about you or what you want or what you think or what works for you or what's right for you. Because there's no more you.

Riley: That doesn't sound like so much fun.

Premodaya: That's what I'm saying. Beforehand, that sounds like, "Who the heck would want that?" It sounds like a loss. That's what I'm trying to explain. It sounds and seems like a loss, and that's what I meant by, "You will be richer," because it's actually the loss of *that*; the loss of 'you' is the gain of everything else. Everything else is only gainable when you disappear—'you' have to get lost. The real shock of the spiritual search is that people enter the spiritual search thinking they are going to find themselves. If the search is persisted in and sincerely engaged in and real things happen, not stories we tell ourselves, there comes a point where a tremendous shock happens. This is for everyone, because you realize it's not about finding yourself; it's about losing yourself. In some form that gets recognized, and then you realize, "I've been tricked! I thought this was going to *improve* my life." It *ends* your life; it ends your life as you know it, because it ends 'you' as you know it. It's really a trick. You think you're going to improve your life. No, you're going to commit suicide.

Another way to say it is: *You* can be there, or God can be there. They can't both be there at the same time. Who would you rather have in the chair where you're sitting: You? or God? That's your choice. Sounds odd, when you put it that bald-faced, but it's the truth. I'm talking to a room full of people who pretty much understand this. It's evident. It's not that you need to understand it better. It's that you need to jump into it; you need to live it; you need to stake your life on it. You need to take it so seriously that nothing else matters. I don't mean in a solemn way—not serious and solemn and all long-faced. I mean serious as: "This is what matters. This is what's more important than what's on TV."

This is a very strange circumstance: A small group of people that I'm assuming pretty much get it, and pretty much know it—and my job is to somehow cajole you, encourage you, exhort you, trick you (whatever it takes) to start living it as the very center of your life; as the very reason that you're here in this life—to get you to commit everything to it, to put your whole totality on the line, with that. To place your bet, once and for all. And then something is possible. While you're hedging your bets, you just go round and round. The alchemy of this is you place your bets once and for all, and then it changes. That's the secret. It's alchemical. But the scary thing is to put down all your chips on "black 22." Then, if you're wrong, it's over—you're busted, you're flat broke, you've got nothing. That's the risk you take. People like me just sit up here and tell you: "The wheel is fixed! Put your money down, and you'll win! Black 22 is coming up—put your money down!" Because the only way, is if you bet it all. In that sense, life is very much like Las Vegas. You only win big, if you bet big. You only win big, if you risk wildly. Staying safe, you lose.

Only gamblers permeate the Mystery. If you can't gamble, you can't get anywhere—you can't enter the Mystery to a greater degree or, become aware of it more deeply. Everyone here, just by the fact that you're here, must be some degree of gambler, some degree of adventurer, some degree of courageous. Maybe you're quite aware of that; maybe you have no idea of what a gambler you are. Maybe you're a gambler that doesn't know they are a gambler. But if you're here, you're a gambler. And you're gambling with the highest stakes there are: life itself, existence itself, the meaning of life. You can't say it's not fun! Gambling is always, if nothing else, thrilling. And I'm not the adventuresome type, so if *I* say that! But that's the whole point: You're already on the thrill ride, whether you accept it or not, or believe it or not, or know it or not. So why not know it? Why not accept it? Why not see it with your own eyes and say, "OK, all my chips in!" Don't save anything. What are you saving it for? What have you got to lose?

Morgan: It's delusion if you think you will have to lose. I realized I can only win; I have nothing to lose. I'm not afraid anymore.

Premodaya: Yes, you don't have anything to lose. Right!—you don't have anything to lose, you never did. It's more specific than illusion: It's false sense of safety, false sense of security; it's trying to build a sense of security around something that has no security. The only security within insecurity is to accept completely the insecurity. That's the best you can do. The best you can do is to recognize the absolute insecurity—then you relax; then you can enjoy it—then you become like a blade of grass. The wind comes—it bends this way; the wind comes—it bends that way. No wind—it stands straight up. The sun is shining intensely—it gets crispy. The rain is falling—it becomes lush.

The blade of grass is not resisting the Mystery; the blade of grass is living the Mystery. You have to be like that—the blade of grass is cooperating by completely being a blade of grass, not trying to be something else. The blade of grass isn't trying to be a tree. It isn't puffed up with arrogance that, "I'm something more than what I am, something bigger. I can control whether the rain comes, I can control which way the wind blows, I can control whether the cow eats me." That's what we are doing most of the time, telling ourselves this kind of story. But if you become like a blade of grass, life turns into something completely different than what you thought it was.

And that's the real life. The simple truth is that it's always right here, right now. The Unknown is no more formidable than this. Because you have never been anywhere else. You're never going to be anywhere else. It's always here. It's always right here. Some moments the taste of it is sweet. Some moments the recognition of it is terrifying. But no matter what the experience, this is it and it's *you*. It's not something around you. It's not something that envelops you. It's you. You come from the Unknown. You are the Unknown, and the Unknown is synonymous with the Divine. How can our little minds really understand the Divine? But it can be experienced. A taste can happen even in a quick moment like this. Whatever is there for you right now—whatever the experience, whatever you're noticing—see if you can recognize that it doesn't have to be more complicated than this. This is the Unknown. This is what's Real. This is You. This is the Divine. This moment can be contacted any time. You can go deeper in any moment, anywhere, no matter what the circumstances.

FACING OUR ALONENESS

Prof. Alex: I have a situation. I have been with my partner for about ten years, and she is a very loving person. She is away at night quite a bit at her job, and I'm alone in the apartment. Now, I don't feel good alone in the apartment. I feel alright, but kind of empty. When I hear the front door go and she is in, I feel "Ahh." I can be reading a book and she comes home, and I feel, "Ahh, that's great."

What I'm asking myself is, "Why am I so dependent on someone else?" Why can't I feel wonderful sitting here reading a book in comfort?

I seem very dependent. I love her very much, but I say, "To hell with everybody; why can't I just be complete?" But apparently, I'm not.

Premodaya: It casts its own light—you said it all. That's a whole Zen— Zen story, right there. Do you really want to hear the answer?

Prof. Alex: Yes.

Premodaya: It means you haven't faced your aloneness. The aloneness that is everyone—you, her, him, her, everyone. One's aloneness has to be faced.

Prof. Alex: And then? [laughter] See, I think it's a wonderful feeling to have someone. I think of people who live alone, and I don't know how they do it? They aren't happy—that's what I think. And maybe it's real. Maybe you do need someone. Everyone needs someone there.

Premodaya: You don't like my answer, do ya?

Prof. Alex: I just think it's unfortunate to be alone. Even though you face it and go through it, and say, "I'm OK."

Premodaya: I'm not talking about loneliness. I'm talking about *aloneness*. The fact that you are alone. No matter how many people are there. The fact that everyone comes into this life, lives this life, and leaves this life, alone. You and I are not young men anymore. Before death comes (and it's getting closer), you have to face your aloneness. Because if you don't face it now, you will have to face it then. And it's much harder, much harder. Face it now, before the physical death.

Prof. Alex: What I'd like to do is feel that good feeling all the time. And that may be looking for enlightenment, or whatever. I'm looking for "the God within."

Premodaya: But you already know you can't have it all the time. You knew that before tonight. Now you have to know more for real, more acutely, that you do have to face the aloneness. It has to be truly dealt with. Truly faced. Truly met. Truly experienced. Not pushed away, not run from. And that's what most of us do most of the time. That's what almost everything is for—television, books, movies, Coca-Cola, everything. You can run away. You can run away with anything. You can run away with your own thoughts. Most of us do. We fill our head—there's a constant dialogue going on, that's all to not face the aloneness. The aloneness *is* the unknown.

It's true. The aloneness is the unknown. That's why we don't want to face it. That's why every fiber goes into terror when we consider really facing it. Because it's falling more into the unknown. And it's, at least for that moment, giving up all the illusions of safety, all the illusions of control, all the illusions that we can hide somewhere and avoid whatever it is we want to avoid.

There's nowhere to hide. This universe doesn't give you anywhere to hide, it just seems that way. You convince yourself that it does, but it doesn't. And when you're trying to hide, everybody sees it but you.

I don't know why, but tonight I'm only the deliverer of bad news. Face the aloneness.

Prof. Alex: It's good news. I know it's good news.

Premodaya: Good. That's a more mature understanding.

CHAPTER 15

FROM SPIRITUAL SEEKER TO *SPIRITUAL FINDER*

Premodaya: Why characterize yourself as "I'm trying," rather than "I'm succeeding"?

Darshana: I don't know.

Premodaya: Partly out of habit maybe and partly because it feels safer.

Darshana: Feels safer?

Premodaya: It feels safer to tell yourself you're trying. It feels safer to tell yourself, "I'm seeking," rather than, "I'm finding." You have been a seeker for a long time; my job is to help you become a finder, and I'm good at my job. You're becoming more of a finder, so now you have to catch up with yourself and admit that to yourself. I don't care about to us, but at least to yourself. You have to do that. You can't stay under the blanket of, "I'm seeking, I'm seeking, I'm searching, I'm looking."

Darshana: Yeah, because coming here—I don't really have any particular—I just enjoy it. I enjoy the space, enjoy the people, enjoy the whole process.

Premodaya: But it's more than that, because when you come here, or think about coming here, or just think about what it all means—in those moments, you are more of a finder and less of a seeker. Now, you have to admit that, because finding is complicated. Finding has its own thrills and its own disappointments. The thrill is: "Wow, this is it!" The disappointment is: "Wow—this is *it?*" [laughter]

You have to face that. This is a kind of trap for those of us who have been seekers for years, and even decades—you start to find, but you somehow remain a seeker. You keep yourself in the seeker position. You don't catch up with yourself and tell yourself, "Wait a minute, *I am* finding." You don't really, fully let yourself have what is happening to you. You stay one step to the side. Seeking is kind of like there is the football player on the field, and there is the fan in the stadium. It's like you stay in the fan's seat. It's time to get out of the fan seat. It's just acknowledging where you've really come to. I have every evidence, and I know the fact, that you have come to something, but you can't keep denying it. It doesn't serve you to keep making that smaller than it is. Sound right?

Darshana: Yeah.

Premodaya: Something in you doesn't want to admit it. Something in you doesn't want to let things expand to where they have come to. Something in you wants to stay.

LET DEEP PEACE CHANGE YOU

Terrence: Giving yourself to the Truth, Reality, or whatever—it certainly seems to me that my life on the external level is falling apart. Things that used to work aren't working anymore.

Premodaya: What's that like?

Terrence: It is painful a lot of the time, and sometimes I feel deep peace, but there is an energy in my head that feels like it's just going to explode, and I'm just wondering, "What the hell is going to happen?" It certainly seems to be connected to giving myself to the Truth.

Premodaya: Before this, was there ever a feeling of deep peace?

Terrence: No.

Premodaya: That is the clue. What will happen if you can ride it and not draw yourself back in as the deep peace expands, and the fear and anxiety and panic and all of the above subsides, it gets replaced by the deep peace. The deep peace takes you over. But you are absolutely correct, it's often a scary ride. In the beginning it's a scary ride. It's a scary ride for two reasons. The first reason is: generally, we have no prior experience of deep peace, so it's all unsettling because it's new, it's different, it's unknown. The second reason is: because the feeling that everything is falling apart *really feels* like *falling apart*. But take a wider view: It's rearranging. If something is changing inside you, if you're getting closer to what's real, if the Truth is happening more for you, how could that happen without some rearrangement? And that rearrangement will feel, more than likely, like a dissolution, like things are falling apart. At its worst it feels like a living hell—if you ask me. At its best it feels like things are really chaos. But what's really happening is everything is rearranging itself so that deep peace can live where you are. What do you think?

Terrence: I think that deep peace isn't really jiving with the way my life is living, the way I make a living, practical things. That's where the chaos comes in, and yet there's still the peace.

Premodaya: Out of the six and a half billion people on the planet, how many do you imagine can say tonight, "It seems that deep peace is happening to me"? Not many. Yes, there's a price to pay. It seems chaotic. It seems like things are falling apart. But there's no way for true transformation to happen without a rearrangement of some kind; otherwise, it would have already happened. Don't be naive and think there is no price; any teacher who says to you, "Ah, welcome to my spiritual meeting; it is all love and light," that's crap.

It's not all love and light; that's ridiculous. It's often painful, it's often terrifying, because that is what's in us, and that is what has to be faced. But you don't transform, you don't become capable of deep peace, unless the conditions are right for it, which means a rearrangement naturally occurs. That can feel like a cataclysm and that can feel like a natural realignment. The more you cooperate with it, generally, the easier it is. When it first started happening to me I was as stubborn and uncooperative as you can be, and for three years I was in absolute living hell. Don't be like me.

What you have to do is be smart enough to remember how many people on this planet can say, "My experience is deep peace—deep peace seems to be happening to me."

Terrence: It is a lot of reason to have gratitude.

Premodaya: That is the real confirmation, when gratitude is felt.

GOD IS STALKING YOU

Premodaya: How about that traffic tonight, huh? Whatever it is! If you made it here despite this traffic, that says something, shows something. That's really the metaphor for spiritual life. There's always plenty of traffic to prevent you. To keep you where you are. To keep you focused on what isn't important—what doesn't really bring you anything. And people get stuck in this. This is what we call "everyday life." You're fighting the traffic, every day. The spiritual life—feeling attracted to, called to, some kind of spirituality, some kind of spiritual path—means and always includes taking your focus off the traffic, accepting the traffic for what it is: traffic. Not giving all your life's energy, all your attention, all your thoughts, all your *self*, to dealing with the traffic, to the everyday, to the mundane, to the worldly.

The spiritual path is a call from the other world. Most people don't go there. Most people don't feel that call, which simply means they are focused on the traffic. If you're here, you have heard some kind of call that isn't about everyday life, that isn't about the trivial. Let's say, it's about the profound. If you've heard that call then somehow, by some grace, by some kind of miracle, proportionately you're one of the few. Somehow, above the sirens and the traffic noise and everything else, you have heard this.

The rest is just about hearing it more clearly and answering it more fully. Everything in spiritual life can be categorized as that. Are you growing in your ability to hear that call? Are you expanding in your ability to *answer* that call? That's really all that's going on. People talk about "spirituality," about "this spiritual path," and "that spiritual path," and all kinds of complicated terms; special jargon for—what's really, simply taking place. Either you're opening more to hearing that call and/or you're opening more to answering that call.

You can gauge yourself at any given time which one is going on, or neither. It's not this esoteric, complex, difficult mountain-climbing kind of road that we tend to think of when we hear the term "spiritual path."

It's just: Where is my attention? Is it on that which is trivial or on that which is profound? Is it on what some people call "Truth"? What some people call "Reality"? What some people call "God"? What some people call "Realization"?—whatever you want to call it. Or is it on something else? Whether it's making more money, whether it's finding a new spouse, whether it's getting healthier—there's every kind of concern that you can put your attention into. But if it isn't about the profound, the eternal, then it's just traffic. You have to ask yourself: Do you want your life energy to be spent on the traffic? Do you want this life to be about how to get through the traffic? Or do you want this life really, truly, to be about flying higher? Certainly, everybody in this room would say, "Yes" to the latter. Or else you wouldn't be in this room; the traffic would have turned you back. You would have said, "To heck with it, I'm going back."

For many people, that's where it stops. That's where it ends—at the point of engaging in the search, looking for the profound, trying to find the doorway that takes you higher. Then, the rest of the lifetime is spent looking for the door, and, as the old joke used to go, "and then, you die." The lifetime was spent playing hide-and-seek—in the search.

This can go on forever. This is the dilemma of the spiritual search. For those blessed enough, lucky enough, having been touched by grace such that they are spiritually searching, the trap—the most common trap is: You search for the rest of your life, and then you die. And this is probably the majority. I don't have statistics, but I could make some up: It's ninety-nine point six percent of all those who search.

If you're not going to get stuck in that trap, you have to recognize that being a seeker, being a searcher, can't be an end in itself, can't be how you get there. It can be the start. It can take you a long way. Absolutely, I'm not disputing that. I'm not denying that. I'm not disagreeing with that. But it can't take you all the way, because searching isn't finding. Searching is searching. At some point a recognition has to happen that it's the finding that counts, not the searching. That somehow a searcher, a seeker, has to become a finder, or else you just stay a seeker forever. This is an amazing phenomenon, because people get very, very on the edge of finding. And they are so attached to searching that they just stay on that edge for the rest of their lives. Or, they turn back, they go back to a more fervent searching. This is so common. What happens is we get attached to the search. The search can be very pleasant, very blissful, very enjoyable. Easy to identify with, "I'm on a spiritual search. I'm on a serious spiritual path. And I'm going to God, by golly! And someday I'm going to get there! If I'm lucky. Maybe."

Finding means at any cost. At any price. Nothing else matters, and it has to be immediately. It can't be "thirty years from now," because I can't take the chance that I'll only live twenty more years. It can't be, "If I'm lucky down the road, I will find." It has to be a change of intention. I admire spiritual seekers; I don't even want to be around anybody who isn't a spiritual seeker. Everything I'm saying isn't a criticism—none of it is. It's an encouragement—a challenge—to recognize that seeking is a stage and if you stay in that stage, you never find. Everybody has to pass through that stage—whether it's one day, one year, or one lifetime.

All I'm saying is: Understand that that stage isn't the journey. It's just a stage along the way. Get out of that stage as quickly as you can. Recognize what you already know beyond any shadow of a doubt. Recognize what your heart is saying to you, what that call from the Beyond is saying to you. Don't trivialize it. Don't pretend it's something other than what it is. Don't let yourself be needlessly distracted, and be willing to actually *be* a finder.

This is the key—the willingness to give up being a searcher and admit to being a finder. To admit to yourself (or maybe even to someone else— but certainly to yourself) that something has already happened. Something has already touched you. To go more deeply, more fully, into that which has already happened. Not something that has to be found down the road but something that is already there, that's already in you, that has already called to you. That, lo and behold, *you have already found.*

Whether you have found it inside of yourself, whether you found it through a book, whether you found it through going somewhere, whether you've always had it, whether you were born with it—however it came, something is already there. Plunge into that. Not in the spirit or the idea of "I'm searching," but in recognition of what has already been found. Whether it's a more open heart, whether it's the radiance of life, whether it's some sense of eternity or infinity, whether it's a feeling of connection with everything and everyone—whatever it is, there's nobody in this room who hasn't already found it. One of those, or something like that.

But you can *not* put your attention on that. You can run around searching. What I'm suggesting is that there comes a point where it's more fruitful, where it gets better results, to switch to the finding mode and see what's already there. The amazing shock is that it's always right under our nose. It's only a shock once you see that for yourself. Until then, it's just an idea. But when you see it, I guarantee you—or if you've already seen it, you certainly have been shocked. The wacky, crazy, odd thing is that nothing can come to you that isn't already under your nose.

You have to become the finder of it, because searching means looking elsewhere. You have to learn the knack of looking under your nose. Looking to what's already there. This takes great intelligence, great insight, to be able to turn the attention in the other direction, and to look at that which you take for granted, and really see the golden nugget in the piece of lead. It takes a lot of willingness. It takes a lot of attitude adjustment because it's saying that you're already sitting on the diamond.

In the beginning, if that's a new idea, nobody wants to believe that. Nobody finds it easy to accept that because it's just too weird. "What do you mean I already have it? I already found it? If I already found it, I would not be here; I would not be reading all these books; I wouldn't be going to all these places." It's a very strange set of circumstances, but the truth is, it's true. And most of us are a victim of it. We stay in those circumstances, and the sincere hearts and open minds keep seeking.

All I'm saying is: See that that could be a trap. I'm not saying don't seek. I'm saying: Understand that, fundamentally, finding is different than seeking. Seeking is no guarantee of finding, but *finding* is a guarantee of finding, and all that can be found is what's already there. It's not like you have to look far; it's not like you have to go to the Himalayas; it's not like you have to take a trip around the world. You just have to be willing to accept that it might already be under your nose, that it might actually be close at hand and always had been close at hand. You have to be willing to accept the possibility that you're far more than you think you are and that you're sitting on something much greater than maybe you have believed so far. Let the singing and dancing begin!

Open invitation: Anybody want to come up and use the chair and work on finding now? Becoming a finder tonight?

Terrence: I don't know why I'm here.

Premodaya: Because you want to be a finder.

Terrence: Something keeps drawing me—has for a long time, to continue coming to satsang, to coming to places like this—and there was someone at home calling me home. The act of—I won't call it seeking, but the act of continuing to go to these things and do "spiritual work" continually seems to put me through emotional hell. It doesn't feel good most of the time. It doesn't make any sense to my mind why I keep showing up to these things, yet I do. It certainly appears like I'm chasing something, and I judge myself for it. And then, sometimes I feel like I'm just drawn. And certainly, it doesn't make any sense to people around me why I would go to these things. I keep it a secret. I feel like a seeker. A secret seeker, because if you bring up anything like this, people just change the subject.

Premodaya: So, are you willing to be a finder?

Terrence: Yes, if I'm not already one.

Premodaya: What have you found?

Terrence: I've found something deeper than seeking things in the material world. Something deeper than achievements and making money. Something even deeper than friendships with people, I guess.

Premodaya: How can you best explain (and we know words are inadequate) what that is? What's your word or your phrase or your paragraph that gives a name to that? That tells the rest of us what that is to you? Give it a name; flesh it out.

Terrence: It's a depth inside of me that seems to be infinite and is greater than me. It's a space around me that is bigger than me, yet it's me. It's a depth and a peace. It's something that's me, and much greater than me, and it's deeper than my mind and my body. And, it's peaceful.

Premodaya: To summarize it, what you're saying is: What I have found is a depth and peace that's inside me and outside me and that includes me and includes everything else.

Terrence: Yes. And I can rest in that whenever I want. Yet I still come to all of these things and continue to do all of this work, as if I need to find it. Sometimes I tell myself I should just cut it out, because I'm trying to make something happen instead of be what I am.

Premodaya: The delusion may be that the idea that you can "rest in it" whenever you want. Could that be not true?

Terrence: "Whenever I want," is not true. When I get emotional and wrapped up, I can't snap out of it, no—but it sounded good. [laughter]

Premodaya: This is what all of us do. You know, we read all of these things; we hear all of these things; a certain kind of phrasing gets second nature to us, and we say things like, "*I can rest in it whenever I would like to.*" That was

Ramana Maharshi, who died in—what? 1950? That's what he always said, "Rest in it." So, it takes this kind of searing self-examination, this kind of self-honesty to question, "What am I really saying to myself? What is really going on here?" What you're saying, with a little bit of questioning is, "I've been telling myself I can 'rest in it' whenever I want, but it's not true." First you have to absolutely accept the truth, which is: I can't rest in it whenever I want. That's what all the searching is about. How to make that the circumstance, that you can be there at will, have it a will, rest in it, stay in it, be in it. That's the actual illusion. That can never happen because then it's a "thing." Then it's a coffee cup. Then it's part of the material world and you can rest in it. It's a bed. It belongs to you. Then it's a possession. And the Truth isn't a possession. It doesn't operate like a possession. It's not material. It doesn't exclude the material but it isn't the material.

I don't have the slightest doubt that you found what you say you've found. But I would say to you that you can't hold it in your hand. You can't rest in it. You can't possess it. You can't keep searching for it and eventually find it—which means finding the way to tame it, to capture it, to lasso it, to have it for your own. If something has to be given up, that's what has to be given up. The idea that it can somehow be yours. What I'm talking about is really, finally, once and for all getting it that what you're talking about "resting in," let's call that getting, can't be *gotten*. Can't be turned into something permanent. Can't be captured, so that you can sit in it whenever the mood strikes. The process is the exact opposite. The process is: You have to be willing to be so un-greedy of it that you actually are willing to trust existence, and let *it* get *you*. You can't get it, but you can allow it to get you. You can allow yourself to be the prey, instead of the hunter, and that's really why you keep coming. To find the way to become the prey. What do you make of that?

Terrence: That makes sense, it does make sense. It appears like I'm such a masochist, because I keep having so much pain, and I keep coming back for more. That's my experience on the spiritual path. That's pretty much eighty percent of the time what I feel. I think that's why.

Premodaya: Could it be the pain of the hunter? See, the hunter is always frustrated. The hunter is always working hard—looking—trying to find the prey. The prey is going about its business. The prey is never frustrated. The prey is gamboling through the meadow. You have to be willing to be the prey. You have to be willing to let something get you—which is very much like death. The prey doesn't know what's going to happen. Maybe it's being caught to be tagged as part of a wildlife program and set free and handed a bunch of carrots on the way out, or maybe it's going to be shot dead and skinned. The willingness to be the prey is the willingness for, "Whatever happens, happens. Whatever this means, I'm going to not try to escape it. I'm going to let the Profound catch me, and it'll do with me what it will. I don't know if it's going to give me dinner and set me free once and for all, or if it's going to skin me alive." That's what all the fear we all have is about.

He who would become a finder rather than stay a seeker, is he who is willing to be the prey and give up the seemingly superior position of being the hunter and become *the hunted*. It doesn't rationally sound right. It doesn't make rational intuitive sense. But you can't get the Truth; you can only let the Truth get you. I will say it again; I don't have the slightest doubt that you have found exactly what you say you've found. *That is* finding. You *are* finding. But that finding has awakened in you as it does for most who find, a desire to hold on to it. To have it be there all the time.

That's the trap of the sincere spiritual seeker and, for better or worse, the successful finder. Most of us would say this, "I have gotten a glimpse." That's the word I hear all the time, "I have had many glimpses," and those glimpses make us greedy to make it our permanent condition, let's say. But that doesn't work. Because then we have turned it into something that belongs to us, and the Truth doesn't belong to anybody. But you can belong to the Truth. You can be swallowed up by the Divine. What that takes is the willingness to be swallowed, which is another way of saying: the willingness to be the prey rather than the hunter. It's the same as the willingness to disappear. The willingness to die. The willingness to become nothing. The willingness to see what it means when the Unknown takes you.

See if right now you can relax into yourself and see if you can shift that longtime mode of the hunter. See if right now you can shift your attitude from hunter to hunted. See what it feels like, rather than sit in yourself as the hunter, sit in yourself as the prey. Meaning allowing Truth to get you in its sights and do with you as it's going to do. Really *be* the prey. Really *be* not the one in the superior position. It's really a humbling, allowing yourself to be humbled. I mean, what's more humble than being the prey? See if that can be accessed and what that experience feels like. See if that attitude shift is even possible.

Terrence: It's a lot of work to be a hunter. It takes a lot of energy.

Premodaya: That's right. The first thing you notice in actually, shifting that attitude, is how much has to go into being a hunter. How much is subsumed in that effort.

Terrence: Wow, it's so simple—a change in attitude. About a year ago, I just gave up on all the spiritual stuff. But then I had this profound experience, and for the last year I have been trying to chase it and grasp it and hunt it down. I can feel it now. It feels softer. It feels more vulnerable. It feels—just allowing, and because of that, a little bit more playful. It's kind of like, "Yeah, whatever."

Premodaya: See, this is the big surprise. That it's a relief accepting the notion of being the prey and giving up the hunt. It's a big huge relief. It feels better to give it up! Now just continue to see yourself as the prey. Continue to accept the possibility that what you have been seeking, is stalking you. And let yourself be captured. Now you can really relax. All this nervousness is the nervousness of the hunter. It's nerve-racking being the hunter. Now you can relax. The prey can go about its business and let the hunter take care of what happens next.

Terrence: Yes, I'm a believer. I get it. Yes, thank you very much.

IT HAS ALREADY FOUND YOU

Premodaya: The most important question is: What are you looking for? The amazing thing is many of us go on a really determined spiritual search and we never really clarify what we are looking for. No wonder that we get frustrated, we get disappointed, we get lost along the way, we find, we don't find. If it's pertinent to you, then you have to really know what you're looking for. Otherwise, you're meandering. Then the corollary question becomes: Why are you looking in the first place? What's behind the whole effort? Usually it's a very short list—what people are looking for: inner peace, happiness, satisfaction in life, God, what is the Truth, Reality. Those last three are pretty much synonymous, in a very real way. And that's pretty much the list.

We're talking about not millions, but billions of people because, certainly, everybody is looking for happiness, and, certainly, most people would say they're looking for some kind of inner peace. The amazing thing is that the list is so short, but this is a clue—essentially everybody is looking for the same thing.

Now, this rules out a whole other category, which is people looking for escape. People looking for a way to get away from themselves. But that's another veer-off entirely. That becomes a question of emotional and psychological issues. That has to be cleared up first before a person in that mode can say, "I'm looking for inner peace." They're really looking for escape. But, probably, if you're here, you aren't looking for escape. You're looking for one of the things on the primary list, or you enjoy the company of spiritually-minded people, and the energy that gets created.

If something is being looked for, searched out, you have to get as clear as you possibly can about what that is. The interesting thing is, the things on that list are findable. There are people who will testify, "I found it." "Suffering ended for me." "I found inner peace." "I found God." "I fell into Truth." "I see Reality." There are people who will tell you that, a lot of people. It's an interesting phenomenon, this spiritualist life, that people go on a search. Some find it—whatever they are searching for. Probably I would say, interestingly enough—I can't offer an explanation—the majority at ICODA do. But the majority, in general, don't. Maybe it's that ICODA attracts the best of the best, which is you. The people who are really ready.

But, in general, there are people who are quite sincere, quite committed, have a very devoted spiritual life year in year out, decade in decade out—and you ask them, thirty years down the road, and they say to you they haven't really found what they're looking for. It's all a very interesting phenomenon. Part of why it's interesting is those who find generally say the same thing. Even coming from many, many different traditions, many different practices, many different experiences—worlds apart, continents apart—completely different philosophies, completely different methods, those who find talk very similarly to each other and almost invariably end up saying something along the lines of, "It wasn't really that I found it; it's due to the search, *it found me*."

This is another clue. Again and again, people will testify, "I realize, now that I found it, that *I* didn't find it. That through the effort I made, I became somehow more available to it. And somewhere along the way, my intention changed. I thought I was entering a spiritual search to find something for myself, and when I found it, it became clear to me it wasn't about myself at all."

It's amazing how many people say this. They can't all be nuts or making it up. When people say it on one continent, and another continent, and one century, and another century, I tend to trust it. It's a clue. There's a whole mode called "Advaita Vedanta." A whole philosophy that comes from India, that's very ancient, that says, "All is one." That's the central idea, the central teaching, the central Truth—all is one. There's no division anywhere. No separation anywhere. There's only one thing going on. And that gives voice to what everybody else, who isn't part of that tradition or that philosophy, seems also to say. It's just that philosophy, which has been worked out over many centuries, is very focused on that one idea, and is very articulate about it, but it articulates something that just about everybody seems to say in one way or another.

A big category of those who never find, those who keep searching and never get anywhere—is a category of people who look in books and in philosophies and in religions and in traditions and who kind of approach it (and I'm not saying there's anything wrong with it, we all start there), but who approach it kind of mentally, philosophically. There's nothing wrong with that mode, everybody starts in that mode, but you can't find anything if you stay in that mode, because you can't think your way to Truth. Even though there's a whole wisdom tradition that's based on the yoga of knowledge, that is the path of thinking your way to Truth—even *that* path says that doesn't get you there, that it just prepares you, that just takes you a goodly way, and then you have to divert on a different path. Even the knowledge path says, "Knowledge isn't enough—can't get you the whole nine yards." It can get you eight yards, but that last yard will take a different kind of approach.

There are great books out there, we all know. Great teachers. Great things have been written; great things have been said. But you can't get it from a book, because a book is in your hands, and if it can come from your hands, you would have gotten it already. A book can be helpful, a philosophy can be helpful, a teaching can be helpful, but it can't get you there. It can't make you a finder. It can't turn you from a seeker into a finder if you only keep looking in books, if you only keep considering philosophically, if you only enter the spiritual realm conceptually.

There are other approaches. There are many yogas. Yoga is just a word that denotes a system for "getting there." Some systems are based on mastering the physical; some are based on mastering the mental; some are based on mastering the heart. Those are the major divisions, but they are all a road that takes you a certain distance. One of the tricks for the seeker is as early on as possible—to get a sense of which road they can travel most conclusively on. Some people are more heart people—the heart road will work better for them. Some people are more mental—the knowledge road may take them a long way quickly.

It helps to have a sense of yourself, of what moves you best. But all these ways, all the practices, all the seekings, all the efforts, all the attempts, all the best intentions and the sincerest motivations are just preparations, just ways of you getting shaped into a more malleable form. If you're the clay, then you have to be shapeable, and we all start relatively unshapeable. We all start fairly rigid, it seems to me. All of these philosophies, all these traditions, all these religions, all these spiritual paths, and all these practices, really serve the purpose of softening the clay, making the clay more malleable, more shapeable so that whatever needs to happen, whatever can happen, can *actually* happen. Because if the clay is hard, and can't be moved, and can't be shaped, and can't be adjusted—then nothing can happen. You can't make a sculpture from clay that can't be manipulated. So if you're the sculpture, you have to be able to be sculpted.

You enter the spiritual path, the spiritual life, the spiritual intention, thinking you're going to get something, wanting to get something. That's normal and right; there's nothing wrong with it. But somewhere along the line, it gets clearer to you that it's not about getting something. It's about softening, becoming more available to what's already out there—*you* becoming more available to what's already available to you. Somewhere along the line, if they go far enough, most people realize that, "What's available, was always available. It was *me* that was not available. I was not soft enough. I was not permeable enough. I was not shapeable enough for it to get to me."

On the one hand, it's important to know what you're looking for, but on the other hand it's equally important to know: are you ready to find it? What I'm really suggesting is that the second one is more important than the first one. If you don't get to the second one, you never get anywhere. Those people who search and search, even for decades, and they never find—they may enjoy themselves; they may enjoy the practices; they enjoy the fellowship, but when you speak to them, they say, "Well, you know, it hasn't really changed me," or "I haven't found what I really wanted to be able to get to."

I was talking to someone like this who told me that he had been practicing yoga for thirty years, starting as a teenager very consistently for thirty years, every day. I asked him, "What have you gotten from it?" Apparently, no one had ever asked him that because he had to stop and think for a minute. He thought about it—you could see it in his face; he was seriously considering the question, and then something came over his face, and he looked at me and said, "Actually, nothing." Nothing! Thirty years—you got nothing? He said, "Well, I guess it's good for relaxing. And it has toned me. I'm flexible, and I'm well-toned."

Well, you can get that at any gym. You don't have to get into yoga. But I know this guy—and it made sense to me that in thirty years, he hasn't gotten anything from his practice, because he has a closed mind. He is not really looking for anything. He is not really sincerely searching. He's hoping it will fall from the sky on top of him, and he doesn't want to open himself. It's a fear-based approach and he doesn't realize he is afraid. And of course, I didn't say any of this to him, because he didn't ask me.

That's a very large category of people—people who practice sincerely, but they've never really asked themselves and gotten clear, "What am I looking for?" They've never gotten to the stage where it becomes evident to you that it's just as much about: How ready are you? How willing are you to receive it? To accept it? To take it in if you found it tonight?

There's another category of people that I have seen who actually find something, who very much get involved in a true transformational process and something happens to them. But they have been so committed to the search mode, to being in search mode, that they don't notice they've found it. It's like the farmer who is looking for a needle in the haystack and really doesn't believe he will ever find it, because the haystack is so big and the needle is so tiny. And then, one moment, he comes across it. He finds it, but it's so unbelievable he doesn't even notice! He just keeps looking. He wasn't really expecting to find it in the first place. This is another whole category of spiritual seekers, people who actually have found something, who have experienced something, who have had a realization of some deep and profound kind, but who keep going in search mode. Who don't switch from searcher mode to finder mode. They are cheating themselves, obviously, but it isn't their intention. It's just they have become habituated to the idea that searching is what it's about. They have forgotten that they are trying to find something, so in a way, they don't even notice when they've found it.

I want to share with you one of the most important things to know, no matter which category you happen to fall into, in terms of classification—one of the most important things you can understand (and you can jump ahead by understanding this better), is the spiritual search isn't about getting something. Although we think it is, in the beginning. It's about *you* softening up. It's about you becoming more shapeable, so that existence can give you what it wants to give you, that you haven't been in the right shape to accept. Somehow, it's been knocking on your door, and somehow, you haven't been answering. I swear to you, this is everybody's situation.

You wouldn't be at this meeting if that was not the case for you. You would be watching TV. You would be at the movies. You would be figuring out your grocery budget. You would be looking at the want ads for a better job. You would be looking online to buy a car at a good price. You would be focused on something other than your spirituality: your desire for Truth, your yearning for what's real, your right and pure motive for happiness. You already know, if you're in this room, that it isn't going to come from a better car or a better job or a bigger house or a fatter bank account. Although those things are all nice. But the real satisfaction isn't going to come from those. You already know that, or you absolutely wouldn't be here.

You have to know that it's about the condition of you. It's about your receivability. Can you receive what life is trying to give you? Can you go where life is trying to take you? Are you ready? Are you willing? And are you able? Those are the requirements. You may be ready and willing, but not able. You may be ready and able, but not willing. All permutations of those three are possible. I'm trying to turn your understanding from, "It's about what I need to get and where I need to get to," towards, "It's about my readiness. My willingness—my willingness to get there, to take the road, no matter what's on the road." In that sense, it's more about you than we tend to realize.

As much as you're trying to find the Truth, as much as you're wanting happiness, as much as you sincerely hope for inner peace—the Truth is looking for you even more than that. I'm not speaking poetically. That's the truth. *The Truth is looking for you—it really is.* You may be looking for God with all your heart and soul, but however much heart and soul that is, God is looking for you far more intently. Because the Truth, God—whatever you want to call it—has a greater capacity than we do for that intent, for the intensity of it, for the bigness of it, and for the purity of it. If you're looking for it, if you desire it, if you have some and want more, whatever the situation is, it's only the case because the Truth was able to find you enough to cause that to be the case. So something has already happened. There's not a person sitting in this room that it isn't true of—that something has already happened. The Truth has already entered enough, found you well enough, that it could spark whatever brought you to this point, whatever brought you to the point you're on in your search or in your intent.

What I would like you to see is not what's possible ahead—but for just this moment—that something *big* has already happened. Get it that, something has already entered your house, the nature of which is beyond anything you can imagine! Or else, you wouldn't care about any of this. Most of the world doesn't care about any of it, because they haven't gotten to a point yet of being malleable enough that something can enter. But you have. You're the rare few; you're not the majority but you're the lucky minority. To the degree that that's true (and it absolutely is), can you see that you're already a finder? Can you see that just that circumstance moves you from the category of, "Well, I'm a seeker, I'm seeking. I'm intently going to find inner peace, and I'm searching the right way." Can you see that that's less the case than, "Something has already found me, and that something must be some aspect of the Truth, the Divine"—whatever you want to call it?

Can you accept what you have already found? Can you receive it, so that you actually get it that it's real? Because it's motivated you enough to actually affect where you go and what you do and who you talk to, and all the rest. It's real; it's not some mind game you're playing with yourself, although at times you may think that. But you have to see—I'm really imploring you—you have to see that something has already found you, that the needle is already in your hand and you can stop focusing so much on the haystack. Start looking at your hand. Somehow you have done enough right or been right enough in some way that it has found you enough; something has already come; something has already arrived, or else there would be no search for you at all.

COOPERATING WITH THE DIVINE

Premodaya: It's not my job to bring you to Truth; it's not my job to bring you to the Divine or to Reality or to Universal Love or whatever you want to call it, because if you're coming to me, that has already happened. Sometimes people come and they don't even realize that that has happened. They don't even recognize that something has happened to them. More often they do, but once in a while, somebody comes who doesn't even recognize it, or fully recognize it, or know what it means.

If the Divine comes to you, if Truth comes to you, if something of the Beyond has touched you, it doesn't mean it's going to heal your personality; it doesn't mean all your problems will be solved; it doesn't mean your anxieties are going to disappear; it doesn't mean life will get easier. Sometimes—actually I would say most of the time—the spiritual search begins for people with those ideas, "Somehow I will be a better person; this will make me better. My problems will get dealt with; my issues will get resolved." So, if the Divine comes to you, then what has happened is:

The Divine has come to you. If something from the Beyond reaches to you, there's no promise in it; there's no guarantee in it of any amelioration of anything (although we like to think that those things can and will happen, but that's our idea). The Beyond really isn't much concerned with our problems. That which is Infinite, that which is Eternal, that which is Profound, doesn't muck around in our issues—that's our playground.

It's good to understand how a deeper connection to the Profound, to the Divine, to Truth, to God (to whatever your word is), it's good to understand that that doesn't resolve things. The better understanding is that your *cooperation* with that touch—your surrender to the Divine's influence on you—if it evolves and becomes complete and sincere and open and full, *can* solve many of your problems, is likely to make you a better person, can end many of your anxieties. It's not that the Divine drops from the sky and solves your problems or evolves you into some better form of human being, but your response to Divine will and to the actual coming of the Profound into your life can have those effects, but it's up to you. It's up to how much you recognize and respond to the Truth that has come to you; that's completely in your control.

It isn't a process of garnering something, the idea that something will be realized and you will gain something—that isn't what happens. But if you really want to gain something, then you have to open yourself; in essence, you have to bow down. It's a process of humbling. You have to become so humble that the very humility, the very right seeing, the very correct understanding, the very heart opening, that's what solves problems, is what cures ills. Not because you were trying to gain something, not because you were trying to grab something better for yourself; but because you cooperated enough, and are learning to cooperate enough, and are practicing cooperating enough that something bigger actually begins to function in your life, actually begins to function through you, actually begins to operate through what you call "you," and then the proportion of things change.

Then the problems that seem so awful don't seem so awful. Then the dilemmas that seemed insurmountable suddenly seem like possibilities.

Then the anxieties that plagued you and the suffering that seemed like it was endless takes on a whole different perspective and suddenly looks much smaller. Those are the possibilities, but not because something came to you for your gain, something came to fix you, but because you shifted your focus from that which doesn't matter, that which is impermanent, that which is going to die and fade away, to that which comes from the Eternal, comes from the Infinite, comes from the seat of Truth. That's why I say my job is not to bring you to the Divine; my job is to encourage you to cooperate. This is why I talk so much about allowing; this is why I talk so much about willingness.

It's really that simple—your willingness is the entire key, the master key. Your willingness to respond to that touch that has already happened and to let it expand in you; to let that touch, touch you deeper; to let that touch influence you; to take that touch seriously. Your willingness determines everything.

The problem is, willingness doesn't have any conditions. Things may come to you that are not pleasant. You may have bodily experiences that are difficult; you may have mental comings and goings, emotional experiences that you would rather not have or that aren't pleasant. The idea people have is, "If I'm touched by that which is Profound, if the Beyond comes to me, it will be all ecstasy and bliss, and I'll feel wonderful, and I'll be high all the time, and life will be great!" Well, nobody's ever led that life yet. Every life has its ups and downs, its triumphs and its tragedies, its health and its illness. So that's the crazy ideal we all carry, that somehow life can be a perfect experience of constant happiness, nothing ever goes wrong, and even if something goes wrong, *we* feel great anyway. But that's not life in the Divine; you will never stop being a human being as long as you're on this planet, and a human life contains difficulties—every human life— Buddha's life, Jesus' life, every life. What's a greater difficulty than being crucified?

We have to grow up and recognize that we are expecting the impossible; we're expecting something that is not the nature of this life. For the

Beyond to come to you, once the Divine has touched you in any way, that process begins—you could say—automatically. You start, whether you know it or not, to move towards the greater understanding that what is, *is*. It becomes a process of purely acceptance. There are days when life will bring you joys and pleasures, and there are other days guaranteed, when life will bring you difficulties and pains. The end of suffering doesn't mean you never have pain again; it doesn't mean things don't go badly—it means you stop expecting the impossible.

As you grow in that understanding you develop an automatic response to whatever comes of first allowing it, recognizing that this is Reality: "I don't control my experience; I don't control what happens in this universe and I don't need to walk around acting as if I do." Then that keeps permeating and metamorphosizes you, so that the day comes, eventually, when you don't add any layer of needless suffering to the experiences that come. You don't infuse life with your idea of what's right and wrong or how it should be for you—and that's the end of suffering. It means if life brings pleasure on Tuesday—OK, and if life brings pain on Wednesday—OK.

Pain isn't synonymous with suffering; suffering is our addition, our answer to the pain, whatever it is, or the difficulty or the discomfort, our response to it that says, "It shouldn't be this way! I don't like this; this shouldn't be happening to me. Somebody else can get cancer, but *I* shouldn't get cancer. Why did the doctor say I have cancer? This can't be right!" This is immature and arrogant, nothing else. If it can happen to anybody, it can happen to you, and probably will. At some point losses increase, usually in the last third of life. Suffering is when you say, "These losses shouldn't be happening; this is wrong; this is not how it's supposed to be for me, maybe everybody else, but not for me." These losses are inevitable.

Suffering isn't because you incurred a loss, suffering is because of how you responded, what your attitude was toward that loss. You can be the holiest person on this planet, but this is L.A.—somebody's going to smash into your car sooner or later. And if you're over sixty, some illness is going to come to you sooner or later. But we all kind of hold this amorphous idea in the back of our heads that, "everybody else but not me." So, I want to encourage you to include yourself in life's inevitable equation, which includes losses. Including yourself in the equation is the end of suffering. Recognizing that not only "it can happen to me," but "it's *going* to happen to me," even if that recognition is nothing else than knowing profoundly, "I'm going to die," which many people push away and avoid feeling.

Usually, somewhere between forty-five and fifty-five their gut prevents their pushing it away and they feel it anyway; mortality becomes quite palpable. If you're under forty it may not have happened yet for you, but just wait. And even that is a great clue, that there are these preprogrammed evolutions that happen in everyone, exactly like puberty; there's a time clock built in. Certain things happen in certain eras of life, in every life, cross-culturally.

If you can drop the idea that you're special, that you're unique, that "hopefully it won't happen to me," you'll be more in reality, because it *will* happen to you. It's immutable and there are no exceptions. When you see yourself as the exception you're not cooperating with reality. When you actually start to understand that you're the same as everyone else and there are no exceptions, not only is that more of a cooperation, but that's more of a motivation for the willingness. Then you start to get smart and you start to understand more and more that how you take what happens is more important than what happens. We want control over what happens, and we miss the point that if there's any control at all, it's over how you take what happens, not over what happens. Life brings what it brings; what is, *is*. So, if there's something to learn, it's how to cooperate, how to not be in a fight, in a struggle with life experience, because it doesn't jive with your preference.

I talk almost daily about the futility of our own preferences. It's a crazy battle that we play inside ourselves, that our preferences, what we hope for, what we like, what we prefer, is going to make us happy, is going to make life good. Just a little examination of that, a little exploration, and it becomes evident, quite quickly, that any time you have gotten your preference (which is probably often, maybe more often than you recognize), any time what you hoped would happen happened, if it brought you happiness, that feeling was short-lived. That shiny new car feels great for about three days. Marrying the woman of your dreams is good for about two years.

It all has to evolve into something else; it all has to plug into what's deeper, what's more real. And the mechanism for that is your willingness to allow what is, rather than be in a struggle with what is—your cooperation with Reality.

My contention is that you have been touched by the Divine. If you're in this room, if you come to ICODA, if you're at a meeting like this, wherever it is (it doesn't have to be ICODA) then there's no doubt, as far as I'm concerned, that something real and profound has already happened to you; otherwise it's impossible for you to be in a group like this, or be in a setting like this, or listen to words like this; it grates. If we pulled somebody in off the street who hasn't been yet touched by the Beyond, they wouldn't be able to sit still in their seat; this would all just be too strange. The words wouldn't compute at all; it would all sound like nonsense. The inner response would be absolute rejection, very quickly. So, if you aren't feeling that, if you're not trying to figure out how you can run out of here, then I guarantee you God has already come to you.

But how much are you cooperating? Despite that fact, how much are you still luxuriating in doubt? How much are you still questioning what, deeper down, you know doesn't need to be questioned? How much are you still trying to control, that which ultimately, if you think about it clearheadedly, is uncontrollable? You don't control life; you *are* life.

See as clearly as you can how any noncooperation is just a mind game. Not out of any bad intention or because you don't get it enough, or something's wrong with you, but simply because that's what the mind does; it plays these mind games. When the Profound is contacted, when Truth is more palpable to you, the mind steps in at some point, right then or three days later or three months later, and says, "Ugh, it can't be real; it isn't true.

It doesn't mean what I hoped it would mean." Or "It isn't enough," or "It didn't change my life," or "It didn't open my heart," or "It didn't heal me." Or whatever! All mind games, all your mind's interpretation of how the Divine should be experienced. Get real, of how God *should feel*. You have no idea of how God should feel; nobody does! You never will. Willingness means you feel whatever you feel—good, bad; it's enough; it's not enough—you don't fall into that trap of believing that those ideas have any weight, mean anything other than a mind game is being played on you.

It's inevitable; it never stops; it can diminish, but sooner or later—it seems now like almost every week I use the example of Christ on the cross: "Father, why has thou forsaken me?" Mind games! If it can happen to him, you think it's not going to happen to you? It's inevitable; it's programmed in. So don't be fooled. It has great meaning to me; it's a great clue—whether there was really a Christ or not, it doesn't matter—it's a fantastic clue. We all think that this should never happen to us, that when we really get it, we'll never question anything. Yet a Christ, a world teacher, more influential than any other, in the last moment of life, complains. Moves into fear, doubts, and we think it's not going to be the case with us. Somehow, we have to get to the point where that doesn't happen. We really think this, everybody, and you'll never stop thinking it but stop believing it. That's what you can do, you can stop believing it, and then the mind game becomes very tiny, and you just laugh at it. You don't live it anymore; you don't spend hours saying, "Ah, nothing has really happened to me" or "It happened five years ago; it doesn't feel as good as it did then; I gotta get it back." You stop all that dissatisfaction, false dissatisfaction, mind-generated dissatisfaction. But if Jesus Christ isn't the exception, please get it that you're not either.

Prof. Alex: Something happened to me. I was driving around the neighborhood; it was very lovely. But this day, I had a lot of worries, and I was enjoying nothing, and I suddenly thought, "I'm sick of being Alex! I'm just sick of it—drop it!" And suddenly, I was in the most beautiful place!

The sun was shining, the gardens were beautiful again, and I thought, "You don't have to go looking for this paradise; it's there all the time! You just have to get rid of the stuff that's going on, let it go." It lasted a few minutes and then there was a phone call, and I was back in business again. But since then, I've been saying, "I can put my attention on Alex, Alex's life—or I can say, I'm sick of it, I'm dead, Alex is dead," and then, hey, it's all there. It was a beautiful experience. I had to get to a pretty desperate state, but it was like the great, whatever, is waiting for us at all times; you don't have to go looking for it. What I needed to do was drop Alex.

Premodaya: Actually, what you're talking about is the focus of attention. It doesn't mean you stop attending to what has to be attended to in life, but it does mean it's a great lesson. What it does mean is: Something else is there that can also be attended to, and you fell into that. You moved your attention. By dropping Alex, your attention naturally went to what's deeper. This is why there are so many wisdom traditions, ancient traditions, where the whole practice that they espouse and live is about how you focus your attention. This is a huge part of Buddhism; it's practically the entire path of Zen, and it's exactly what we're doing when I say to you, "Know what you already know more fully." You're giving the everyday example of it, the practical day-to-day way that it works.

But people have this idea (it's almost inevitable for everyone) that there's a dichotomy; there's a split between my regular life, my daily life, my worldly life—and my spiritual experience, my spiritual life, my ability to be in contact with the Profound—as if one is a trade for the other. The idea behind that, the hope, the preference, behind that, the mind game behind that is: less of one, and more of the other. It doesn't work that way. Life will always be life; the world will always be the world; as long as you're here you'll always have things you have to take care of. It's not that you'll spend less moments with your attention there, and more moments with your attention on the Divine; it's that you will cooperate enough; you will surrender enough; you will stop trying to control that which can't be controlled enough, so that they will go on at the same time, that your attention to the practical, to the worldly, to the material won't so much distract you from the Profound. You will see more fully and more readily that they're not separate, and you won't kick yourself for forgetting. Same example, last moment, it's Christ on the cross, he forgot. The anguish was so great—for a minute he forgot.

Deborah: When you were saying that everyone in this room has felt the Divine, or has been touched by the Divine, I feel uncomfortable by that because I feel it feeds my ego, like I'm really special. Then I feel like that's wrong, and I get really angry at myself for feeling that way. Even though I do really agree, I do feel very much in touch with something, I don't like the feeling that other people aren't.

Premodaya: It's like everybody in the world is walking down the same road, and some people are at mile one and some people are at mile ninety-three and some people are at mile fifty. And those people who haven't been touched by the Divine (let's say everything from mile zero to mile fifty is not touched by the Divine) aren't better people or worse people. The people at mile eighty aren't better than the people at mile fifty, or mile forty, or mile ten; it just hasn't happened yet. If you understand that it's a question of perspective, distance—not who is higher, who is lower, who is better, who isn't better—that's the right understanding. The person who has walked further isn't better than the person who hasn't gotten there yet.

It's the truth. There is nothing special, if you've been touched by the Divine and now you're saying you recognize that; it doesn't make you better than anybody in any way. It just means you've gotten to mile fifty-one. Maybe you didn't even walk; maybe somebody carried you; I don't know. There's no way to take specialness from it, but the mind can take specialness from anything—anything. You can have a humiliating experience, and the mind will tell you it's because you're special, in some way, some devious way. It will turn it into that.

So, what I would like to say to you is, that's great news that you recognize that mind game. The problem would be if you didn't recognize it. The fact that you recognize it means it's not a problem. It means it's going to take care of itself through your own understanding. I wouldn't worry about it; I would keep noticing the tendency of the mind (which is not your mind, which is *any* mind) to aggrandize, to inflate and to tell ourselves, "I'm something." Just the fact that you see that, the antidote is already operating.

ABOUT THE AUTHOR

Bodhisattva Shree Swami Premodaya is a spiritual teacher, and Western Guru in the Eastern tradition. He is known to seekers around the world for his wit and wisdom, and real effectiveness. Holding degrees from New York University and Antioch University, he is the former director of Outpatient Psychiatry and Psychology at Cedars-Sinai Medical Center in Beverly Hills, California. Prior to that he was Western Regional Director of Clinical Services at National Medical Enterprises, overseeing treatment at thirteen psychiatric inpatient, outpatient and specialty programs, in six different states. Later he became CEO of his own psych company, Behavioral Health Resources, Inc., which provided management and consultation services to a number of psychiatric hospitals, outpatient clinics and rehab facilities, in California, North Carolina, and other states.

Premodaya was born in Germany in a 'displaced persons camp' after the war. He immigrated to the U.S. with his mother and stepfather when he was four years old—three refugees, who spoke no English. At age 31, a subsequent series of intense mystical experiences transformed him from ardent atheist to spiritual advocate. In 1983 he was formally initiated as a direct disciple of Osho (1931-1990), who named him Swami Premodaya ("Love Rising"). Premodaya remains his faithful devotee to this day. Premodaya also considers himself a disciple of American spiritual teacher, Gangaji (even though she does not offer formal discipleship initiation). His own spiritual work with others does not reference either of their voluminous teachings, and is not based on any particular religion, tradition, practices, philosophy, code of conduct, or belief set. Rather, he helps, encourages, and guides individuals to experience Truth directly, in whatever way serves their unique individuality and spiritual growth.

International Centers
of Divine Awakening

ABOUT INTERNATIONAL CENTERS
OF DIVINE AWAKENING (ICODA)

The mission of ICODA is to offer profound life, love, peace and truth-affirming transformational work for individuals and groups. Founded in 2004, ICODA is the vehicle through which Swami Premodaya carries out his God-given mission of spiritual guidance, education and upliftment to any and all spiritual seekers. ICODA is an incorporated church (International Church of Divine Awakening), better known as International Centers of Divine Awakening—as well as a 501(c)(3) non-profit organization.

CONNECT WITH ICODA

Join online Satsang with Swami Premodaya

Website: www.I-CODA.org

Facebook: www.facebook.com/InternationalCentersofDivineAwakening

PremodayaTV: www.Premodyatv.com

email: info@I-CODA.org

phone (USA): 310.497.1899

70372274R10227